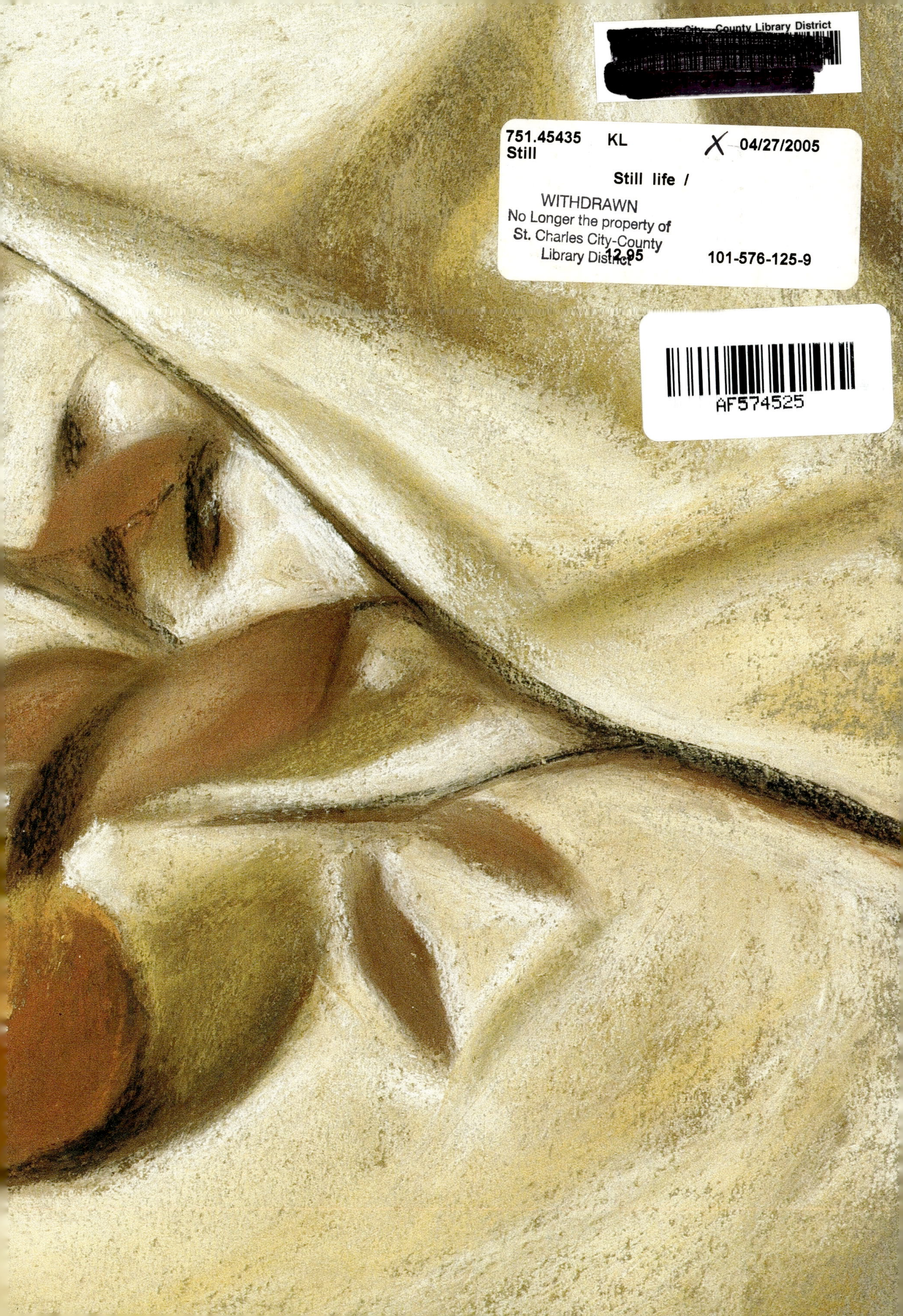

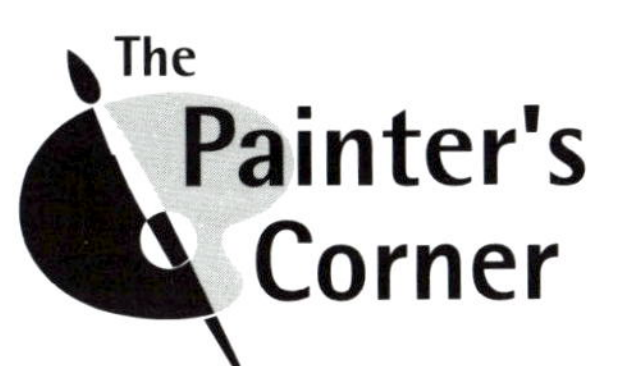

STILL LIFE

BARRON'S

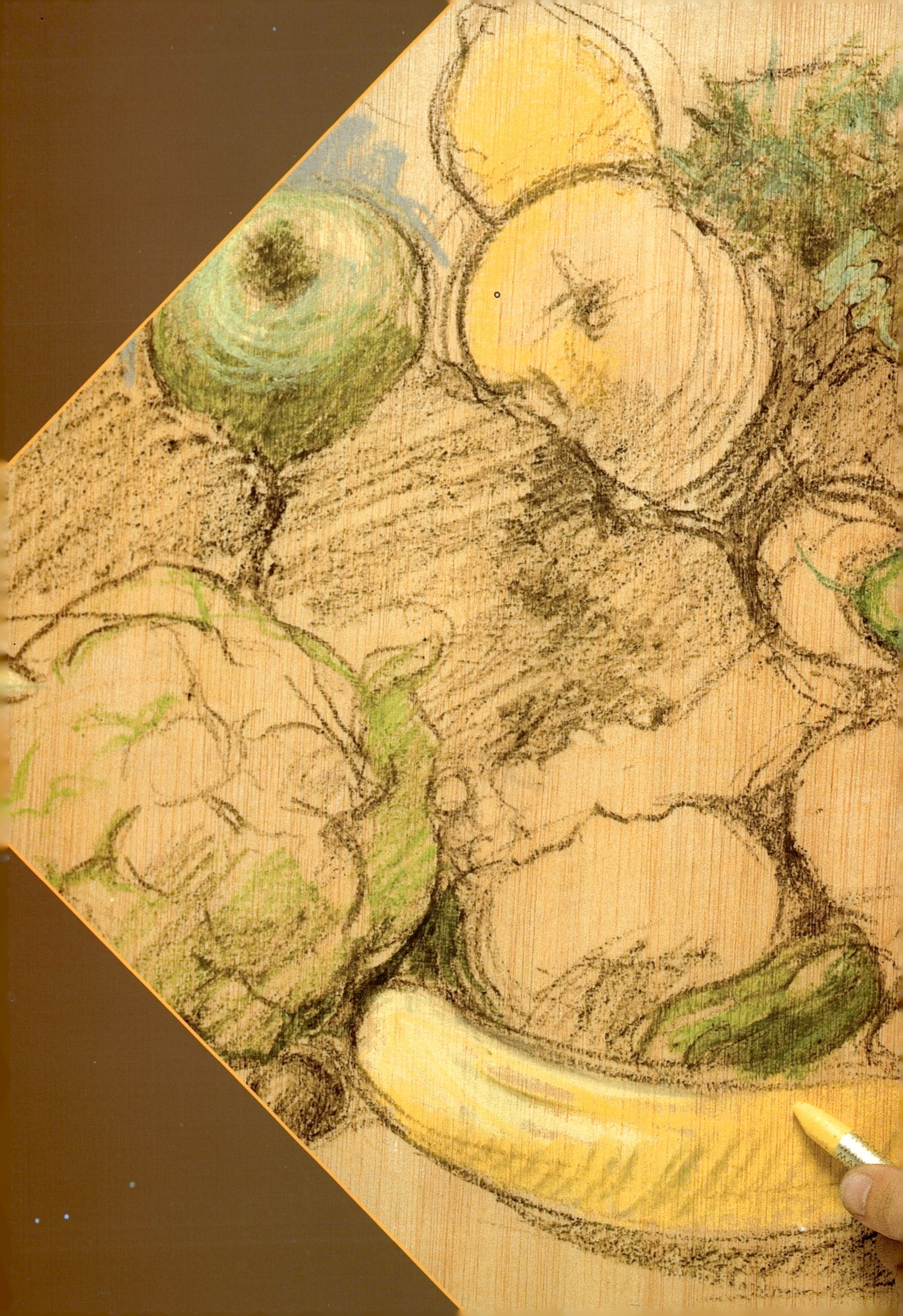

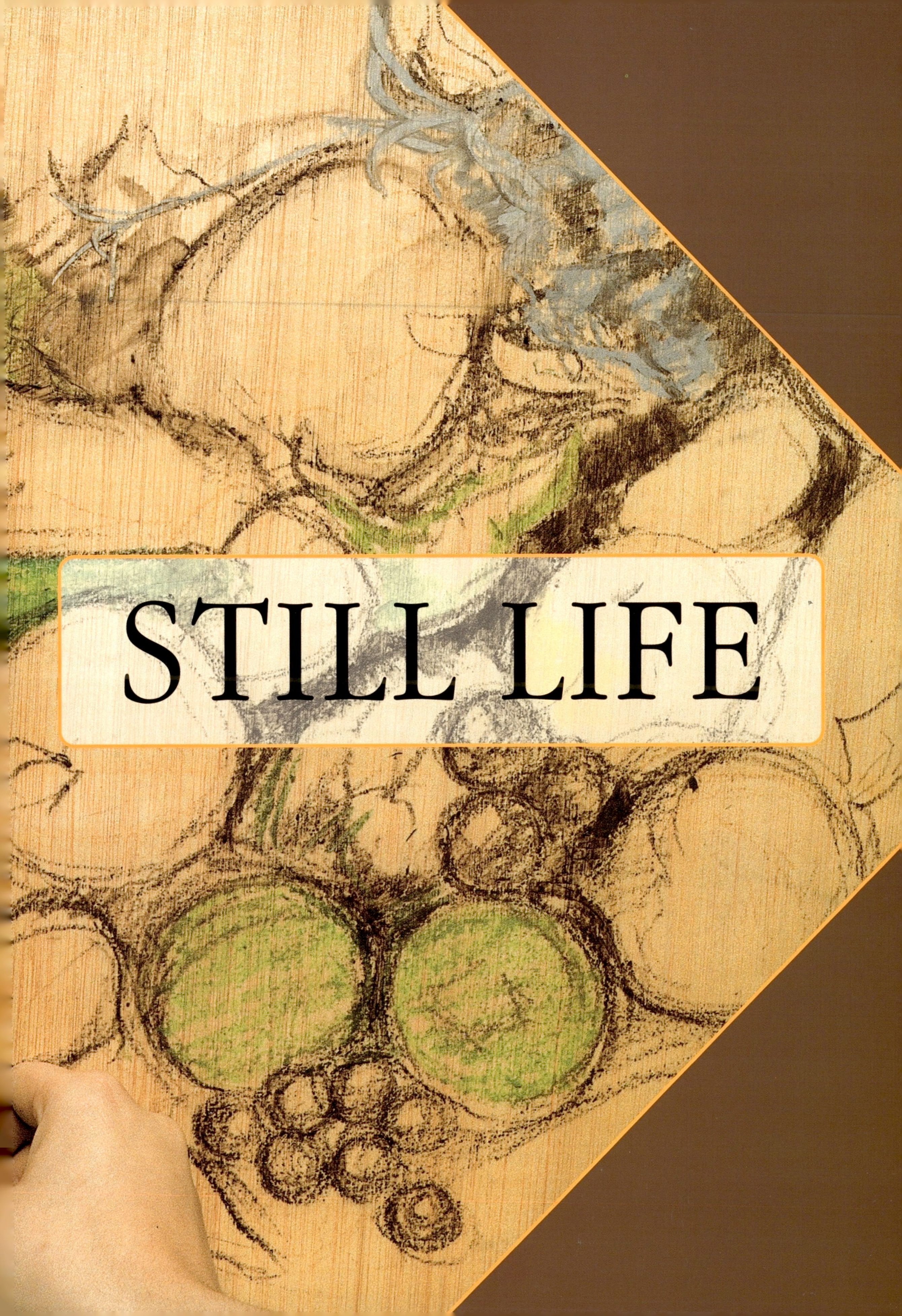
STILL LIFE

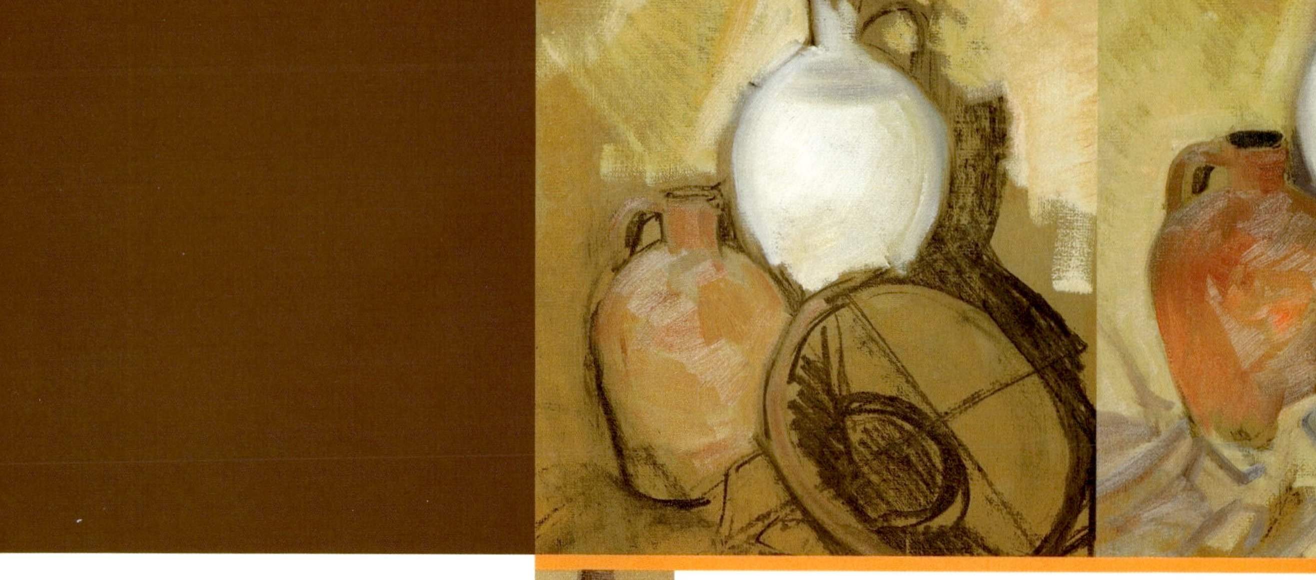

Original title of the book in Spanish: *Bodegón*

Published by Parramón Ediciones, S.A., Barcelona, Spain

Authors: Parramón's Editorial Team
Editor in Chief: María Fernanda Canal
Photography: Nos & Soto
Text and Coordination: Josep Asunción
Book Design and Layout: Josep Asunción
Projects: Josep Asunción, Vicenç B. Ballestar, Myriam Ferrón, and Yvan Viñals
Production Director: Rafael Marfil

All inquiries should be addressed to:
Barron's Educational Series, Inc.
250 Wireless Blvd.
Hauppauge, NY 11788
www.barronseduc.com

International Standard Book No.: 0-7641-5707-8

Library of Congress Catalog Card No.: 2003107538

Acknowledgments
Parramón Ediciones, S.A., wishes to express its gratitude to the following people for their kind collaboration: Arturo Solari, Gemma Guasch, Melisa Vallmitjana.

Printed in Spain
9 8 7 6 5 4 3 2 1

Contents

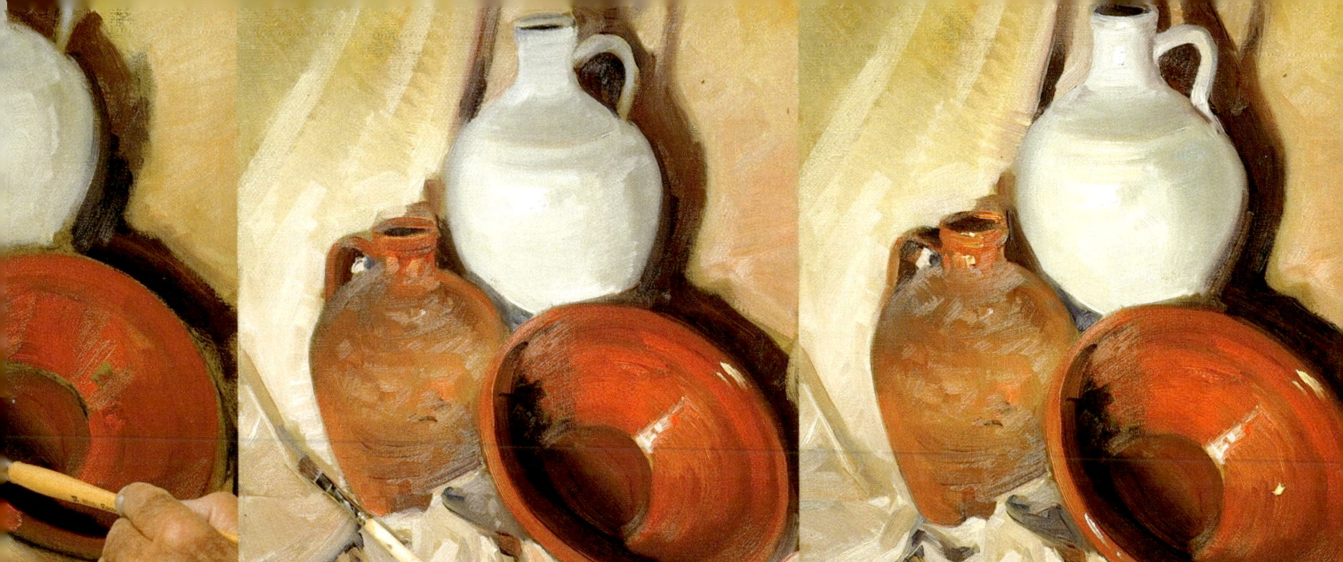

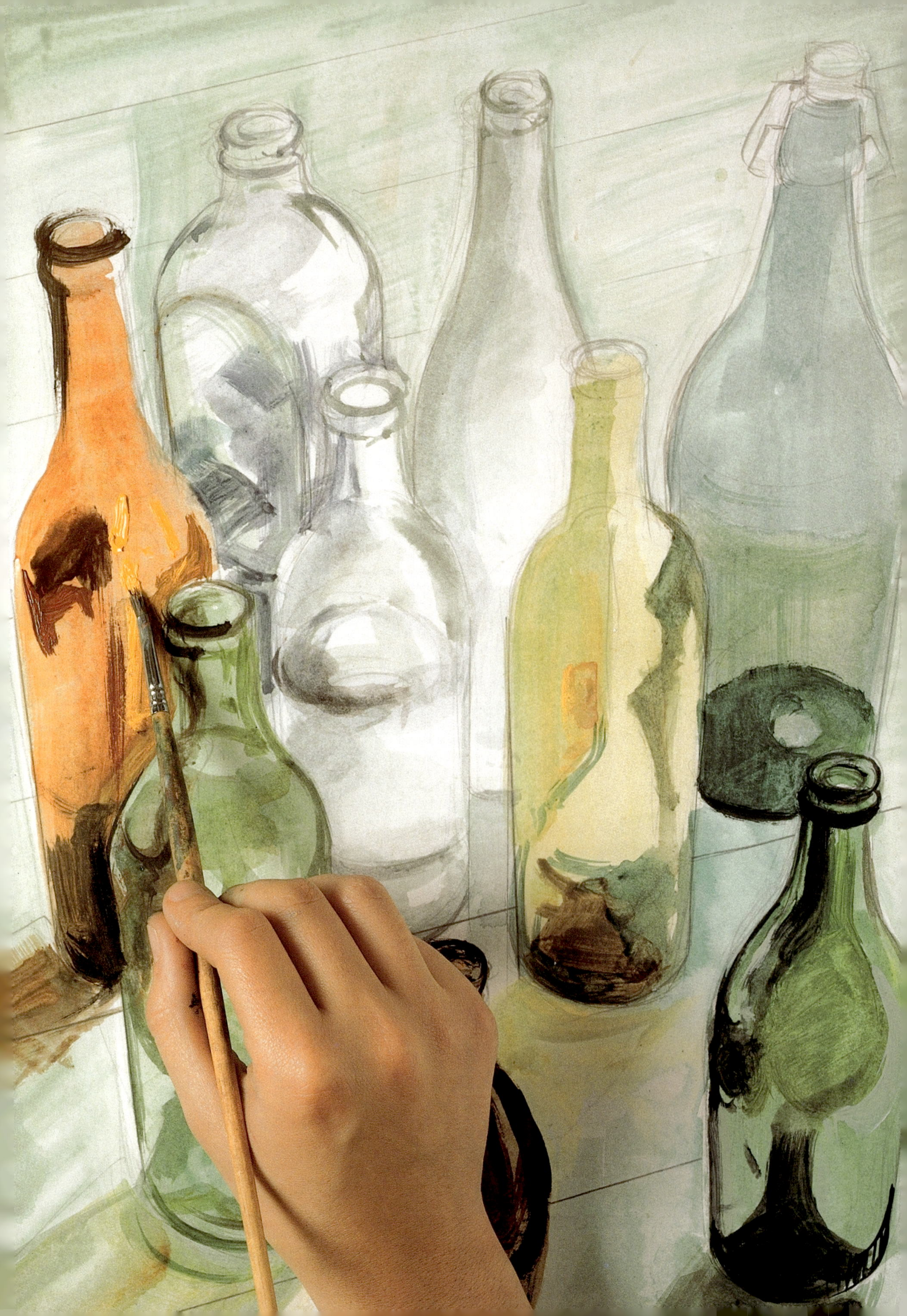

Introduction

Still life is the most popular of all the painting genres. In the last five centuries of the history of art, still life—from its appearance as a genre—has been one of the major fields of exploration for thousands of artists. It is the ideal subject for a foray into painting; this is why beginners choose still life over all other learning subjects. Still life proves that the most mundane and simplest objects are good models for producing personal creations of enormous beauty and expression.

The first half of this book is devoted to the basic theories needed to paint any still life. The first pages include an introduction to its history, which will help the reader understand the conceptual, psychological, symbolic, or emotional messages conveyed by a still life representation at any given time. Next, we will cover the basic concepts of the creative process. The first three subjects in this section—color, form, and space—explain how to create the image, that is, how to compose the scene, apply perspective, define volume, and blend colors. The next two subjects—texture and style—show how to use different media, how to be expressive with lines, or how to incorporate the materials.

The second half of the book takes the reader through ten very different still life exercises. In each one of them, we will analyze step-by-step the technical and expressive process for each painting. These ten examples are a valuable learning asset for the variety of styles and techniques that they offer.

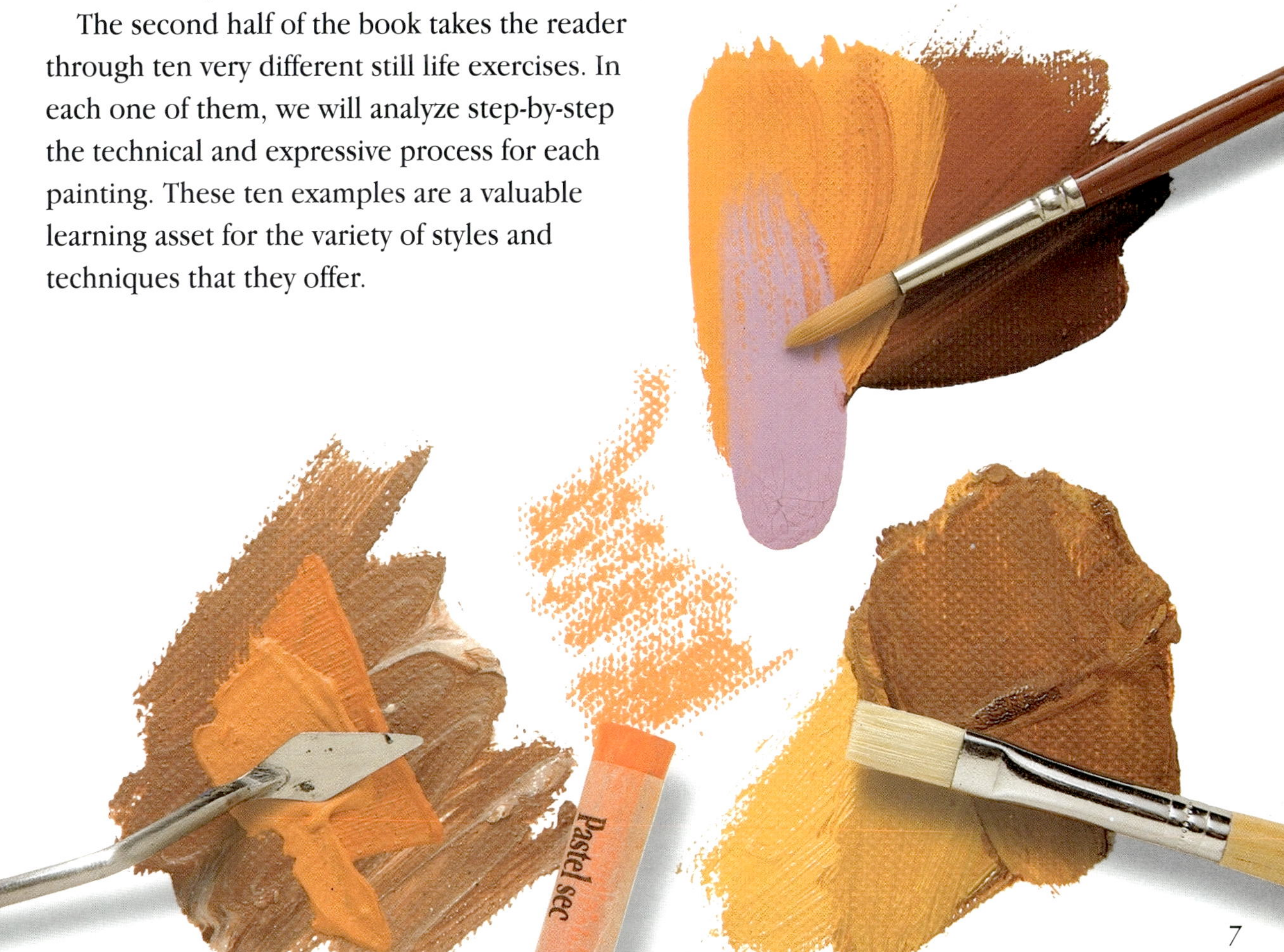

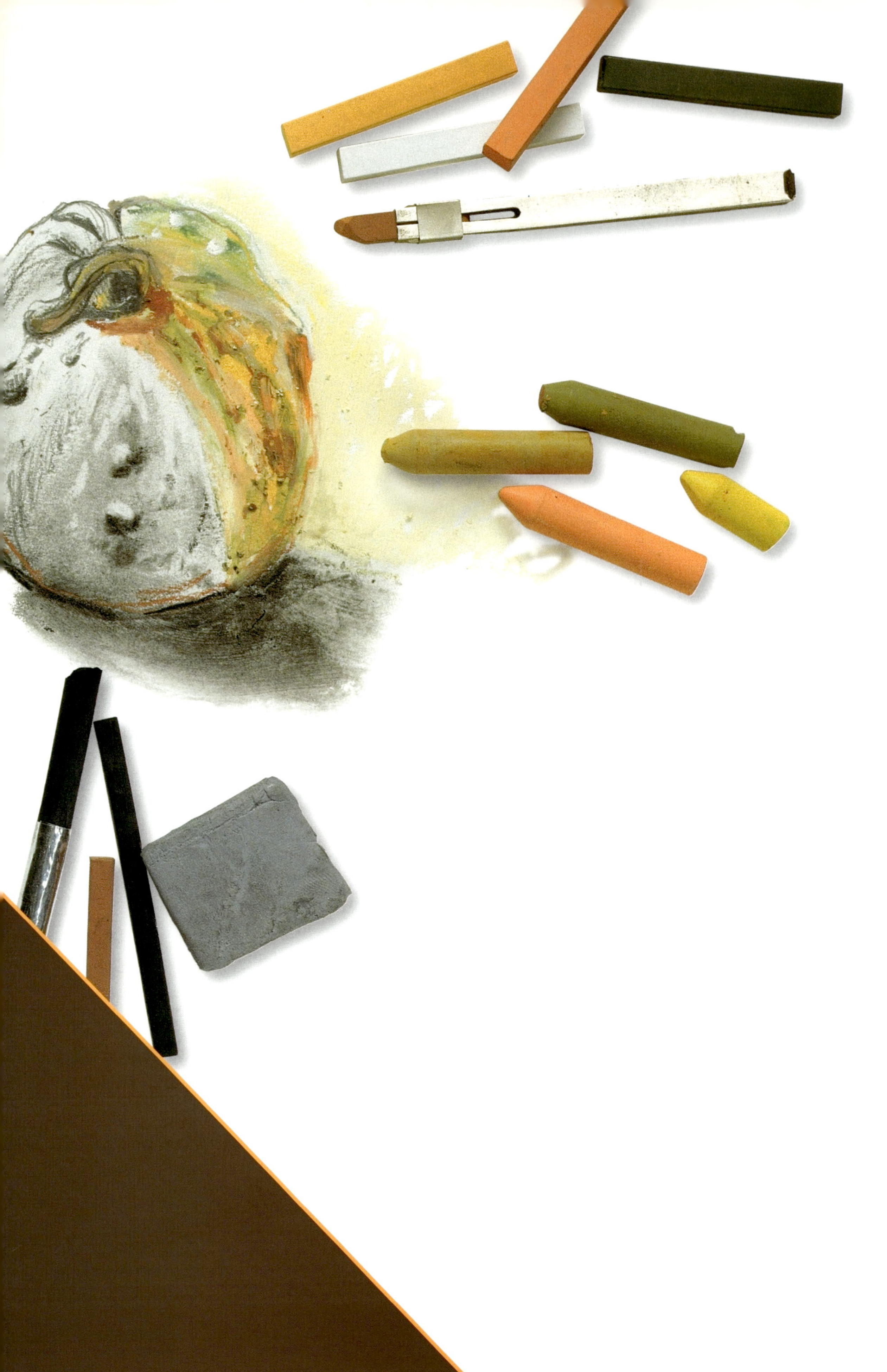

Still Life in Painting

Of all the subjects covered in this collection, still life is perhaps the only one that every painter has experimented with in his or her formative and creative process. Just a few elements arranged in a small space have the power to motivate the artist and to inspire beautiful works of art.

We are dealing with one of the most popular genres in the history of painting, for the simplicity and the possibilities that it offers the artist at every level. The birth of still life as an art genre took place toward the end of the sixteenth century, and it was closely linked to the sentiments of baroque artists. This style instilled a new vision in the reality of the moment, which was disturbed by the changes that took place in the religious, economic, and social scenes. From that moment on, still life has served to exalt the value of simple and everyday things. Through the exquisite still life paintings of Chardin, the observer may feel transported to the magic of a moment in time, something as natural as a morning breakfast in the life of a family.

We can appreciate the language of painting and its potential for experimentation at the hand of pioneers like Cézanne, Picasso, and Matisse through the representation of objects like a chair, a few apples, or a fish tank on a table, or we can let compositions by artists like Dalí, Magritte, and De Chirico lead us into virtual and dreamlike worlds. Each still life representation, through the selection of the elements, its composition, and the way it is painted, reflects the artist's individual personality, the particular way he or she sees the world, a unique and one-of-a-kind message. It is not necessary to create large paintings to be able to express great ideas or passions. In the words of Paul Cézanne at the end of the nineteenth century, "A simple apple can amaze Paris." From this perspective, in painting, creativity does not consist of inventing new forms, colors, or themes but of expressing a personal point of view about something that already exists with the poetic and emotional charge that comes from the most inner spirit of the artist. The following pages will take the reader inside the meaning and history of still life to understand its evolution and to enjoy the magnificent works of art that have been created from something so simple.

◆

Still life is one of the most popular genres in the history of painting, for the simplicity and the possibilities that it offers the artist at every level.

◆

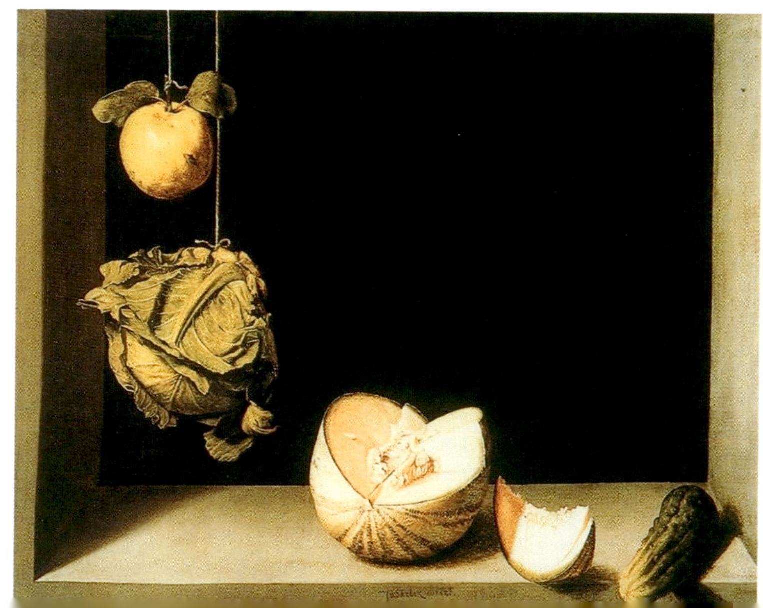

Juan Sánchez Cotán, Cabbage, Melon, Cucumber, and Quince, *c. 1602. Museo de Bellas Artes, Granada (Spain). Sánchez Cotán is considered the first Spanish baroque painter. The paintings of this Carthusian monk are very realistic and delicate. They search for the transcendence of the real nature of objects to become a bridge between the natural and supernatural, transforming them into images for contemplation.*

What is still life?

The words *still life* refer to the painting of an inanimate object or group of objects. Many household items can be used for this purpose, like plates, pots, vegetables, fruits, and so on. However, with time, the subject matter for this genre expanded to include other objects as well. Nowadays, still life can consist of any object of manageable dimensions, placed in a small scene, which may include the presence of animals and flowers. A still life is, in brief, a staged reality.

VAN GOGH'S CHAIRS

By the end of 1888, Vincent Van Gogh had finished two paintings of nearly identical dimensions. In one of them, we see his chair, and in the other, Gauguin's. These paintings represent a very personal way of handling still life. Van Gogh's choice of a chair as a model is due to the symbolic meaning of this particular piece of furniture. The chair acts not only as a support, but interacts with the body sitting in it. Thus, the empty chair personifies its owner, and Van Gogh uses this popular metaphor to express the visions he has of both himself and his friend Gauguin.

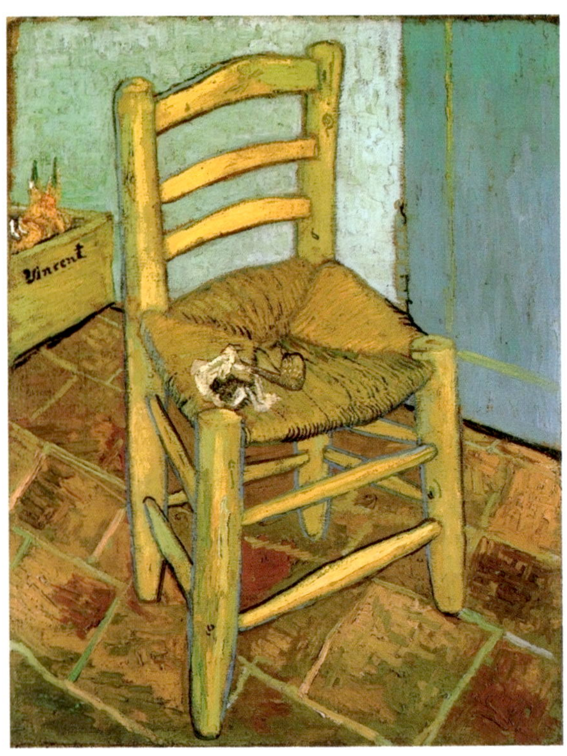

Vincent van Gogh, Van Gogh's Chair, *1888. The Trustees of the National Gallery, London (United Kingdom). Van Gogh's chair is humble looking and is placed on a simple and rural background: the tiled floor, the door, the box full of onions. . . . Very personal objects have been placed on it: a pipe and the tobacco pouch. Van Gogh, who was always looking for the ordinary and for maximum simplicity by choosing a humble life, must have painted this humble-looking chair, his chair, as a sort of self-portrait.*

Vincent van Gogh, Gauguin's Chair, *1888. Rijksmuseum Vincent van Gogh, Amsterdam (Netherlands). Gauguin's chair has arms and is more elegant. The two novels that rest on it depict the symbols of culture. The lighted candle represents the deep admiration that the painter professed for Gauguin, because Van Gogh considered him a source of inspiration. Some historians see in the empty chair the omen of what was about to happen a month later: Gauguin's departure and the breakup of the artists' relationship.*

The predecessors of the genre

Many examples in art that predated the baroque already showed an interest in incorporating objects into paintings. This is due to two reasons. First, a relationship exists between the symbolic value of certain objects and the narrative, normally ritualistic, magical, or religious in nature. Therefore, objects like swords, a chalice, an anchor, eggs, fish, a plumb line, books, clocks, a skull, keys, a ring, or the palm of a hand charge the composition with significance, representing a profession or the social status of a person or the metaphysical concerns of the time.

The second motivation is the depiction of virtuosity. The interest in making a scene credible finds painting objects a perfect subject matter because of their richness of textures, forms, and colors. The ties between the observer and the image are very strong because the spectator is familiar and identifies with them, making them his or her own.

Hans Memling, Vase with Flowers on a Shelf, *1470. Thyssen Collection, Lugano (Italy). For many centuries, painting was completely subject to a hierarchy of themes that gave historical and mythological scenes the highest priority, while still life enjoyed the lowest. This still life was painted on the back of a canvas.*

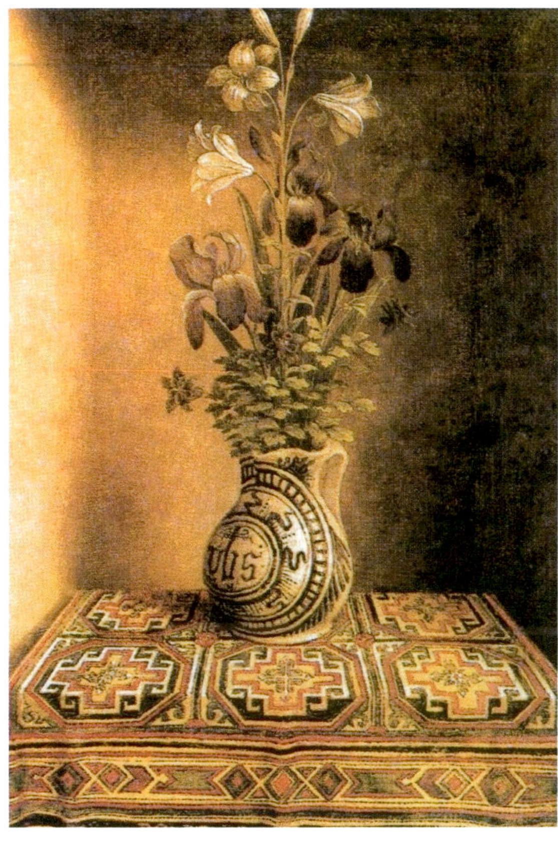

A GRAPHIC DOCUMENTATION
In a still life, we can see the typical objects of the historical time in which it was painted. In this sense, this genre provides first-hand graphic information that helps us know that culture better.

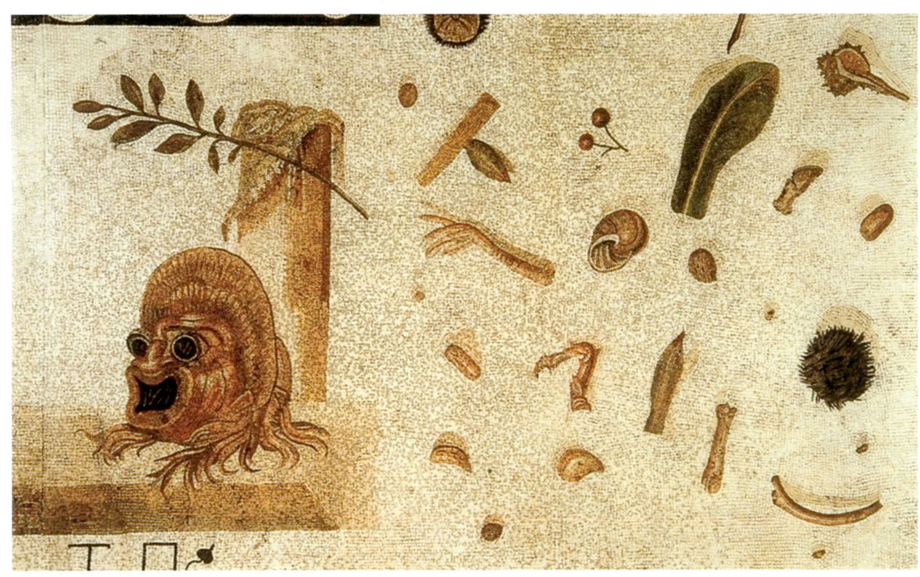

Decorative mural in the house of Julia Felix, first century A.D., Pompeii (Italy). The walls of a Roman house already displayed beautiful images like this one 1,600 years before the genre is considered to have appeared. It is not part of any other composition but, rather, an independent work of art, a true still life.

The first baroque still life paintings, intimate and contemplative

In 1596, Caravaggio painted what is considered the first still life in the history of painting. A few years later, still life had extended throughout Europe. During the seventeenth century, Spain and The Netherlands (Flanders and Holland) were the two main centers of still life production. In the eighteenth century, the leadership shifted to France.

Until the middle of the seventeenth century, still life was quite austere; it had an intimate air and normally depicted a few well-chosen elements where the artist tried above all to convey a personal sentiment. The precursor of this type of painting in Spain was Juan Sánchez Cotán, together with Zurbarán and Velázquez. All three treated the subject matter with extreme realism, great sensitivity, and respect. Each plate, jug, and cup become items of nearly sacred quality, and a cabbage or quince become objects of extraordinary beauty.

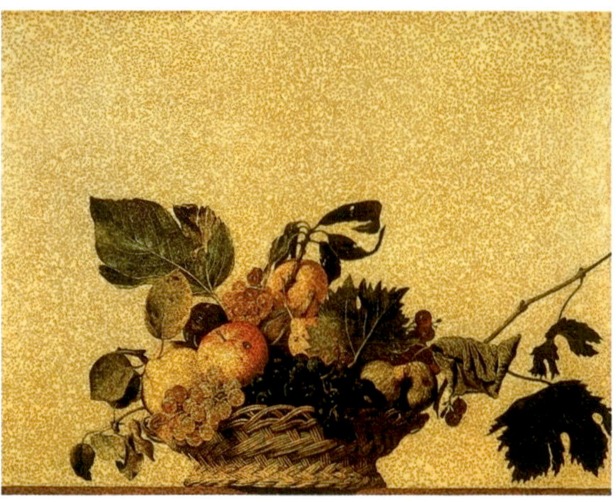

Caravaggio, Basket with Fruit, *1596. Pinacoteca Ambrosiana, Milan (Italy). This still life is considered to be the first of the genre. The subject of a still life gives its own meaning to the painting. If we look closely, though, we will see that the true interest, which was present in Caravaggio's entire body of work, is light. To represent light, any piece of fruit is as valid as a human form.*

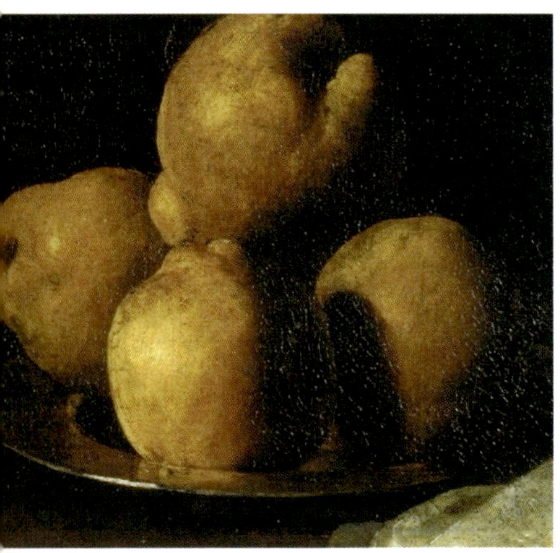

Francisco de Zurbarán, Still Life with Quince, *c. 1630. Museu Nacional d'Art de Catalunya, Barcelona (Spain). This still life by Zurbarán is the maximum expression of simplicity. Light defines the objects in a dark environment, which gives the composition a very special mystical appearance, a legacy of Sánchez Cotán.*

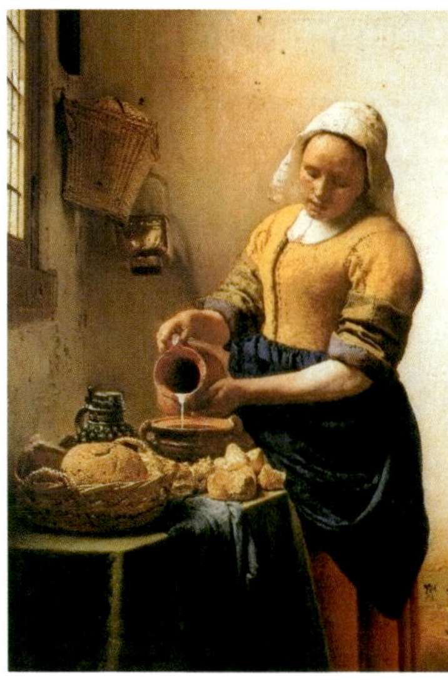

Vermeer de Delft, The Milkmaid, *c. 1660. Rijksmuseum Vincent van Gogh, Amsterdam (Netherlands). The mention of Vermeer is inevitable when talking about still life. His view of simple things is absolutely magical. His treatment of light, color, and texture is exquisite, and the result is a painting devoid of drama and charged with poetic meaning.*

THE REFORMATION
In northern Europe, the Protestant Reformation had a profound influence on painting. It demanded new themes that depicted sacred subjects without using the religious iconography of the Catholic faith (Christ, the Virgin Mary, saints . . .). The two great Counter-Reformation baroque artists who painted charming themes were Rembrandt and Vermeer de Delft. Their work was very much in line with the Spanish school, which had an affinity for simplicity and everyday subjects that resembled religious contemplative themes rather than being commercial and decorative.

Lavish and virtuoso still life

During the baroque period, the salons (the closest thing to an art gallery) became very popular, together with a bourgeois population that was fond of paintings. Toward the middle of the seventeenth century, art was no longer being commissioned exclusively by political or religious institutions, and there was a considerable public demand for paintings. Having paintings in the house was synonymous with prestige and social status. Their quality was measured by the level of realism with which they were painted.

Furthermore, if the still life made a reference to the owner's financial and social status, it had to depict pantries full of food, tables with succulent dishes, and expensive jewelry. The artists that followed this line of reasoning were Frans Snyders, Georg Flegel, and Willem Kalf.

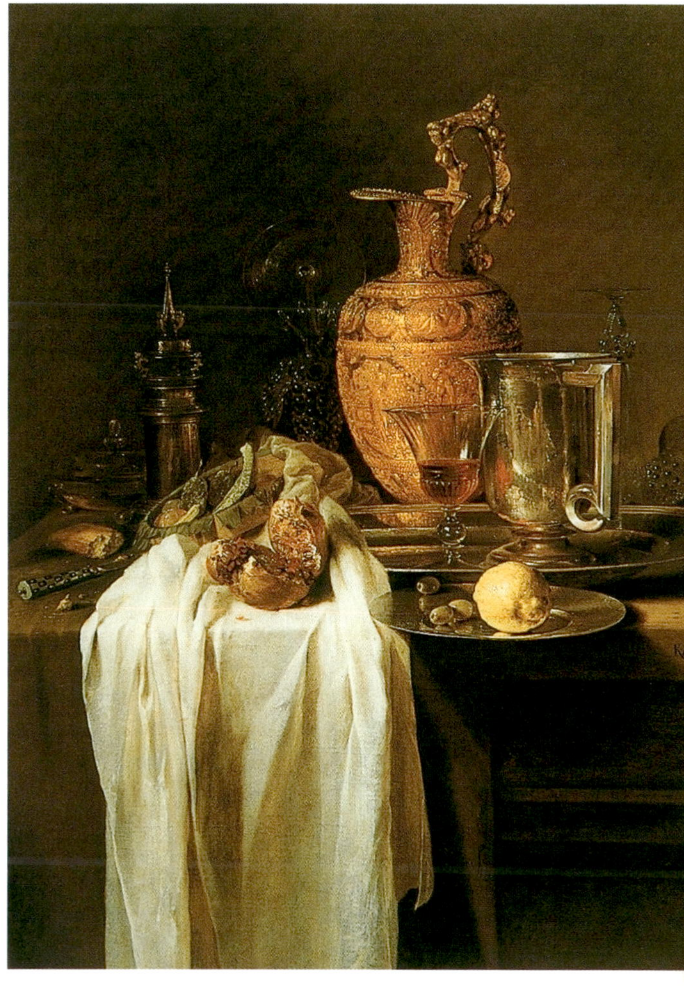

Willem Kalf, Still Life with Pomegranate, *1640. John Paul Getty Museum, Malibu (United States). The still life paintings by Kalf exude special elegance and refinement. If you observe carefully, you will discover that in reality the still life is not the true theme here but an excuse for expressing certain aesthetic values, typical of a thriving capitalist society.*

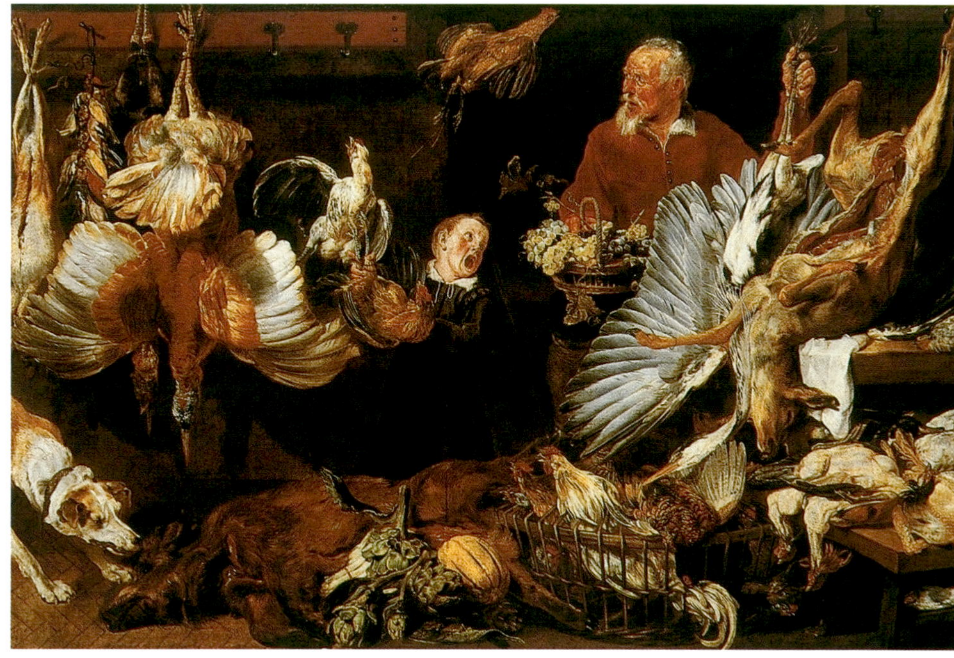

Frans Snyders, The Game Merchant, *Nasjonalgalleriet, Oslo (Norway). If the intimate still life invites the viewer to contemplation, the lavish still life invites recreation and consumption. The compositions are dynamic, with diagonal configurations, foreshortening, and oblique planes, without symmetry. Colors and textures are organized superbly, as in a symphony where many different instruments take part.*

The beauty of common objects

In the eighteenth century, all artistic effervescence in still life that had taken place in Holland was transferred to France. Jean-Baptiste Siméon Chardin was considered the main still life painter of the century, together with Jean Baptiste Oudry and Anne Coster-Vallayer, among many others. In Spain, the most significant representative of the genre was Luis Eugenio Meléndez. Until the time of the French Revolution in 1789, the entire century was marked by a social system with great contrasts. The aesthetic taste of the dominant nobility was pompous, which favored absolute displays of wealth and luxury. It was based on adornment, appearances, and the superficial and decorative, all of which reached their maximum expression in the rococo period. French still life artists of that century, on the other hand, were the proponents of refined aesthetics without exuberance, in search of beauty in normal, daily life.

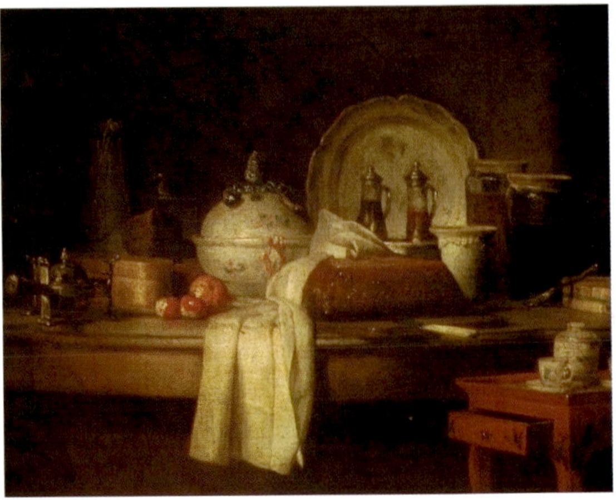

Jean-Baptiste Siméon Chardin, Kitchen Table, *1756. Musée des Beaux-Arts, Carcassonne (France). The light that illuminates Chardin's paintings is always soft and satiny. His compositions are well thought out, always searching for asymmetrical balance, avoiding great tension. It is worth observing the quality of the texture, so naturally and brilliantly applied to the objects.*

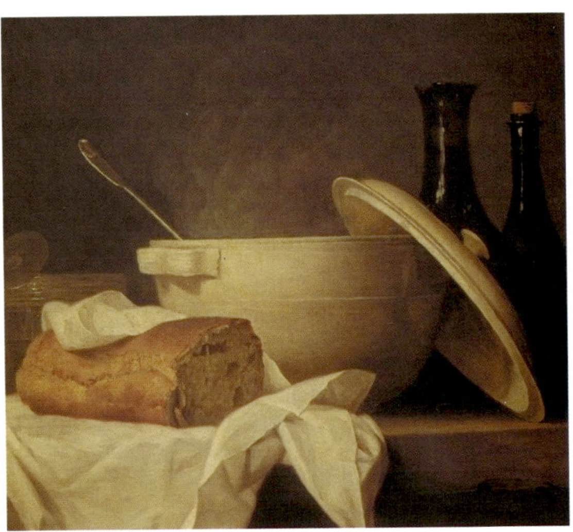

Anne Coster-Vallayer, The White Soup Tureen, *Private collection. The superb work of this French painter, who has been so often compared to Chardin, looks like a symbiosis of the magic of Vermeer and the mysticism of Zurbarán.*

THE NINETEENTH CENTURY

After the French Revolution, a very culturally popular period began, the Enlightenment, which focused its energy on the education of the populace. None of the three artistic styles of the nineteenth century—neoclassicism, romanticism, and realism—gave still life the credit that it deserved. The Academy propagated the idea that still life was a lesser genre, that it was "less cultured" and therefore useless. Regardless of this, artists like Delacroix, Manet, and Fantin-Latour depicted it magnificently in their paintings.

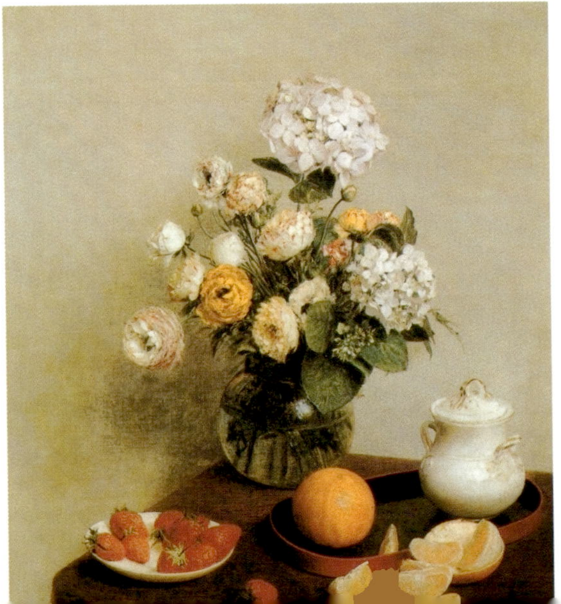

Henri Fantin-Latour, Still Life with Dahlias and Vegetables, *Toledo Museum of Art, Ohio (United States). Fantin-Latour followed the most perfect style of the academicians. The Academy was based on a classical cannon of perfection and beauty. Four years later, the first exhibition of impressionist paintings opened, and a freer style of painting was proposed, more colorful and personal, without canons.*

The impressionist influence

Impressionism, which was born as a reaction to the prevailing academic sentiment, caused a real revolution during its time. Artists, provoked by the advances in photography, felt the need to explore other areas that did not involve the exact representation of reality, which could be captured with a camera. Painting was in need of new grounds. Many artists created work that was not always welcomed openly by the "official" group formed by Degas, Seurat, Signac, Monet, Renoir, and others. They were called the nabis, which included many great artists that worked independently: Toulouse-Lautrec, Cézanne, Van Gogh, and Gauguin among others. The two postimpressionist artists that most frequently painted still lifes were Cézanne and Van Gogh.

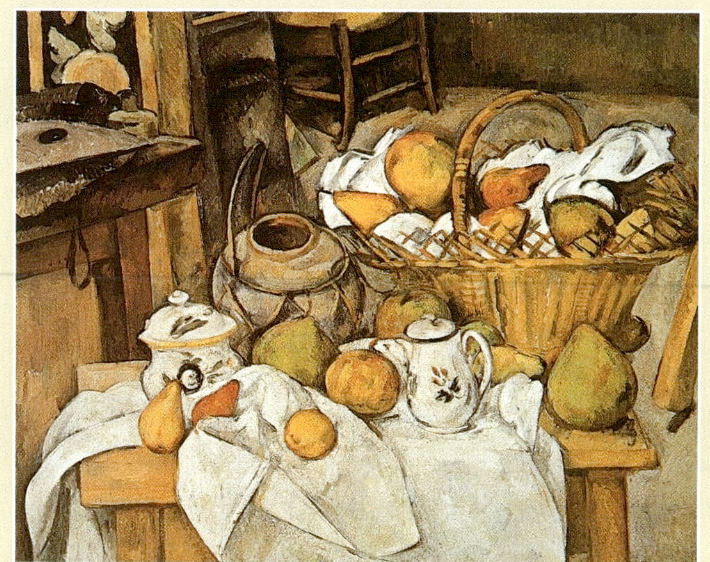

Paul Cézanne, Still Life with Basket, *c. 1890. Musée d'Orsay, Paris (France).*

PAUL CÉZANNE

Cézanne is considered the precursor of cubism because of his free treatment of space and form, his great variety and combination of rhythms, the distributions of planes, the different layers of definition, leaving even some areas unfinished, and the superposition of different plane views captured from different levels. In Cézanne's work, the background and the objects are integrated with harmony through constructive brushstrokes, more resembling a block of paint than a line.

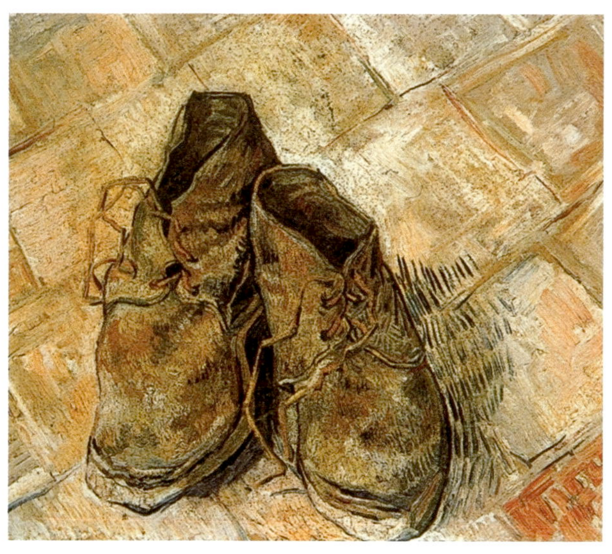

VINCENT VAN GOGH

The peculiar painting style of Van Gogh, with vigorous strokes of very intense colors and a precise and simple drawing style, make him unmistakable. Although he is a contemporary of the impressionist artists, because of the enormous expressive charge of his paintings, he can be considered the father of expressionism. His selection of subjects—personal objects, flowers, vegetables, and so on—always showed an interest in representing things in their most natural state, with the greatest possible emotional charge.

Vincent van Gogh, Boots, *1888. Private collection.*

Still life at the beginning of the twentieth century

Impressionism opened the doors for the investigative development of painting. In a few years, practically in the first third of the century, a phenomenon unique until then erupted, the coexistence of many new styles: fauvism, cubism, futurism, constructivism, neoplasticism, dadaism, surrealism, and many other "isms" that presented themselves as artistic movements with very defined tendencies. The artist was one more piece of the puzzle in the European intellectual mind.

Still life went from being a lesser genre to a major one. It became a popular subject among most artists, especially those who studied the specific language of painting, like color, form, space, and materials, because the theme was in reality nothing more than an excuse to paint. What mattered was not what was painted, but how it was painted.

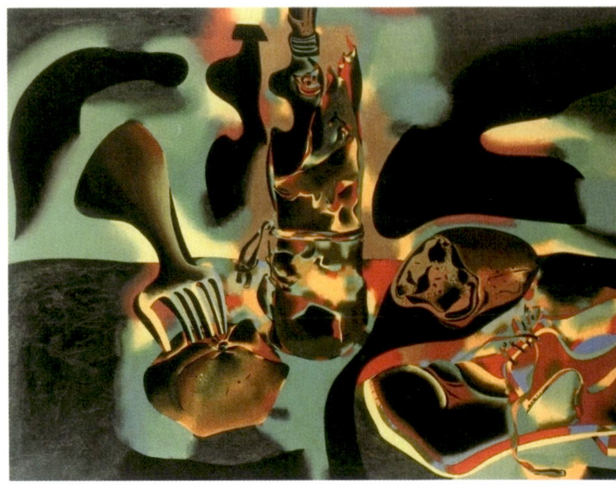

Joan Miró, Still Life with a Shoe, *1937. Museum of Modern Art, New York (United States). Miró developed a very personal and lyrical surrealism. He used still life to represent his passions and desires.* Still Life with a Shoe *is one of the first psychedelic paintings. The forms and colors of reality are modified according to the deepest perception of the artist, which in this case is conditioned by hunger.*

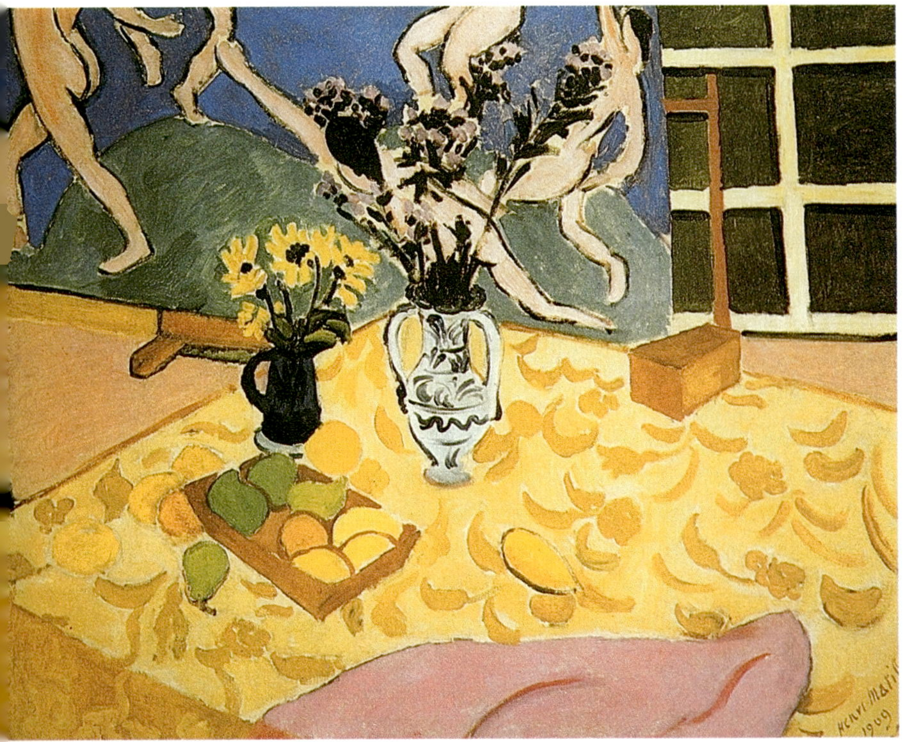

Henri Matisse, Still Life with "The Dance," *c. 1909. The Hermitage Museum, Saint Petersburg (Russia).*

THE FAUVES

The term *fauves,* meaning "wild beasts," was coined by the French critics of the first exhibition of this movement's painters. Fauvist painters pushed the expressive capability of color to the limit. Matisse was one of its most noted representatives. He played with colors in an original and absolutely unorthodox way, taking chances with his compositions by presenting asymmetrical and angled views that were completely flat in favor of chromatic impact.

Cubism and surrealism

Painting has always pursued three-dimensional representation, or depth. Cubism, on the other hand, restored the two-dimensionality of the canvas as a surface for creating art while representing depth with flatness and changing the object's point of view, disregarding the laws of perspective. Still life became the genre par excellence of the cubist movement, so much so that the entire bodies of work of Braque and Juan Gris consisted of still life scenes. Picasso also employed still life in his cubist paintings, although he did not limit himself to them but ventured into other genres with the suggestive and powerful landscape of Horta de Sant Joan. Surrealist painters considered art an ideal channel to represent the experiences that take place in the subconscious. Their goal was to create tension in the observer by depicting deformation, ambiguity, and out-of-context themes. Still life, because of its dramatic nature, lent itself to the creation of new virtual realities extracted from a world of dreams.

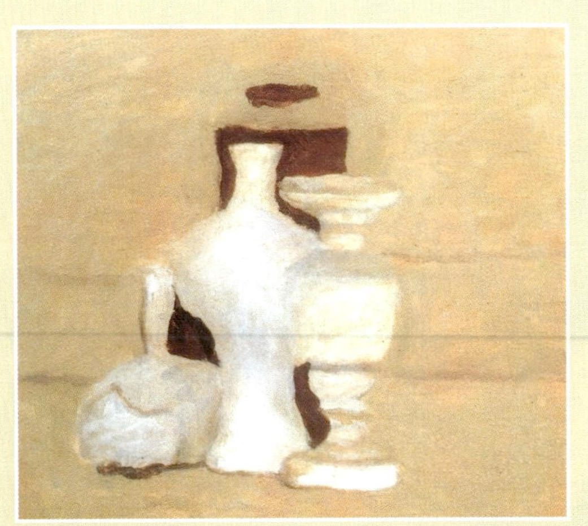

Giorgio Morandi, Still Life, *1963. Private collection.*

GIORGIO MORANDI
After World War II and up to the middle of the twentieth century, the "isms" continued to lose power and people began to value the personal work of the artist in an environment of greater culture. Giorgio Morandi deserves special attention. For many years, he limited himself to painting bottles and jars on a table. His work, of great sensitivity and beauty, always depicted elements with a low level of tension. Colors are delicate, and sometimes a simple nuance sets one bottle apart from the next. His soft and delicate brushstrokes express the vulnerability of the human being.

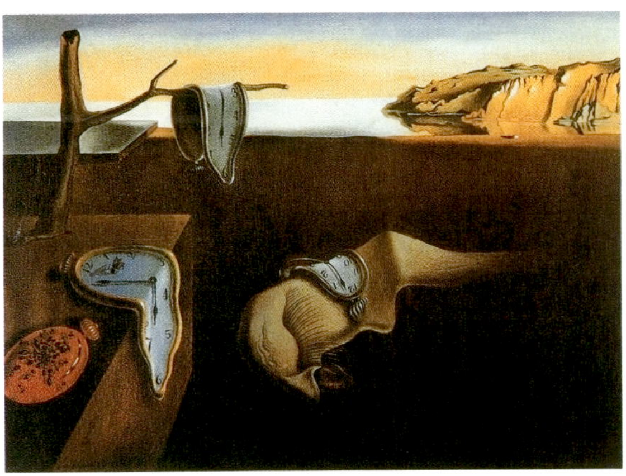

Salvador Dalí, The Persistence of Memory, *1931. Museum of Modern Art, New York (United States). Dalí created scenes of great tension by incorporating numerous symbolic elements that came from his dreams and from his deepest secret desires. The famous painting with melting clocks speaks of the theory of relativity of time and energy, which are neither created nor destroyed but transformed.*

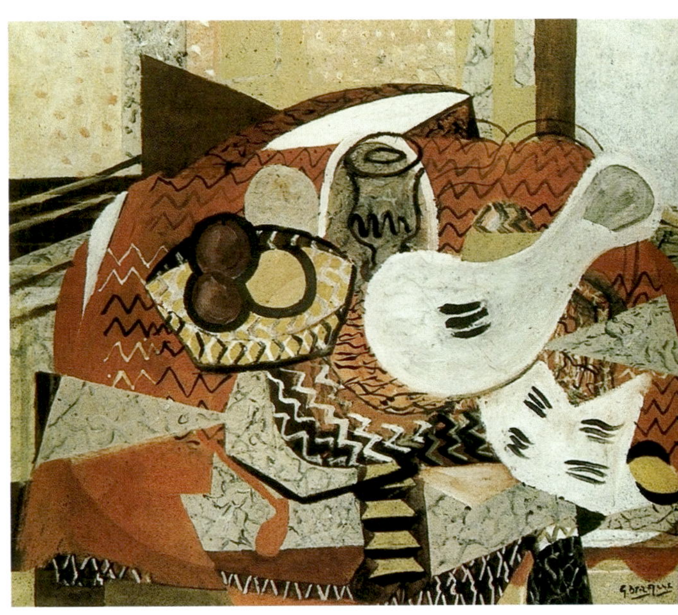

Georges Braque, Still Life with Red Tablecloth, *c. 1936. Private collection. Cubism broke away from the painter's submission to the model, opening the potential for the manipulation of the still life's space and forms at will.*

Contemporary still life paintings

Contemporary still lifes as a part of painting are inscribed on the second half of the twentieth century. They differ from those of previous decades because other procedures and nonpictorial techniques are incorporated. Painting is considered one more medium among all those that can be used by an artist, including photography, the printing press, video, and in the last two decades of the twentieth century, electronic and computer resources.

Following the abstraction and lack of formality of the fifties, pop art made its appearance at the hands of Andy Warhol and Tom Wesselmann, among many other American and European artists. Pop art opened a new door through which many artists entered. Behind a superficial aesthetic appearance, there is a strong hidden connection of the artist with his or her cultural time and immediate environment. Pop art images correlate with what is happening in the streets; that is why the paintings look like publicity, because they often resort to graphic design, industrial and advertisement images.

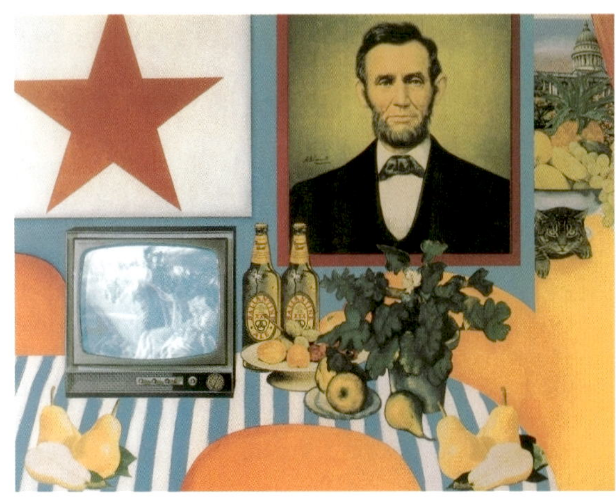

Tom Wesselman, Still Life, *1963. Private collection. If Chardin painted a French breakfast scene of the eighteenth century, Wesselman painted an American one of the twentieth century. There does not exist such a great conceptual difference. For an American, this would represent the purest form of realistic still life of the sixties.*

Miquel Barceló, Soup with Red Plate, *1992. Private collection. Barceló's work of the nineties updates the classic still life with food found in the baroque. Barceló's style is very casual, and he incorporates formal elements of wild and primitive feeling. His paintings show great interest for the subject matter, which is resolved with the use of relief and the incorporation of different textures like soil, cardboard paper, and so on.*

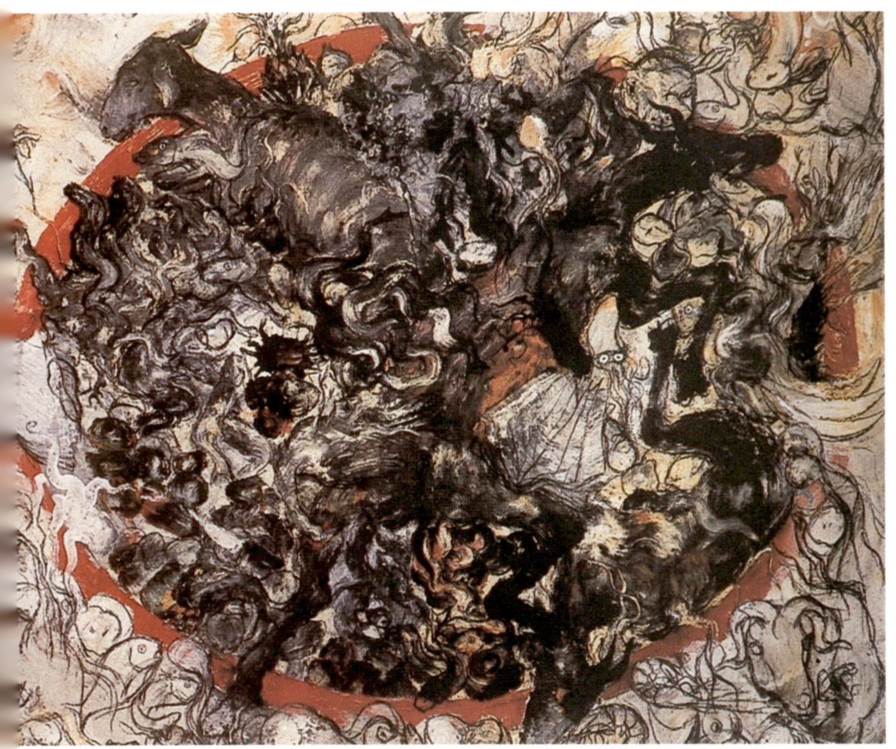

THE VALUE OF OBJECTS
Some contemporary artists have confronted still life through the material aspect of objects. Antoni Tàpies, Anselm Kiefer, and Miquel Barceló, among others, have resorted to the incorporation of objects (painting them or gluing them directly onto the surface) to create paintings that require specific references of cultural symbolism to be able to connect strongly with the observer.

The subject matter

When an artist expresses feelings and emotions through an image, he or she not only achieves this with the way the work is executed but also through the meaning of the image. With still life paintings, the way a theme is treated is as important as the theme itself. Each element evokes a different emotion because of the significance that the object has for the artist and for the person who views the work.

The elements of a painting are always connected to the author; they are born from his or her expressive intention. Those elements may sometimes be expressed very clearly. Most frequently, though, that is not the case because painting constitutes an impulse or an irrational need to express oneself through color, shape, and brushstrokes. . . . In any case, the selection of the subject to be represented is an expressive decision that responds to a personal intention. The knowledge of those expressive contents is acquired as the artist matures in his or her own creative process. The selection of a theme is an important decision because it is closely connected to countless emotions: aesthetic, cultural, ideological, psychological, sociological, biographical, and so on.

The selection of a theme is an expressive decision that responds, in a lesser or greater degree, to a conscious personal intention

There are two general important criteria for the selection of the subject. It can be ideal for its significance, as would be the case of Van Gogh's imagery, which acts as a graphic documentary of a visual autobiography. It can instead be chosen for its physical characteristics—color, form, texture, rhythm, and so on. This is the reason why Cézanne chose apples and baskets. Cubist artists selected musical instruments, and Esther Olivé de Puig chose a cabbage and a few eggplants cut in half, as shown in the picture below. These two factors normally coincide in the same theme, although the interest of the painter may focus more on one than on the other. This chapter will approach the model from both perspectives and will present a few practical points.

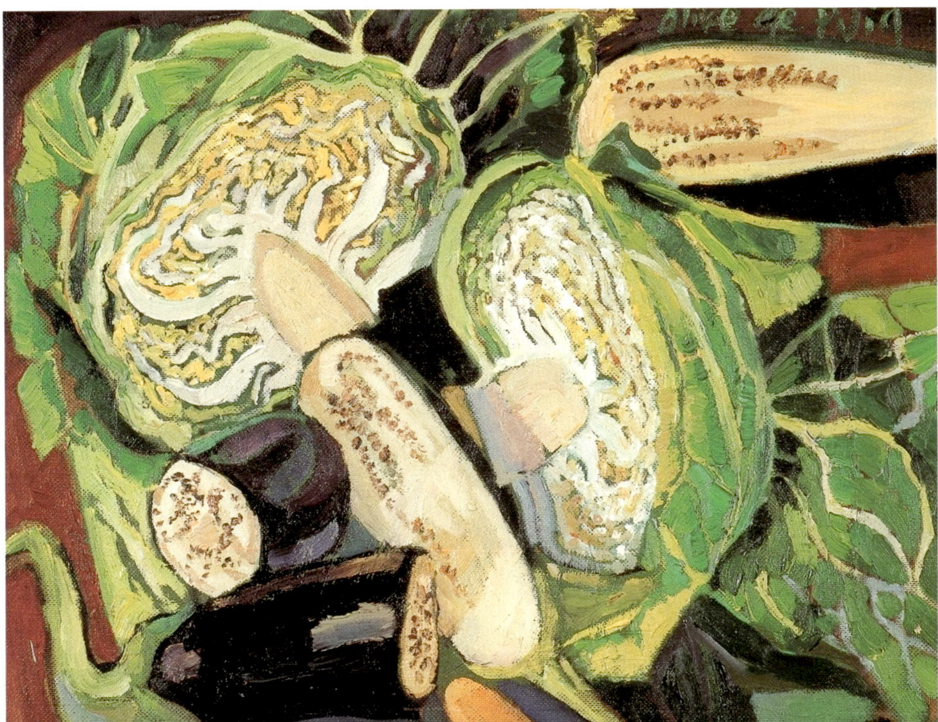

Esther Olivé de Puig, Cabbage and Eggplants, *1996. Private collection. The interest of Olivé de Puig for a still life whose expressive strength focuses on its two-dimensionality and a play of sinuous lines and folds led her to choose the inside of a cabbage and some eggplants.*

The most recurrent themes

If we take into account that a still life is the representation of objects that are not very large in size placed against a background, we can think of many items that fit that requirement. However, some have been used over and over again throughout the history of painting. They include

Containers: ceramic, metal, glass . . .
Tools: working tools, brushes, kitchen, writing . . .
Personal items: watches, jewelry, clothing, boxes, mementos . . .
Printed material: books, maps, diaries, prints . . .
Food: fruit, vegetables, animals, bread, beverages . . .
Flowers
Indoor objects: furniture, fireplaces, mirrors, lamps, other paintings . . .
Allegorical items: *vanitas,* the five senses, professions . . .

Usually, these subjects are intertwined so that a still life with flowers always has a vase. In an allegorical mention of the five senses, we will find books (eyes), food (taste), flowers (smell), musical instruments (hearing), or playing cards (touch). However, there is always a leading object, a more significant theme, that gives meaning to the composition.

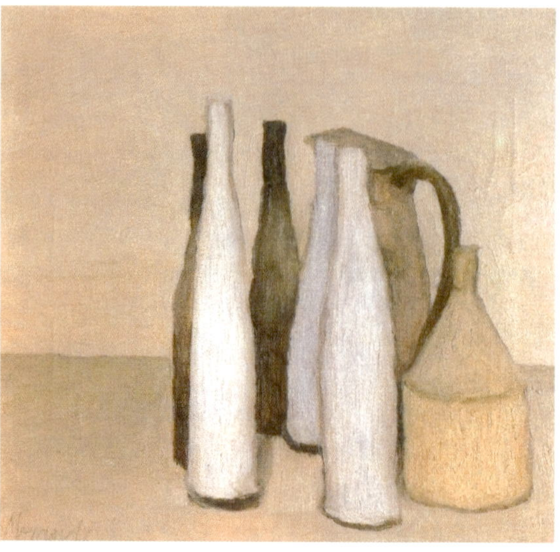

Giorgio Morandi, Still Life, *1951. Calleria Comunale d'Arte Moderno, Bologna (Italy). Painting containers is the most common theme. Bottles are significant because they express fragility and produce subtle tones of light and transparencies. Ceramic containers are good for chiaroscuro, metal gadgets for reflection, and so on. Morandi was able to create a painting of great personality from a group of simple bottles and containers.*

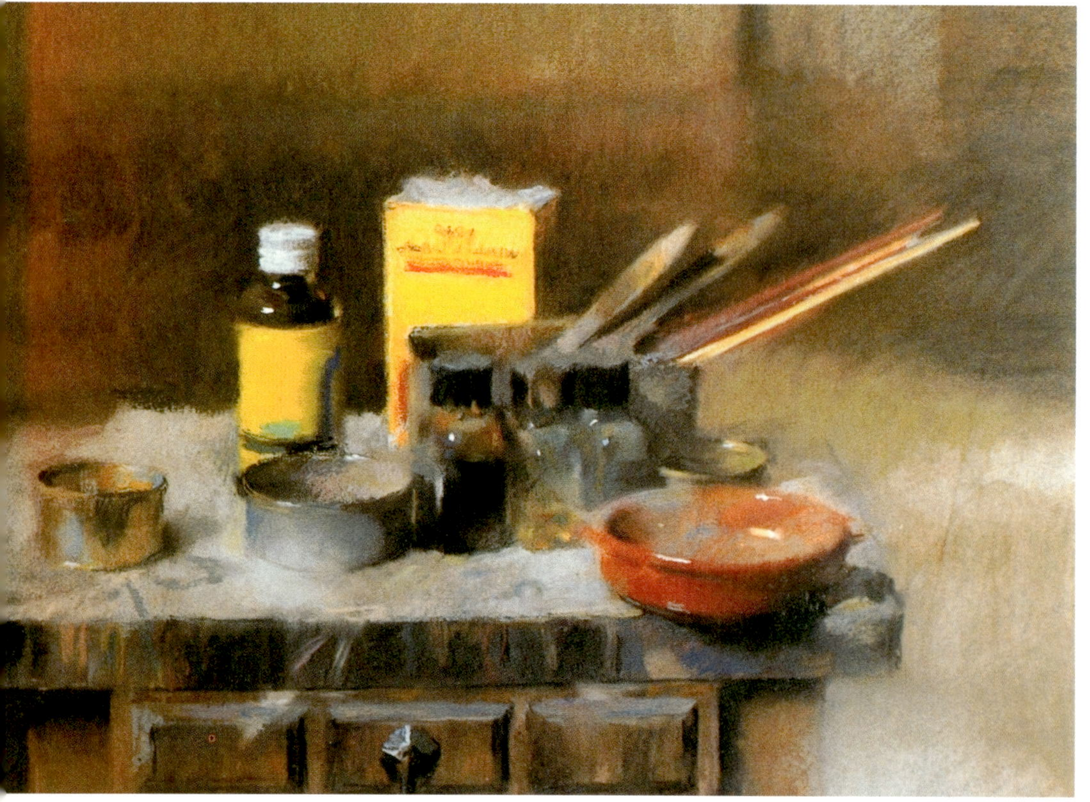

Felipe Santamans, Still Life, *1950. Private collection. Some objects carry the emotional charge of the person who uses them. They offer the natural presence required by still life to avoid falling into an artificial representation with a simple decorative meaning. The artist's own tools can be a perfect model to get started.*

Still life with food

Food has been present in still life paintings from their inception. The phrase still life makes reference to inanimate objects, like scenes with food and beverages. The most common elements are fruit, vegetables, game, wine, and water but also baked goods, breads, soups, cheeses, and sweets (something very common in eighteenth century still life paintings). Still life with food always conveys the feeling of immediacy. Contrary to a piece of furniture or jewelry, food must be eaten. Therefore, it depicts a moment in the present and invites the viewer to enjoy or to reflect about things that expire and things that are forever.

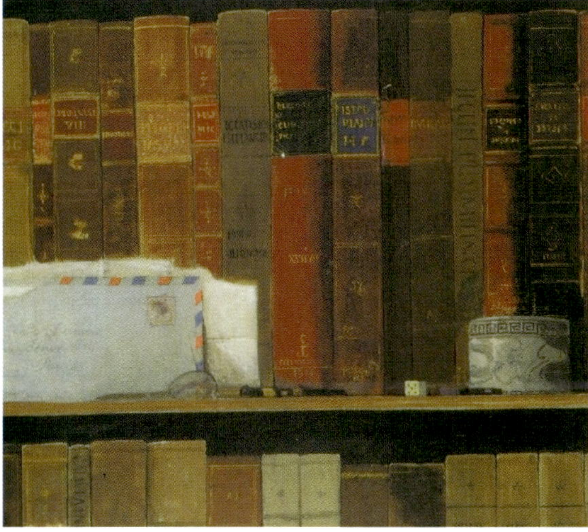

Luis Marsans, Library, *1985.*
Private collection, Paris (France).
Books symbolize culture and thinking, and their incursion into still life happened at that level of significance. Later, though, other artists like Luis Marsans and Miquel Barceló painted books for their physical appearance.

Esther Olivé de Puig, Clothes on a Hanger, *1996.*
Private collection.
The idea of representing pieces of clothing on a hanger gives the painting a natural and spontaneous feeling that makes establishing a relationship between the observer and the image easier.

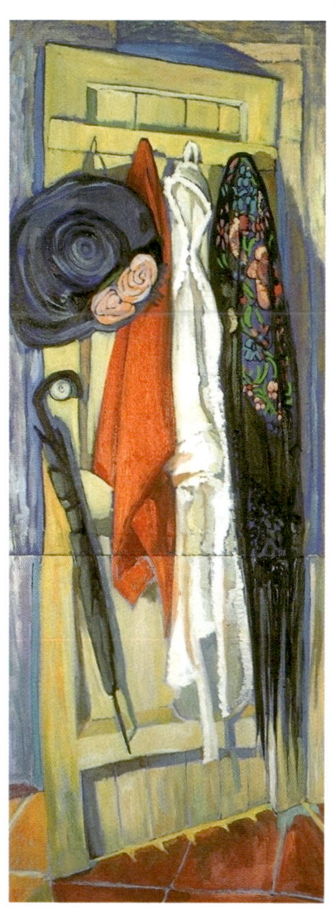

PERSONAL ITEMS

We can consider personal items a variable or an extension of tools because they often consist of objects that are used, like clothing, jewelry, fountain pens, watches, pipes, and so on. However, they have an intimate aspect—a feeling of personal and exclusive relationship is established between the person and the object. Clothing is something very personal; it has been chosen and used by somebody. That is why somehow it defines the person who wears it.

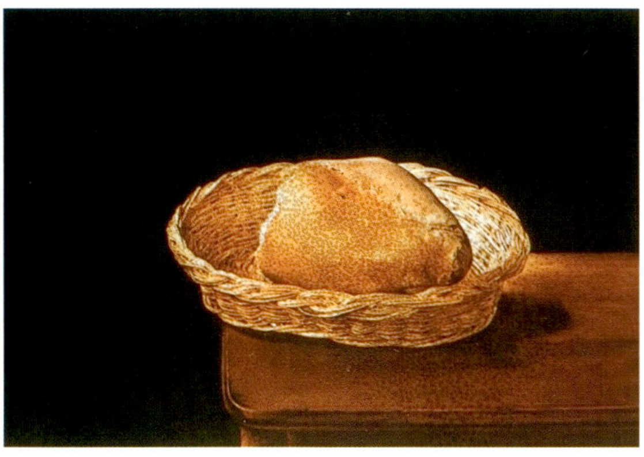

Salvador Dalí, Bread Basket, *1945.*
Teatre Museum Dalí, Figueres (Spain).
This painting by Dalí is a tribute to the first still life paintings with food by Spanish baroque artists (Zurbarán and Sánchez Cotán) who treated this theme with great elegance and a spirit of austerity that sets them apart.

Furniture in painting

A still life painting of furniture does not exclude the presence of other elements. Typically, the furniture is there to hold other objects, like Van Gogh's pipe on his chair, for example. However, furniture not always acts only as a support, but it plays an important role; that is, it is a vital element with its own significance. In *Red Studio* by Matisse, there is a perfect integration of objects and furniture and paintings. This type of model for still life scenes pursues a global and integral image of still life, to capture the scene, the place, not so much the details. Background and figure are one and the same: a painting.

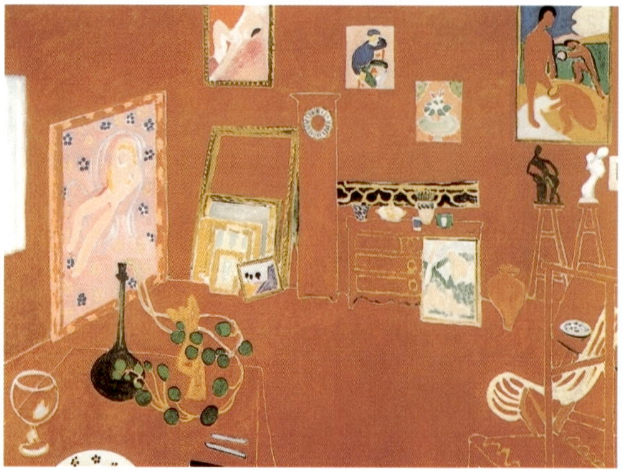

Henri Matisse, Red Studio, *1911. Guggenheim Museum, New York (United States).*

Flowers

Flowers offer the possibility of brushstroke freedom and color freedom because they do not require excessive formal attention. On the contrary, they are very forgiving of errors, disproportion, changes, experimentation, and so on. Also, the great variety of forms and colors present in this type of element allow the artist to create as many different compositions as desired without repetition. Paintings with flowers are very decorative. In fact, Van Gogh painted them to hang in his house and to enlighten his torturous life with their view.

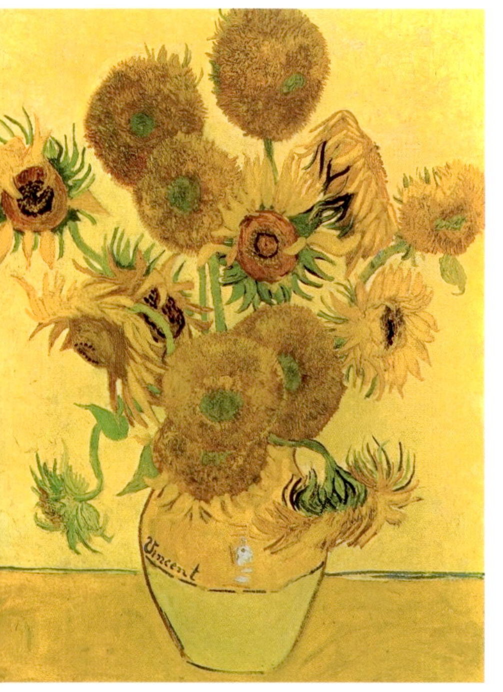

Vincent van Gogh, Vase with Sunflowers, *1888. National Gallery, London (United Kingdom). Van Gogh painted many flowers because to him flowers were a gift from nature that generously gave themselves for the shear pleasure of our eyes.*

VANITAS

Of all the allegorical themes, the one that is most commonly painted is the still life with a skull. They are called *vanitas* for the reference they make to the text in the book of Ecclesiastes: vanity of vanities. The skull confronts the spectator with his or her own condition, as a mirror. It is also a reminder of the uncertainty of the future and of sudden death, inviting the viewer to resolve whatever pending matters he or she now has without leaving them for later. The skull materializes the anguish in the face of the unknown, the unseen. This message, hard but real, has motivated a great many artists to paint *vanitas*.

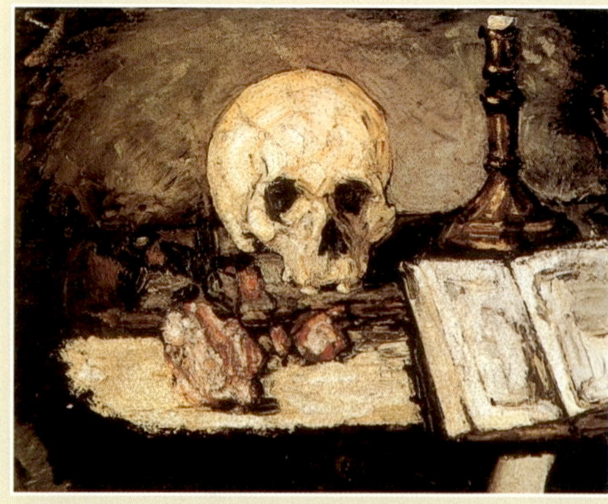

Paul Cézanne, Skull and Candelabra, *1865-1867. Private collection.*

The planning

One of the main characteristics of the baroque period is the theatricality. Baroque paintings resemble scenes of a movie or moments in a theatrical representation frozen in time. For this reason, still life found in this movement the perfect ground for expansion and development. Because a still life scene is put together, designed, and organized as if it were a theater piece, it has a stage created by the painter.

Organizing a still life forces the artist to make a series of decisions: Should it have many or few elements? Where should they be placed, on what support, at what height? What lighting environment do I want to create? Natural, artificial, soft, contrasting? How important should the background be; should it be ambiguous or defined? Do I want to create several planes or treat it all as one? All these questions are crucial since they arise at that particular time, not when the first brushstrokes are applied. When the still life is in the planning stages, it is somehow as if the artist has already begun to paint.

SIMPLICITY AND POETRY

For a still life painting, like the one created by Esther Olivé de Puig, which takes full advantage of space and light, it is necessary to have a very simple, austere arrangement with very few elements—an apple in this case—against a special background that almost becomes the scene's sole protagonist. Here, the curtain in the background becomes a key element for the soft light and color that it generates and because of the soft tension of its folds.

Esther Olivé de Puig, Composition with Angles, *1996. Private collection.*

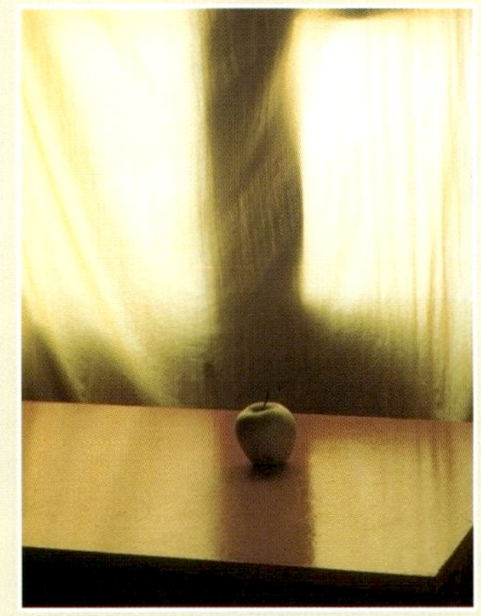

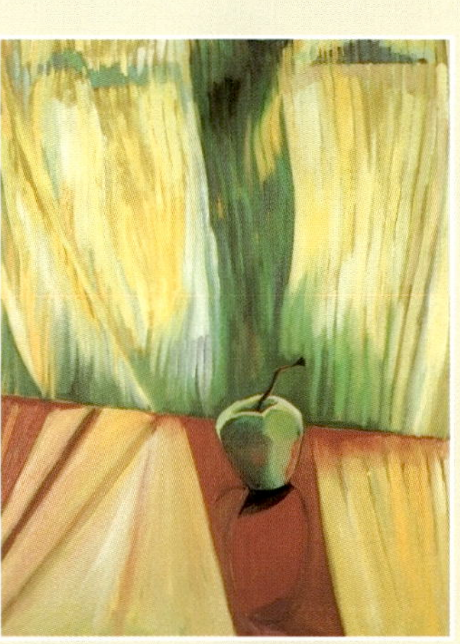

DYNAMISM AND EXPRESSION

The same artist and the same warm lighting, but in this case Esther Olivé de Puig has created a completely different arrangement. She has chosen more objects of various textures and forms, she has even twisted and extended them in some cases. For a dynamic result like the one this artist was looking for, it was necessary to create a small compositional chaos, even exaggerating colors and deforming objects, very much in line with the magnificent still life paintings of the fauvists.

Esther Olivé de Puig, Dynamic Composition, *1996. Private collection.*

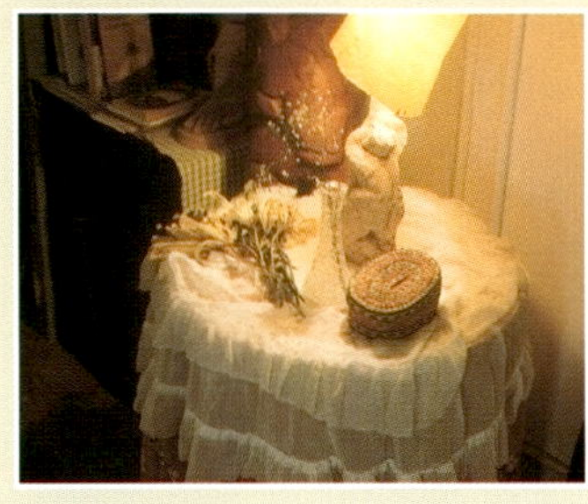

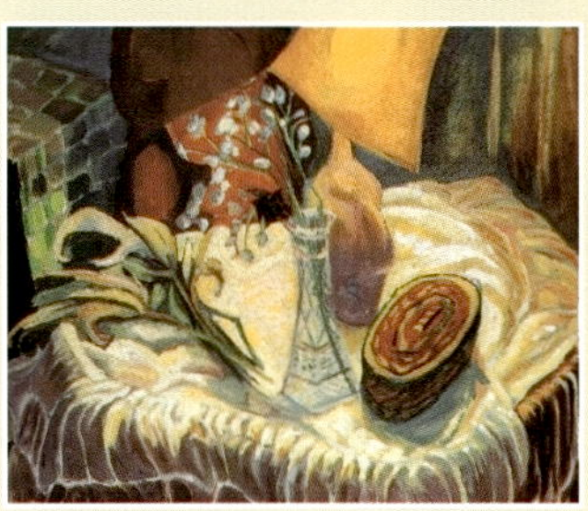

REAL MODELS AND VIRTUAL MODELS

Working with a real model is as legitimate as is working with more intimate, personal views that are born in the artist's imagination.

Light

Light is what defines the image. Technically, without light there is no visual perception. Therefore, we must learn to work with it to be able to create an image that will be seen by the observer. That image is born at the moment the arrangement of the still life begins. All of the artistic elements of the scene (form, color, space, texture . . .) will depend on the light that illuminates them. Furthermore, light creates the mood of the painting and provokes a psychological state of mind in the viewer—excitement, reflection, calm, mystery. All of these principles are applied in cinematography and theater. That is why when we illuminate an arrangement, we are acting the same way a lighting technician would in a play, looking for the appropriate intensity and direction to express the aesthetics of the moment.

Natural light

Natural light does not change the colors very much, it only creates a bluish tone in the shadows. From the beginnings of impressionism, painters have exploited this effect by adding blue to the shaded areas. If natural light is not direct, it will be soft and will create soft shadows that are rich in nuances. If the light is direct, it will be very harsh, without shape, and will create great contrast. The only inconvenience of this type of light is that it changes according to the time of day and weather conditions.

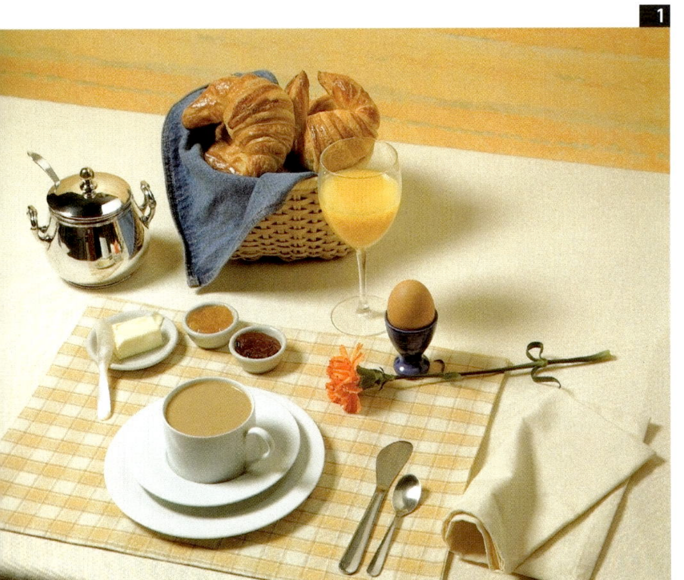

1. Natural indirect light
Natural light creates soft outlines, without harshness or reflections, with a very natural color shade and cool shadows. The mood is very relaxing and fresh, without tension in light or color.

2. Natural direct light
When sunlight illuminates the objects directly, the contrasts are harsh, the shadows reinforce depth and space, and the colors change as a result of excessive light and shadow contrasts. They lose the rich quality of textures, but they gain in expressiveness and energy without being overly dramatic.

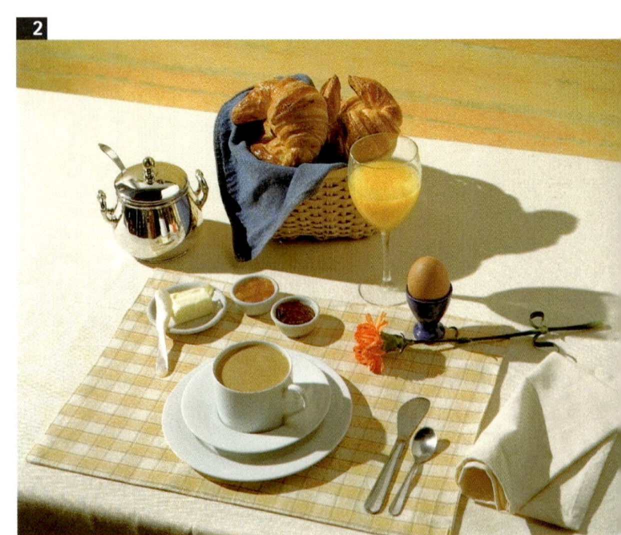

FACTORS THAT AFFECT LIGHTING
These are things to keep in mind when lighting a scene:

- type of light: natural or artificial;
- the intensity: semidarkness, soft, medium, strong, or full;
- the quality: harsh, normal, diffused;
- the direction: from the side, from the sky, against the light, heavy, or ambient;
- the purpose: directed (to a single point of the scene or to several), partial (one or more illuminated areas), or total (the entire scene).

3. Frontal artificial light

Frontal light eliminates the shadows, reducing the feeling of depth. Here, the color, not the chiaroscuro, defines the forms. That is why many impressionist painters, like Cézanne and Van Gogh, used it in their still life paintings.

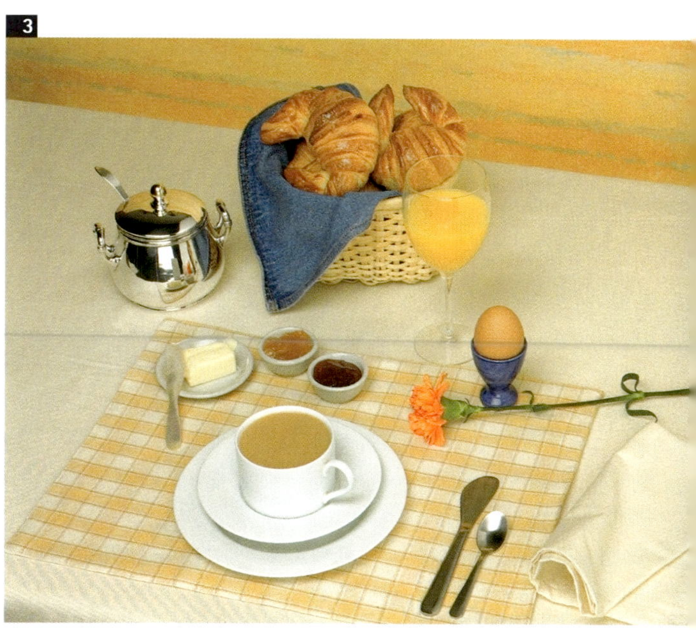

4. Lateral artificial light

This is the classic type of lighting for still life, the one used by baroque painters. If the background is too dark, there is a morbid feeling to it, where forms seem to appear from nowhere and a perception of very strong light is created due to the effect of contrast. Some light sources add a tinted color that is very expressive to the objects, for example, candles and oil lamps that painters used until the invention of the electric light.

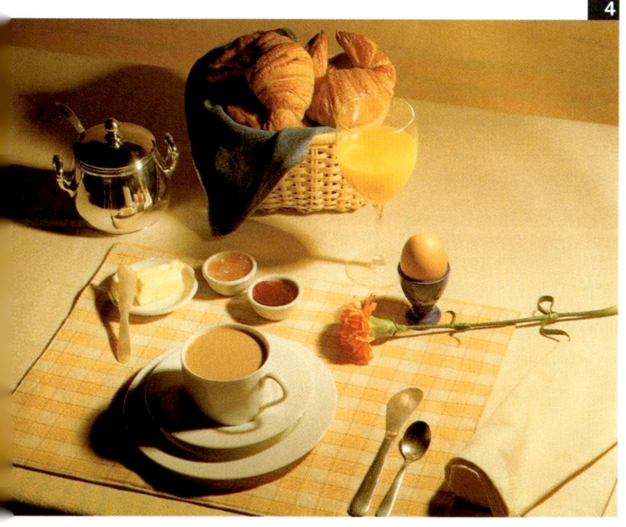

EFFECTS AND COMBINATIONS

The results will be very different if we resort to lateral lighting (very baroque), frontal (very impressionist), emphatic—from below—(very Goya-like and expressionist), or backlit –from behind the model—(in the style of Bonnard and other Impressionists). Obviously, we can mix lighting from several directions. The most common is to combine a source that comes from the side with any one of the other types, especially from the sky—from above—creating a very natural and general effect while reinforcing the feeling of volume.

Artificial lighting

Artificial lighting is the most commonly used type for still life paintings because they have indoor themes. It can come from different sources: incandescent, halogen, fluorescent, combustion (candles, gas, oil . . .). The sources all have many variables that modify the object's color and effect, making the outlines and details softer or harsher. Experimenting with different types of light is very interesting, even combining them to take full advantage of their possibilities.

The direction of light

Natural light can be modified with filters (curtains, screens . . .), but it cannot change its position or be brought closer to the model. This presents a disadvantage if compared with artificial light, which can always be directed and moved at will. If we move the source of light closer to the model, we will be able to apply strong chiaroscuro with harsh shadows and very bright reflections on shiny objects. On the other hand, if the source is moved farther away, the objects will present gradations and they will be richer in shading and textures, with no harsh contrasts.

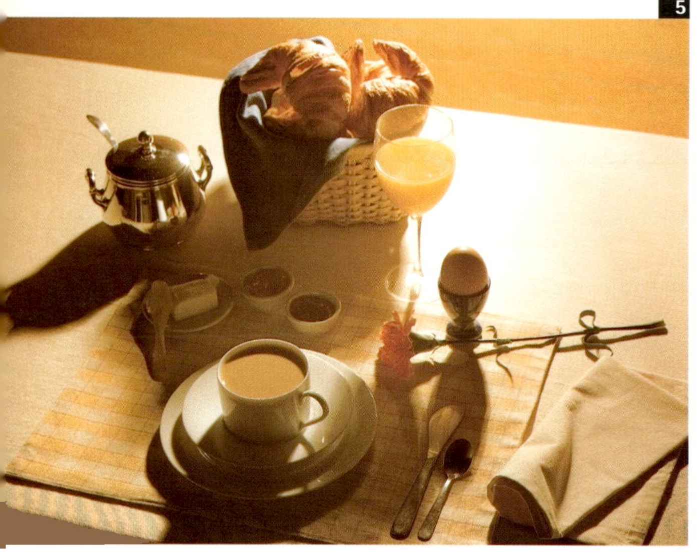

5

Intensity and quality

Intensity and quality are factors that depend on the number of light sources that are used, their electrical output, and their proximity to the objects. Filters and screens can be placed in between (a simple sheet of paper can work as a diffusing surface) to produce softer light and to avoid glare or to illuminate the grouping with ambient lighting. If the light source is natural, fabric, used as a curtain or as a screen, can be used to achieve this effect.

5. Backlight

The volume and the color of objects placed against the light are hard to see. This type of effect is used to exaggerate contrasts because it mimics the light at sunrise and sunset. It is ideal, used in conjunction with side lighting, when painting glass because the light that it creates, even on the shadows, increases the feeling of transparency.

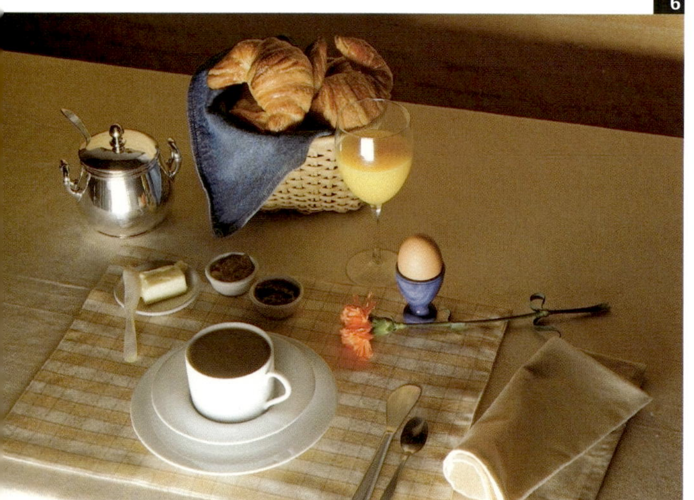

6

6. Emphatic Light

This type of light is the most dramatic of all because the position of the source is completely forced, making it obvious that it is not the result of a natural effect. Because this kind of lighting deforms the objects excessively, it should be used in combination with side lighting, some type of ambient source, for example fluorescent, which softens the shadows.

7. Spotlight

When the source is specifically directed toward one area, the objects in that area receive more light than the rest. This can be done from outside the scene, with a floodlight, or from within, integrating the light source—a lamp or a candle—in the picture. This creates a magical atmosphere.

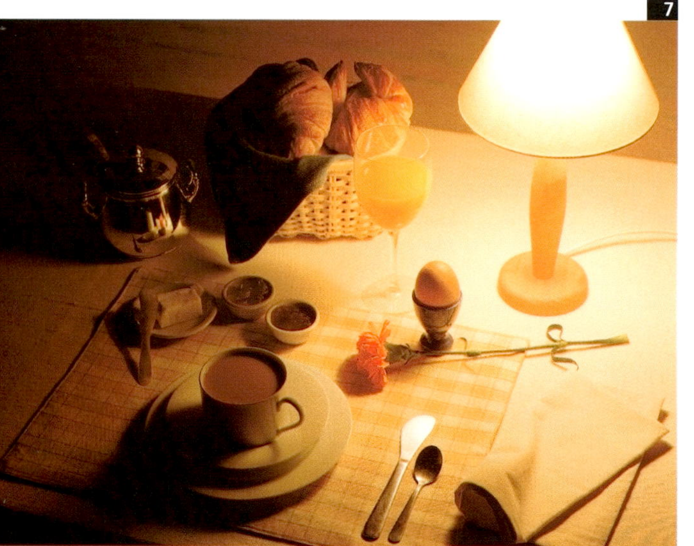

7

THE OBJECTIVE
In terms of the objective, we must consider whether we want to illuminate the entire area or to leave some parts in shadow. If the intention is to highlight a particular object, floodlights or spotlighting can be used, like candles or lamps, incorporating them as part of the still life composition to create a focus of greatest contrast or an especially illuminated area. This approach is used to create an intimate and private feeling.

The language

The same way we learn grammar, vocabulary, and language syntax if we want to communicate with words, we must also learn and understand the use of creative language—form, color, space, texture, and techniques—if we wish to convey precisely that which moves us to paint.

Painting is an act of communication. As such, it involves a communicator, a message, a channel, and a receiver. The communicator is clearly the artist, the channel is the canvas, the receiver the spectator, and the message is the content of the painting. It is similar to any other type of language. In a sentimental poem, for example, the words, the tone, and the rhythm would be the signifier, the communicator, while the sentiment would be the true meaning or content.

Visual language is made of elements that gain significance in accordance with the composition. In the same way as language, where words acquire meaning in a sentence and sentences in a text, visual language consists of an alphabet and syntax. The alphabet of painting is the color, form, space, texture, and techniques used. The first three elements (color, form, and space) are related to the image and the last two (texture and technique) to the physical aspect of the painting. The syntax is composed of those basic elements of the painting. If we compare it again with the spoken language, color, form, and space would be the words, the expressions or sentences. The technique and texture would be the tone of voice, the speed, and the emotional charge of the person speaking those words. To convey the proper message, choosing the words is as important as knowing how to use them.

◆

The first three elements (color, form, and space) are related to the image and the last two (texture and technique) to the physical aspect of the painting.

◆

In this chapter, we will introduce the reader to the world of color, form, and space, to understand how they work, building up the image on the canvas. In the next chapter (the media), we will discover the techniques and textures.

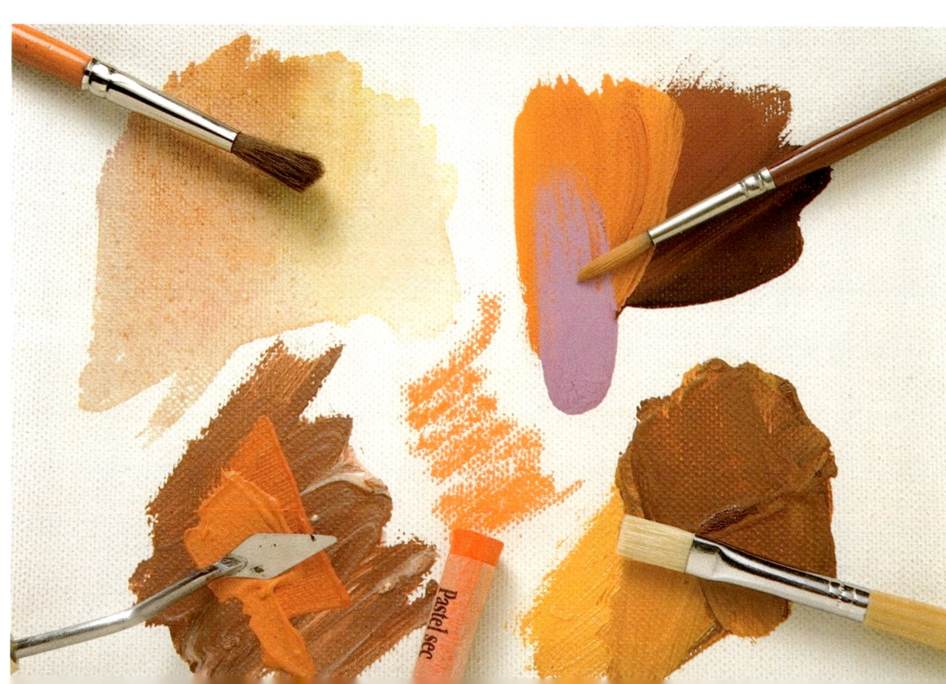

The same way we look for the appropriate words for each act of spoken communication, we must also find the proper color, line, and tool to express ourselves artistically.

Basic principles of color

Let us review the composition of the color wheel. Of all the pigments that are used for painting, there are three basic ones from which the rest originate. They are called primary colors: yellow, red, and blue. By mixing these three colors, we get the secondary colors: orange, violet, and green. Mixing one primary color with a secondary will produce the tertiary colors: blue-green, yellow-orange, and so on. You can continue changing the tone of each color—that is, the tint—to expand the color wheel. You can also create new colors by adding white or black, changing its value, which consists of making a color lighter or darker.

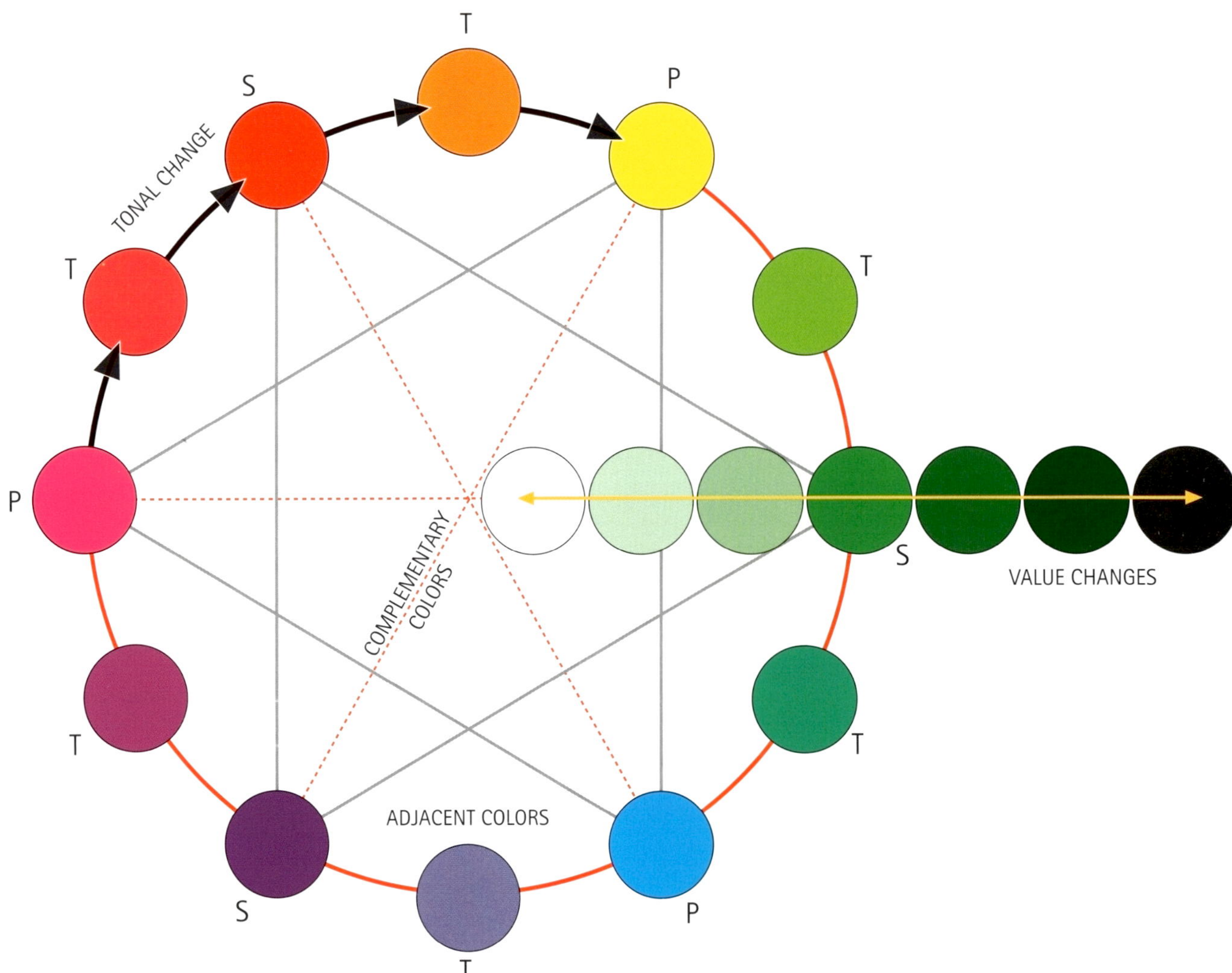

COMPLEMENTARY AND ADJACENT COLORS
There are two types of relationships between colors in the color wheel: complementary and adjacent. Two colors are complementary when they are located opposite each other in the circle—green and red, blue and orange, yellow and violet. Adjacent colors are those found next to each other—red and orange, yellow and green, and so on. These two relationships are the foundation for mixing colors; that is, they tell us how to change the color hue, making it darker or grayer.

How to obtain the desired color

A particular color is defined by three aspects that define it: tone or hue, saturation, and value.

• Tone is the quality of the color. It defines the color's position in the color wheel: green, blue, violet, yellow, and so on. Changing the tone or hue describes the direction in which the color goes in the wheel, making it bluer, redder, more orange. . . .

• Saturation describes the intensity of the color. A saturated color does not have any presence whatsoever of either its complement or black. It is a pure color. On the other hand, when the chromatic intensity is reduced, we say that the resulting color is neutral. A neutral color is a passive color that has a grayer tone, which is created by mixing a color with its complement.

• Value defines the degree of luminosity. White is added to make a color lighter without changing its tone, and black, or its complement, to make it darker. We recommend darkening some colors that are naturally very luminous, like yellow and orange, with earth tones, otherwise they will lose intensity or become too gray and look muddy.

STILL LIFE WITH DANCE *BY MATISSE*

Since each color has a particular tone, level of saturation, and value, we will be able to create any color by adjusting those three aspects on the palette. Let us see how Matisse created some colors in his *Still Life with Dance.*

This is a salmonlike pink, therefore it looks slightly orange. It is made lighter by mixing vermilion or carmine red with white and then adding a little bit of yellow.

This is a neutral green (grayish). To create it, the color has been mixed with its complement (red) and a small amount of white to lighten it.

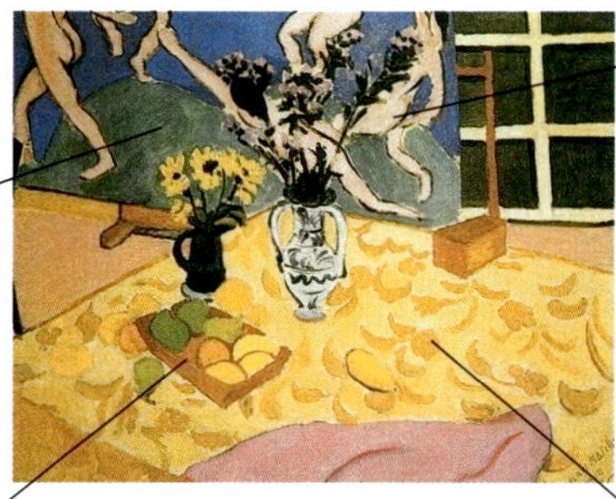

This orange has been darkened with raw umber. The earth tones include the dark oranges, some redder, others more yellow. They can be used to darken warm tones without making them gray.

Orange has been neutralized with blue to produce this brown tone, and then a little bit of black has been added to darken it.

DARKENING AND NEUTRALIZING

Notice that when a color is neutralized, it always turns darker. White is used to make it lighter, whether by adding it to the color or by diluting it to let the white of the background show through.

Adding black to a color makes it darker. Black neutralizes it because black contains that same color plus its complement. However, this is done the quick way, and the resulting colors are always similar.

If we darken a red with black, we will always get the darkest red, but the same maroons will be obtained in the process. If, on the other hand, we choose to darken the red with green, we will get similar results but the intermediate maroons will be more brown (if the green has a yellow tint) or violet (if more blue). The latter approach produces richer hues.

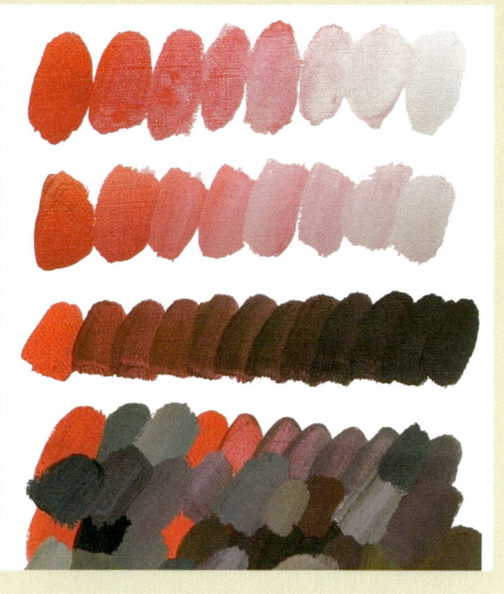

Color harmony for still life

In one of the letters that the poet Rilke wrote to his wife in 1907 about Cézanne's work, there was a very graphic description of what harmony is.

"(. . .) As I have already written about, everything is reduced to a relationship between colors; one is contained when compared to the other, or highlighted before the other, or asserts itself. (. . .) In this swaying movement of a thousand mutual influences, the painting vibrates, elevates itself, falls on itself, and no part of it is still." (October 22, 1907.)

The concept of harmony is as applicable to color as it is to music, to shapes, or to flavors. To harmonize is to organize what is in disarray, to create a unity in variety, to plan a structure that unites diversity. As instruments in a symphony, which intervene at a particular moment, some for the length of the piece, others for parts of it, that is the way colors work in a painting.

Next we will see the harmonious structures that have been most frequently used in the history of painting.

HARMONIOUS MONOCHROMATIC SCHEME AND DOMINANT TONE
Choose a single base color, and all the rest of the colors are generated from it. If only one color is used, it is called a monochromatic harmonious scheme. In this case, black and white can be used, if desired, to darken or lighten the color, because they are neutral. If other colors are introduced, the range is said to be of a dominant color. In this case, the chosen base color is mixed with others to change its hue as long as the personality of the chosen color is maintained. For example, to harmonize a blue, many types of blues can be used (cyan, Prussian, cobalt, ultramarine . . .), also blue-greens (incorporating yellows), and violet-blues (with reds). Gray-blues can be created as well by mixing blue and orange or earth tones (not too much) and black or white. Examples of the use of very light dominant colors are Picasso's blue and pink periods.

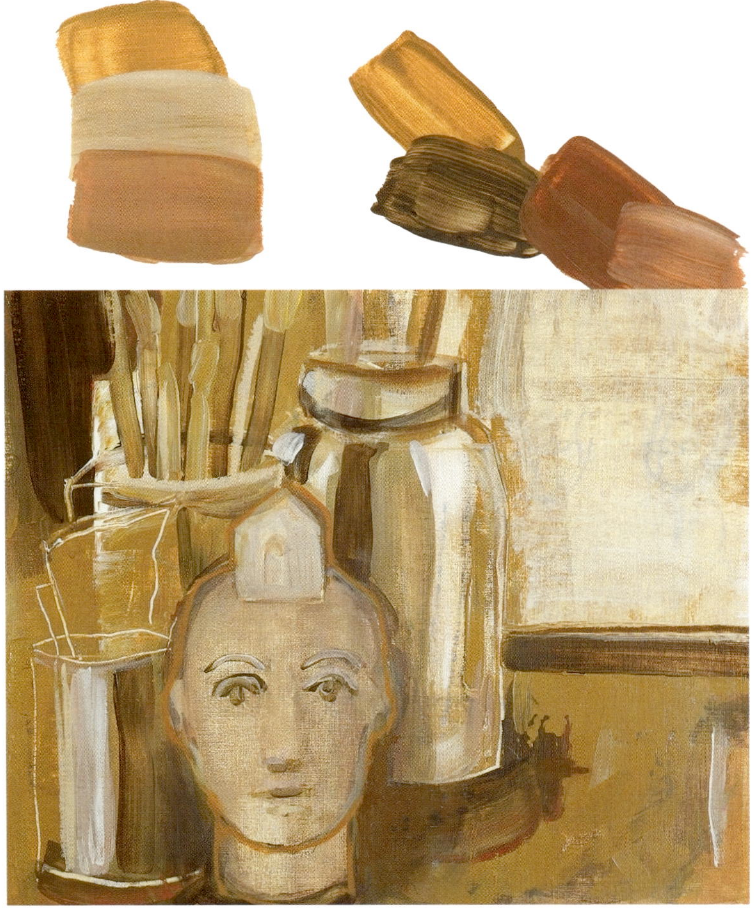

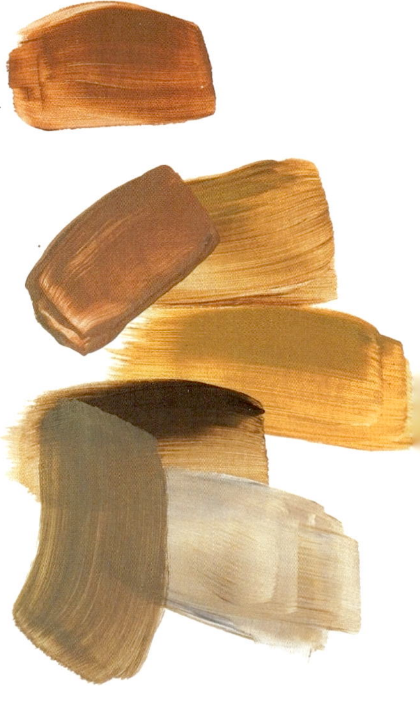

A harmonious scheme of earth tones.

Warm colors and cool colors

Another classical order of harmony is to work with warm colors and cool colors. It has been discovered that certain colors are warm and others cool. This is a subjective phenomenon that is produced in our minds when we perceive color, associating it with previous experiences or objects that have that color (fire is orange, snow is white, fresh grass is green . . .).

The colors that are considered warm include the entire range of reds, yellows, oranges, earth tones, violets, and the greens that contain a lot of yellow. Black, although neutral, is also considered more warm than cool, the same as very dark colors, because they absorb light and retain it. Cool colors are the blues and greens, some violets that are not very red, light grays, and white, although the latter can be included in a warm composition without abusing it. Harmony is almost guaranteed when we work within one of these two ranges.

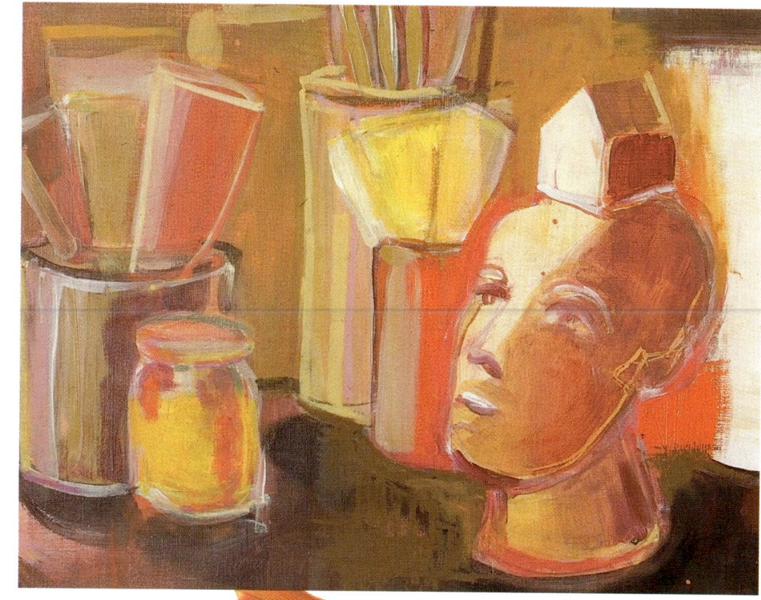

A warm range.

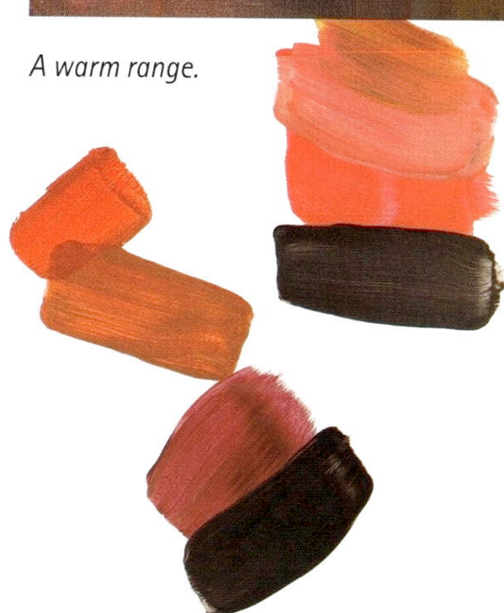

Neutral scheme, suggestive grays

An old slogan among Romantic painters went, "When you don't know how to fix a painting, add fog." It refers to the unifying and harmonizing capability of grays. The most difficult task in a composition is to make many full-intensity colors, that is to say, saturated colors, work together in a pleasing way. The personality of each color comes through with full force, and finding a way to make them interact involves some risk. However, when we neutralize a color, we modify and subdue its specific personality and energy. By harmonizing with neutral tones, colors no longer interact in terms of their proximity but of their mixture, and they all become very similar. Contrasts are not so much based on the color hues but on their value, some are lighter and others darker, but they are all more or less neutral.

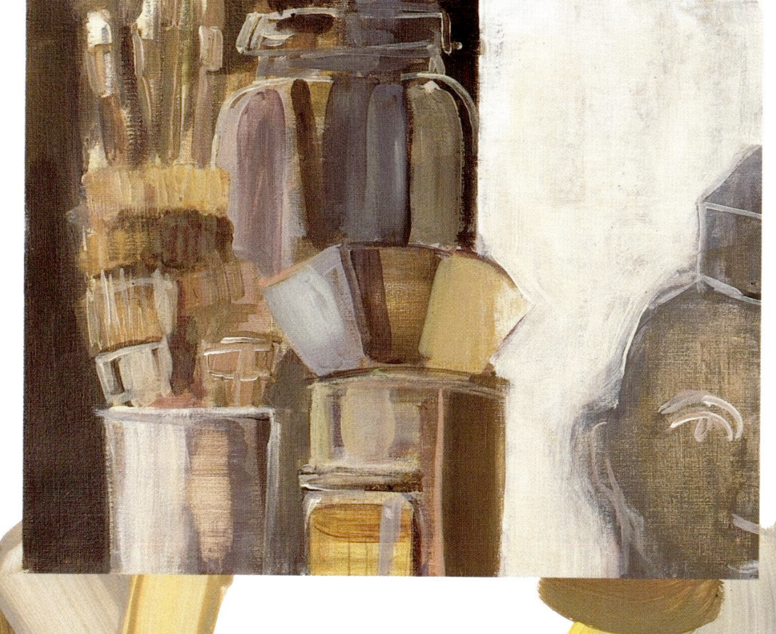

A neutral range.

Harmonizing with complementary colors

Working with complementary colors implies working with the fullest color contrast. Saying that one color is the complement of another means that they are completely different, that they do not have any color in common. To understand this point better, let us think, for example, of the difference that exists between something sweet and salty. One color would be the sweet food and the complement the salty one. If we eat something sweet and seconds later something salty, the flavors would stand out to their fullest, their effect would be exaggerated on the taste buds. However, if we mix the sweet food with the salty in a blender, the mixture will be neither sweet nor salty but, instead, something without personality, with a weak flavor, almost inedible, similar to when we put salt in coffee and sugar in a salad by mistake. Working with complementary colors is very similar. Two complementary colors together vibrate too much and, when mixed together, cancel each other. This type of harmonization was common practice among expressionists, fauvists, and even pop artists due to the color impact that can be produced.

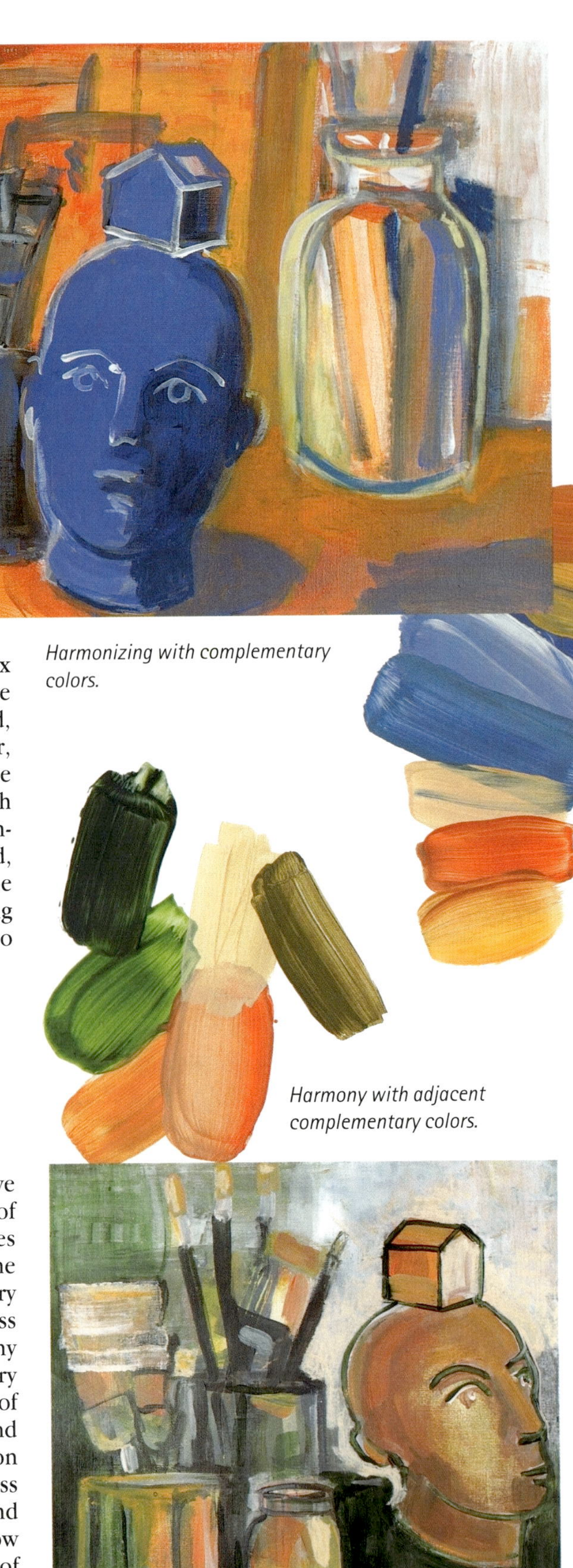

Harmonizing with complementary colors.

Harmony with adjacent complementary colors.

Harmonizing with adjacent complementary colors

To produce vibrant harmony without excessive contrast, we can resort to the combination of adjacent complementary colors, which are the ones located near the complementary colors. If red is the complement of green, their adjacent complementary colors would be orange and violet (more or less red). Therefore, an example of this type of harmony would be a base of greens and oranges—very common in landscape painting because the group of oranges includes the earth tones—or greens and violets, or yellows and blues, and so on. Based on the colors we choose, the result will be more or less dynamic because certain colors are more active and energetic. For example, the combination of yellow and red will be much more dynamic than that of green and violet.

Harmonizing with three and four colors

To achieve a three-color harmony, we will apply the same principle of adjacent complementary colors but add a third color located at the same distance from the other two. When connected, these three colors will form an equilateral triangle in the color wheel. An example of a three-color harmony would be yellow, blue, and red (the three primary colors), or green, violet, and orange (the three secondary colors), or greenish yellow, violet-blue, and orange-red. To form a four-color harmony, four colors forming a square or rectangle will be involved, which can be rotated over the color wheel to define the final four colors.

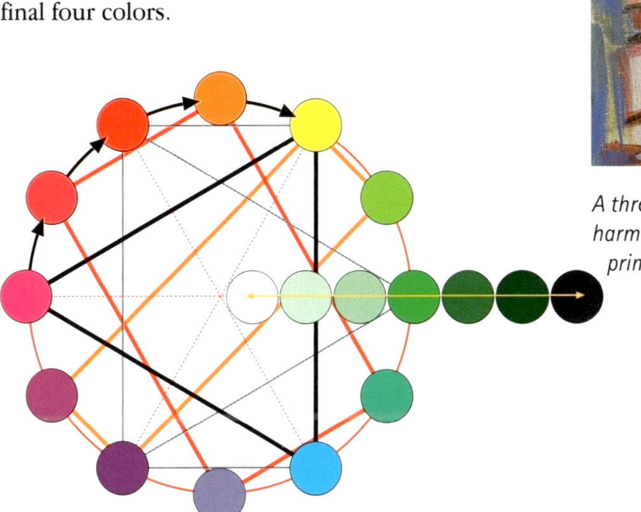

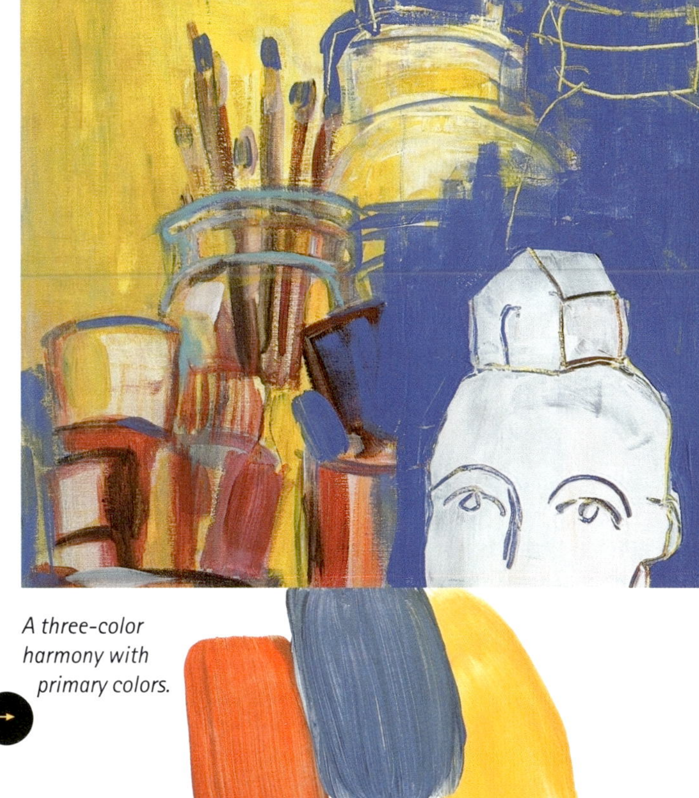

A three-color harmony with primary colors.

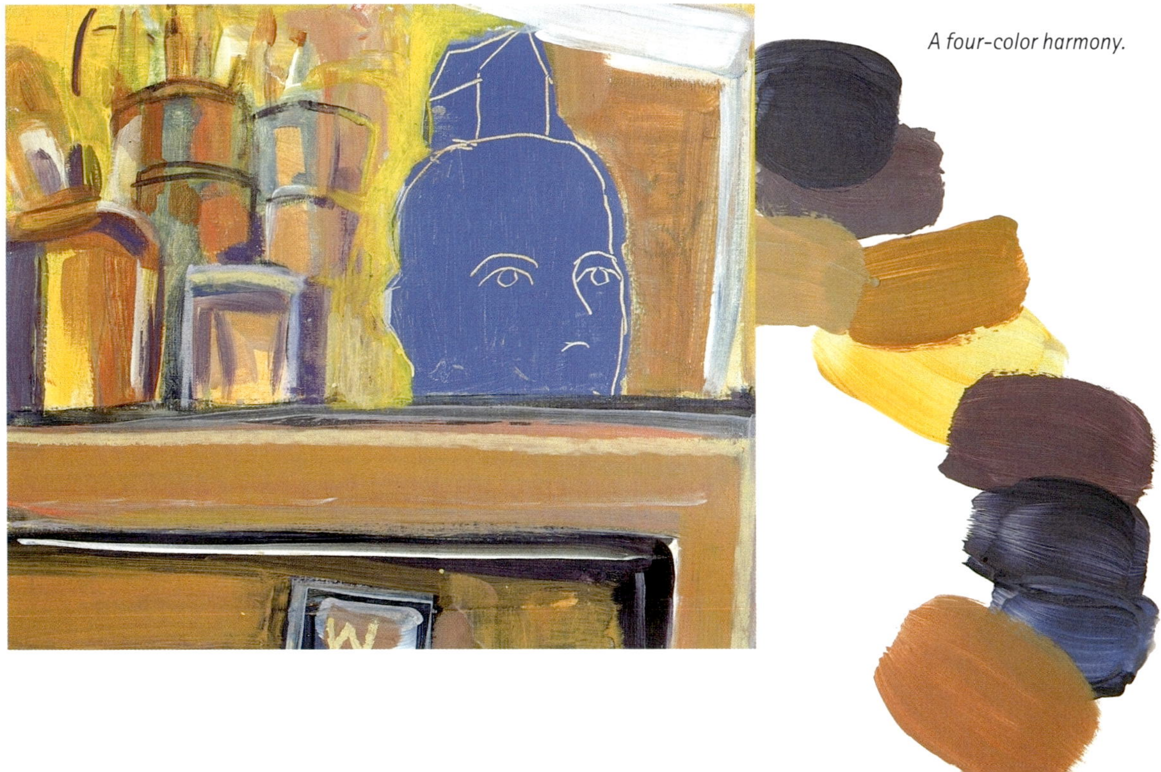

A four-color harmony.

What is form?

To define form, two very different properties of objects must be taken into consideration:

- The real limits that the artist establishes: mass and volume.
- The structural skeleton created by the perception of those forms, which coincide with it.

If the material form of an object is defined by its boundaries—the ones the object is made of and the space it occupies—so is the visual form. That is why when a visual object has no boundaries, or they are not well defined, it is perceived as flat, as a mass of color, as space or texture, but not as a form. Form can always be isolated from its context. It can normally be identified (a table, a bottle, an apple . . .) even when it is not figurative or narrative (a trapezoid, a triangle, a dark mass of curved shapes . . .).

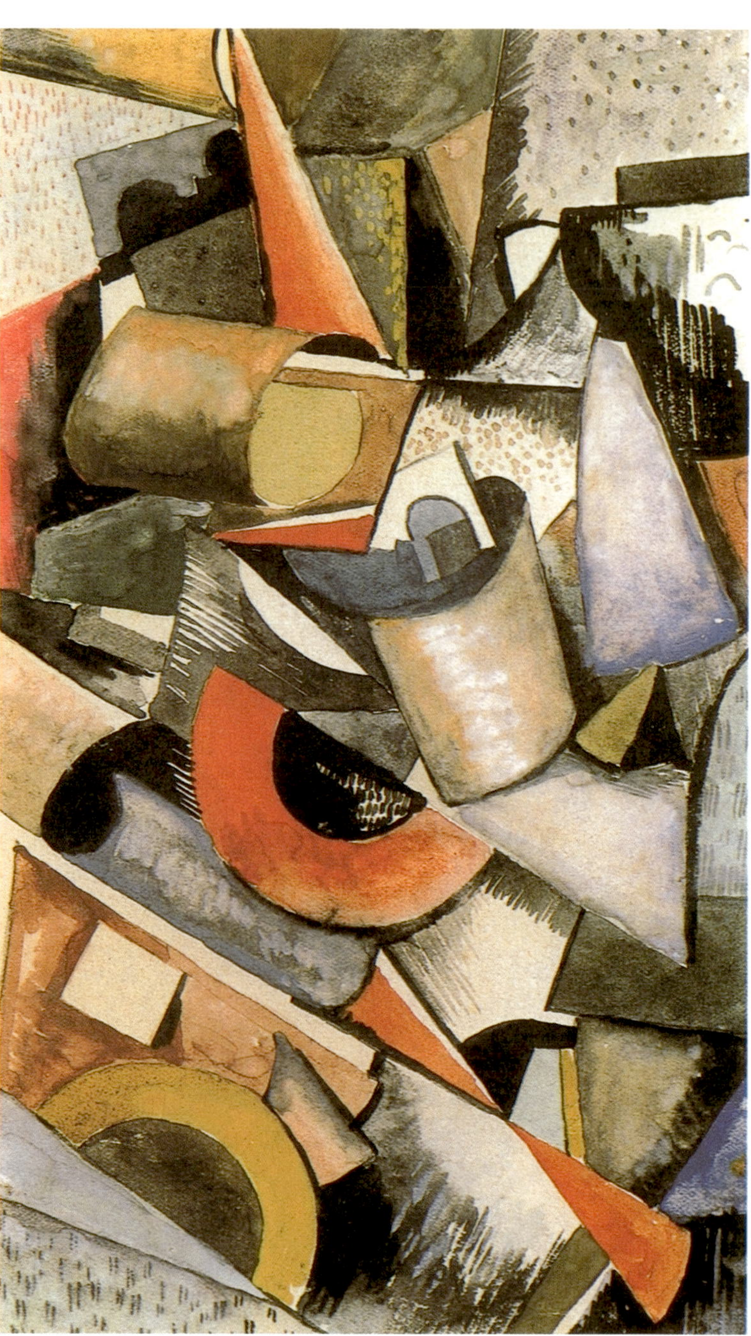

Alexander Rodtschenko, Cubist-Futuristic Composition, *c. 1914. Wilhem Hack Museum, Ludwigshafen (Germany). Many artists were especially attracted by the formal qualities of the subjects. Rodtschenko, like other constructivist, cubist, or modern artists, used still life themes to develop true studies of form.*

STRUCTURAL SKELETONS
Structural skeletons are the internal forms that give shape to the external forms that we see. The same way the human body has a skeleton that cannot be seen but that holds its shape, a lemon has an oval for skeletal structure, a sea star has a pentagon, a bottle has a central axis, and so on. We can continue analyzing every object that we encounter and discover its internal structure, which does not necessarily have to be physical (like the bones in the body) but visual or imaginary.

Blocking in shapes

Blocking in shapes is like putting them into "boxes," in other words, finding an overall form or shape (circle, square, triangle, or irregular lines) that encloses the elements, which will later be defined in detail. Not all shapes are equal, though, nor do they occur the same way. There can be flat or voluminous shapes (like smoke or the foliage in a plant) and very linear or very geometric shapes. Each shape requires a particular study and a different blocking system. Let's see the most common blocking methods according to the type of shape to be represented:

1. Around the axis of symmetry.
2. Blocking in with basic geometric shapes: squares, circles, triangles.
3. Creating a structure from symbolic shapes (a cross, the moon, a scythe, a rope, a spiral . . .) or from the letters of the alphabet (M, L, T, X, H . . .).
4. From intersecting curves: ellipses, ovals, ovoids, arches, and so on.
5. With line sketches, as if you were carving a block of wood.
6. With tentative applications of color blocks, as if you were modeling clay.
7. With linear perspective.
8. With gestural lines.

1. *Many elements have a very strong structural symmetry. They should be blocked in from the beginning, parting from their axis and continuing to organize them proportionately in the space within the structure.*

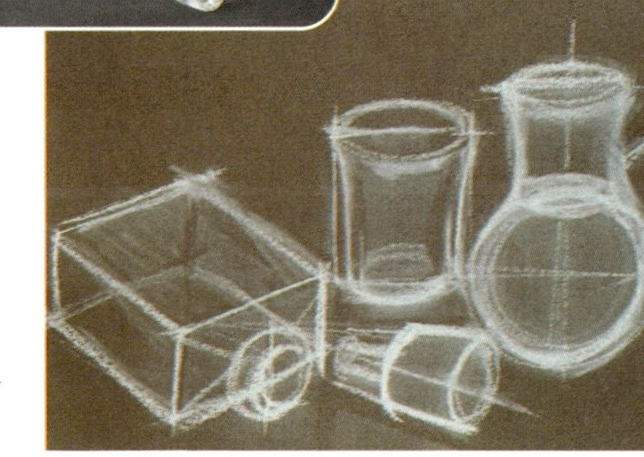

2. *Paul Cézanne used to say that all objects can be drawn from basic geometric shapes: cubes, spheres, and cylinders. Some shapes fit in perfectly, others require the combination of two or more shapes.*

3. *Linear and other symbolic structures that are often used when drawing the human figure can be used to block in objects as well, especially when they are foreshortened, occupy oblique planes, or are complex perspectives. This still life can be blocked in with a crescent moon.*

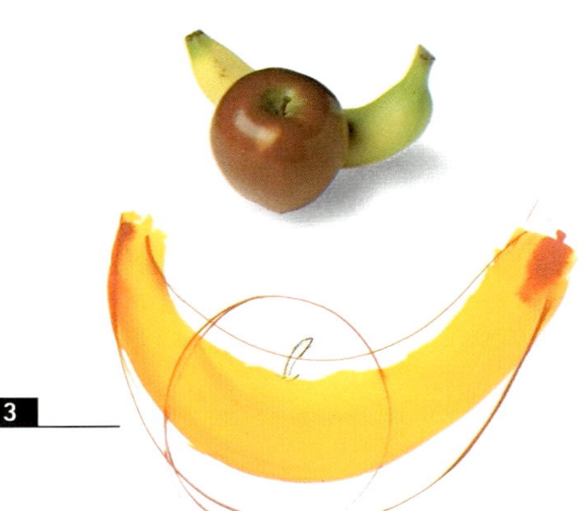

4. *Many natural objects have an internal structure based on curves: spheres, ellipses, ovals, ovoids, spirals, curves, and so on. Often, those curves are combined to define organic, sinuous, or irregular volumes. Drawing them is more practical than finding an internal structure or hidden axis.*

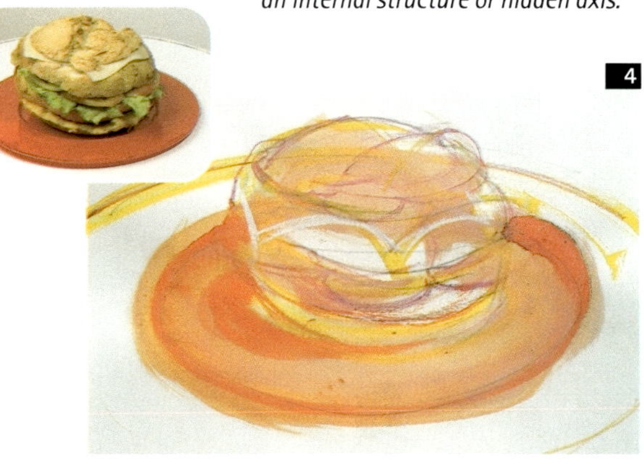

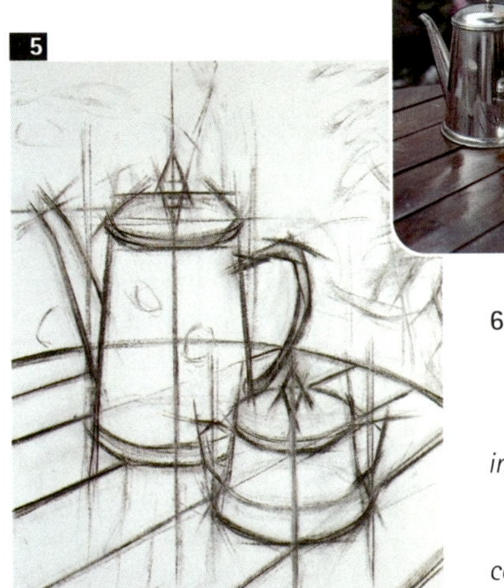

5. *Although in reality still life objects have practically no lines, the artist may resort to them to define the boundaries of the object, the intersecting points of the planes, and so on. Drawing many lines intuitively helps organize the image and helps define an approximation of the boundaries of objects.*

6. *Color is, together with line, the other great graphic resource for blocking in objects. By superimposing blocks of color and varying their intensities, the image is gradually defined according to light values, texture, or color. Many still life paintings respond better to a color block approach (flowers, clothing, areas that are transparent or have reflections).*

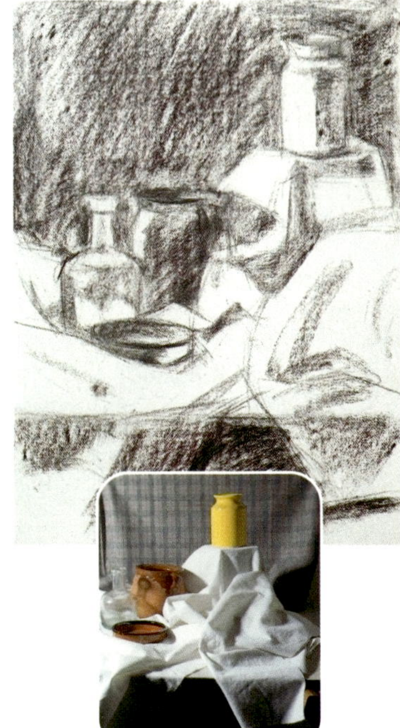

7. *Perspective is the law that organizes our perception of depth. Certain still life objects have a linear character marked by their parallel planes (boxes, suitcases, floor tile, windows, furniture, and so on). The best way to draw the image is to establish the edges following the principles of linear perspective.*

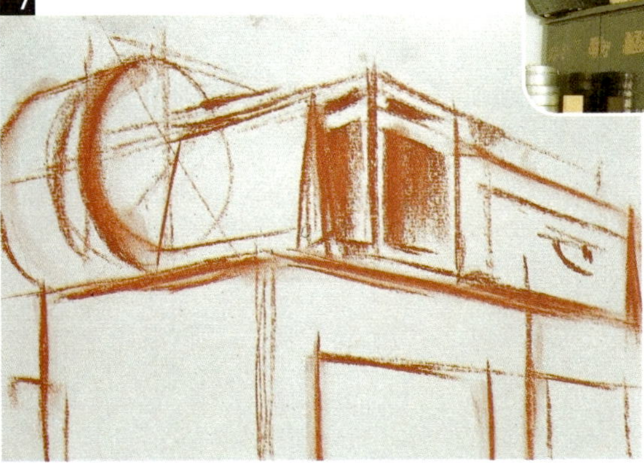

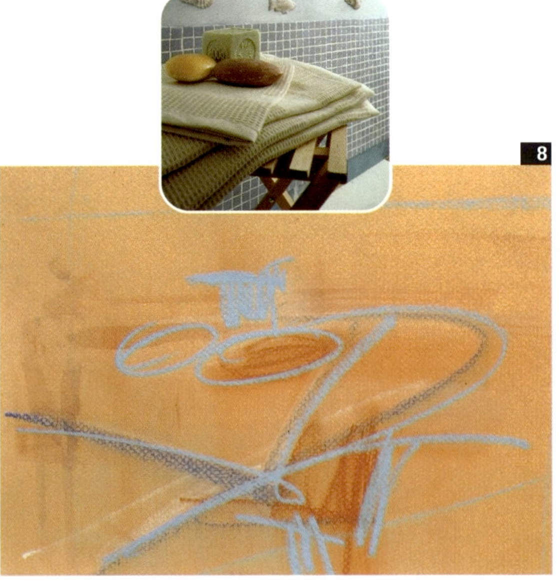

8. *Many artists work better intuitively, without following measurements or calculations. They establish masses, spaces, and tension lines with simple sketches or blocks of color. These first impressions on paper or canvas will define the entire image as well as any other method would.*

The proportions

Proportion is a relation of size among two or more parts. When we say that something is in or out of proportion, we are referring to the relationship of the parts to each other or to the whole. If that relationship is correct, we will say that the image is well proportioned, and therefore it will more closely resemble the real object. The mastery of proportion and its representation is vital for working on realistic still life, and there is only one way to achieve it, observation. To do that, we should faithfully observe a golden rule, "Spend more time observing than drawing." We can use different objects as tools to help us understand the subject matter (a pencil, brush, ruler, graphing paper, and so on). However, the goal is to develop a keen sense of observation to the extent that the artist would be able to perceive the objects proportionately with just a simple movement of the hand in the air before laying out the first lines.

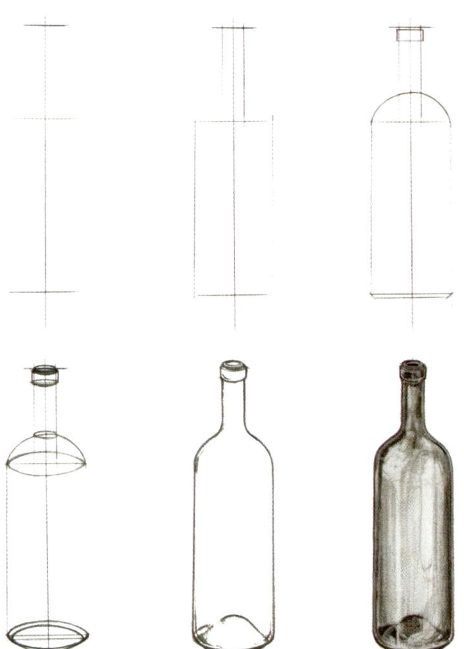

A simple wine bottle has a relationship among its parts that sets it apart from a water, juice, or any other type of bottle. To define it, first we will draw the main parts proportionately (body-neck) in height and width, and then the rounded sides will be drawn. Finally, its mouth and any other details will be defined. This method allows the artist to correct mistakes immediately, while the work is still in progress.

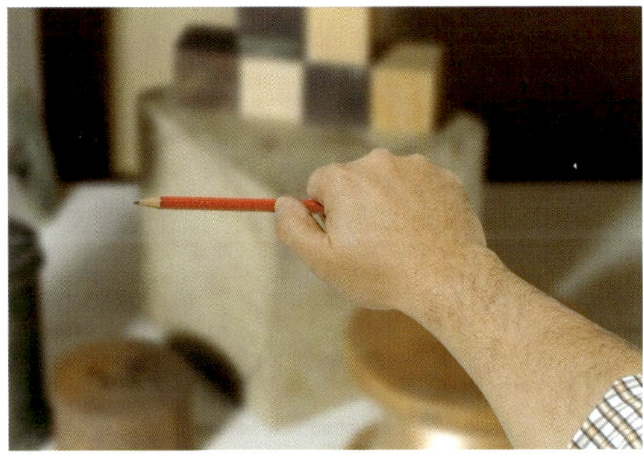

To take a measurement, first close one eye and, with the arm extended, mark on the pencil, brush, or ruler the measurement desired to transfer or to compare the height, width, thickness, or distance. That measurement can be compared with the object to see how many times it is contained in another and to thus understand the proportional relationships.

CLOSING ONE EYE

An important characteristic of the human vision is that the images registered by each one of our eyes is transferred to the brain separately. The brain then organizes the perception of the spatial depth in all its detail. When we close one eye, we lose a good portion of the sense of depth (we go from "stereo" to "mono," if you will), and that lack turns into an asset for comparing the dimensions of what we see, in other words, for applying proportions.

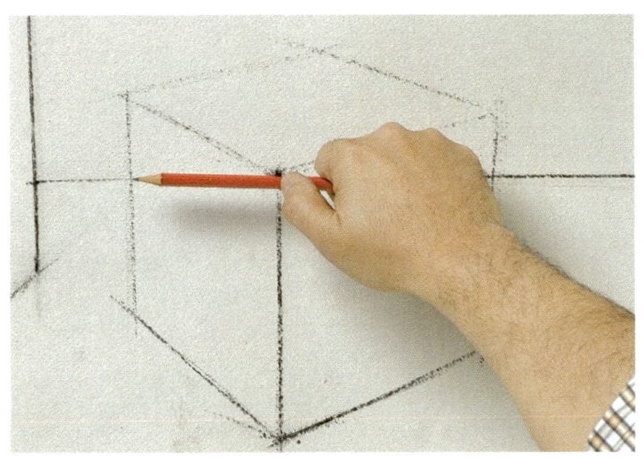

While staying in place with the arm extended and one eye closed, we will visually transfer that measurement to the drawing. The two images, the real one and the one on paper, will be compared as often as necessary.

Light and shadow model the volume

Remember how in the previous pages devoted to the model we saw that proper lighting (especially lateral light) helps the perception of the volumes of the objects. The same principle can be used to set up the model. If we do not wish to work with two-dimensional images nor to create volumes with color contrasts, like the impressionists or fauvists did, then we will have to represent all aspects of that light, which are

- Background or spatial lighting, by areas of greater or lesser definition.
- Modeling of the object: correct light and shadow.
- The shadows projected by the object.
- Light effects derived from the surface of the object and its surroundings, if it is shiny, matte, or transparent (reflection, highlights, transparencies).

All these aspects are translated onto the painting in terms of areas, blocks of color, hatching, or lines with concrete values of light, from pure white to the darkest black, with intermediate colors in between.

ADAPTING THE MODELING TO THE SHAPE
When we model a shape, we always do it with a tool (pencil, charcoal, brush, and so on), drawing the lines or applying the color with certain rhythm and direction. This constructive and gestural aspect of modeling is very important for avoiding awkward shapes. An effective method for understanding how to apply this modeling technique is to imagine that the object in question is in the rain and that we have to guess how the water flows off. The direction that the water follows is the way the lines should be drawn.

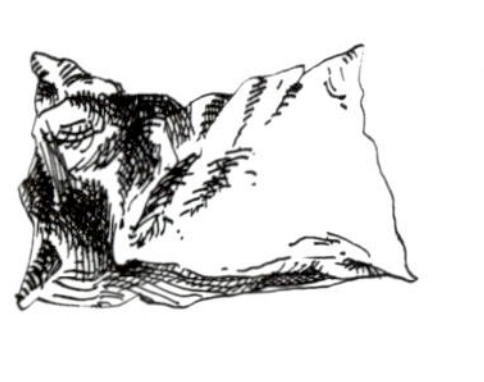
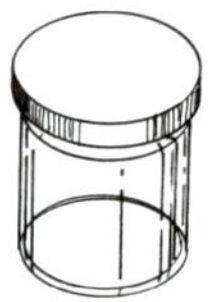
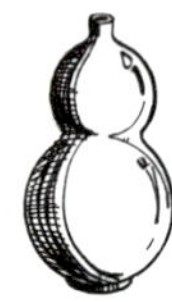
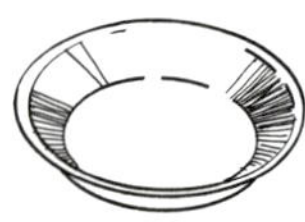
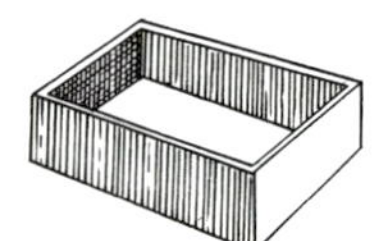

Each shape requires a different direction for the brushstroke according to its anatomy. It is important not to force that natural feeling. Notice how the planes have no gradations or modeling of any kind. Lines should be parallel if we do not want the objects to look irregular or awkward.

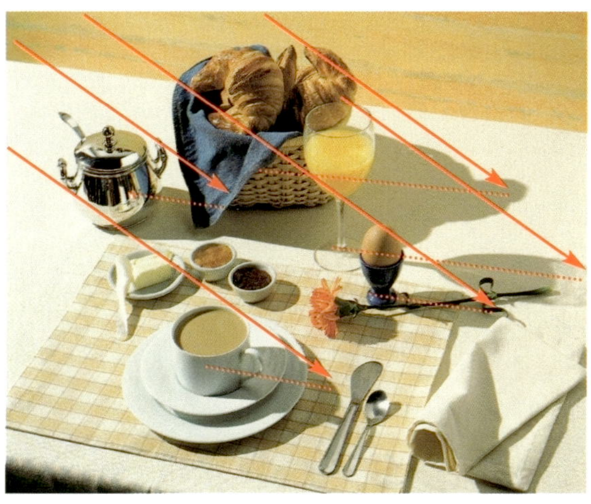

Since the sun is located far away, the shadows projected are parallel. The lower the sun (in the early and late hours of the day), the longer the shadows will be.

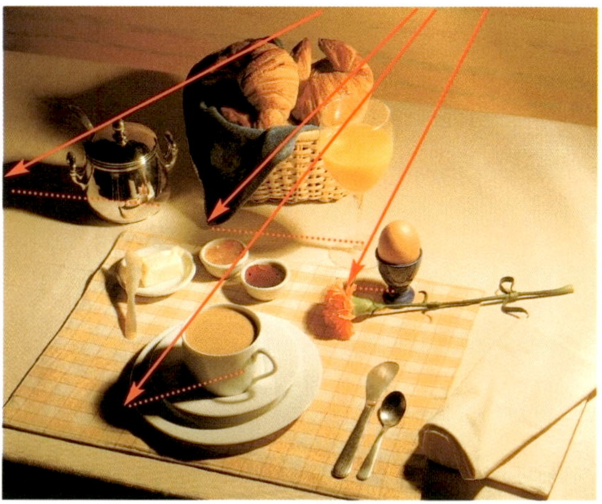

In this still life, the artificial light source is closer to the objects; that is why we can perceive the more or less divergent rays that indicate the proximity of the source with respect to the object. The projected shadows will be divergent.

Transparency and reflections

When an object has a matte surface or is made of a material that absorbs light, its volume is defined with a diffused gradation, more or less subtle, according to the texture. However, when an object is polished or is made of a more reflective material, new elements will be in its representation, new forms: the reflections.

Basically there are two types of surface reflections. One, the reflections of the light source, is called highlights. The other is the reflections from the items that are next to the object and in the general area. The reflections adapt to the shape of the object, distorting the image and maintaining the approximate color of the reflected object.

Transparent glass has highlights, as many as there are sources of light in the room (in this case from a single window), whose shape adapts to that of the object. Other objects or elements are reflected, distorted, or reduced to simple streaks of their own colors.

Antonio de Pereda, Still Life with Sweets, Dishes, and Ebony Bureau, *1652 (Details). The Hermitage Museum, Saint Petersburg (Russia).*

When light goes through glass, it can be seen on the projected shadow. The presence of that light in the shadow greatly reinforces the feeling of transparency. On the other hand, light penetrates the material and spreads to its edges, making them visible in the form of very bright or very dark lines and contours.

When metal is not polished, it is modeled the same way other objects are, with soft diffused touches for the shadows and for the faint reflections of light. For this copper utensil, Pereda applied rough brushstrokes with thick paint to evoke the marks made by the artisan when working the metal.

A polished metal surface can reflect what is around it as if it were a mirror. The shinier the object, the clearer the reflected image. The colors will also have cleaner and sharper contrasts, without gradations. In this case, the plate appears a little worn and the reflections look more diffused.

The textural quality of objects

Every object has different textural qualities on its surface. A visual representation evokes the tactile experience of that material (coarse, smooth, warm, cold, soft, hard, and so on). That is a very important factor in creating a realistic representation of a still life, because it makes the image look almost tangible.

The key to representing textures and materials successfully is, as has been mentioned in previous pages, observation. The artist must carefully examine if there are hard contrasts or soft diffused areas, if there are accidental marks, worn-out or dirty places, what forms have wrinkles, and so on. Also, it is a good idea to practice the effects that we are looking for on a separate piece of paper, using different tools (a wet or dry brush, a sponge, a rag, the fingers, spatulas, rasps, or any other implement). Normally, the different effects can be created simply by changing the thickness or hardness of the brush or charging it with more or less paint.

Jean-Baptiste Siméon Chardin, The Jar of Apricots, *c. 1756–1760. Art Gallery of Ontario, Toronto (Canada). Although Chardin painted all his scenes with a soft light, creating this way a very intimate visual unity, he was very good at depicting different textures and materials within the same scene. In this beautiful painting, we find glass, bread, fresh and preserved fruits, metal, porcelain, paper, a cloth, a string, and even the steam of a hot beverage. Observing each detail carefully is the best lesson that we can learn from this eighteenth-century master.*

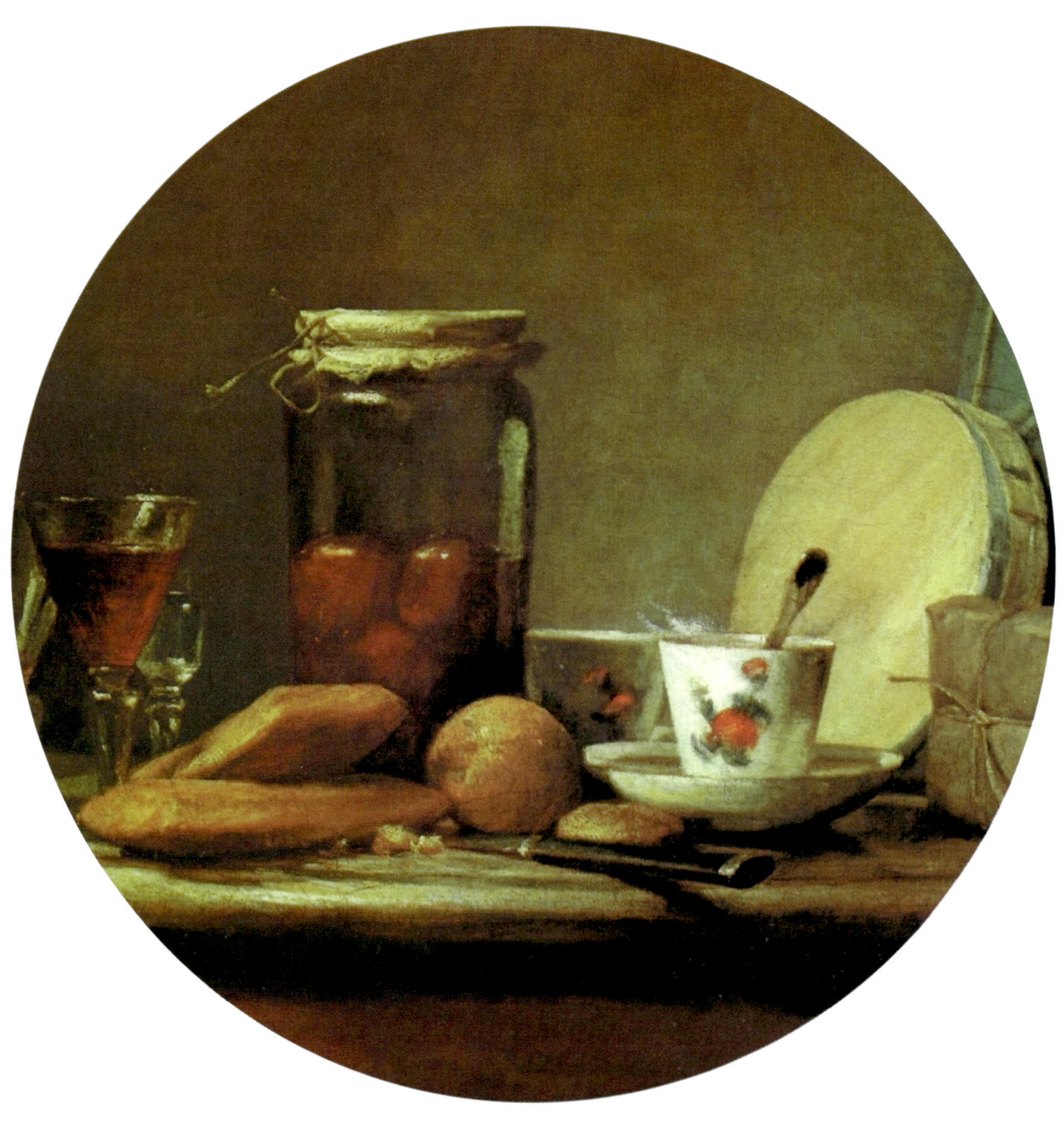

The background and the figure

The dramatic character of still life poses a classic problem in this genre: the relationship between the background and the figure. This does not happen with landscape painting, or with indoor scenes, and even less so with portraits. In the first two cases, the space is an important part of the subject. In portraits, the main theme is always clear, and the background is almost always very neutral to emphasize the figure.

When faced with this problem, the first thing that must be done is to decide from the beginning where the communicative strength of the painting is going to be, in the object or the scene. Therefore, if the strength resides in the object, it should be isolated using color, light, or meaning (by not including other subjects that will interfere with its delivery). If the emphasis resides in the scene, every element, from the background wall to the object's most minute detail, will have to be integrated in the picture. When this question is not resolved from the start, the background ends up looking monotonous and dull.

Joan Miró, The Table (Still Life with Rabbit), *1920. Private collection. In this still life, everything has equal importance. Everything is subject to the same overall criterion: a decorative aesthetic based on geometric forms that Miró applied to the furniture as well as to the feathers of the hen and to the napkin. The triangle is the formal link between all the different parts.*

Francisco de Zurbarán, Agnus Dei, *c. 1635–1640. Museo del Prado, Madrid (Spain). This is a still life of a living creature with great symbolic charge. A tied lamb ready to be slaughtered, an Agnus Dei, an allegory of Christ that deserves no treatment other than a dark and heavy background surrounding a gray sacrificial altar.*

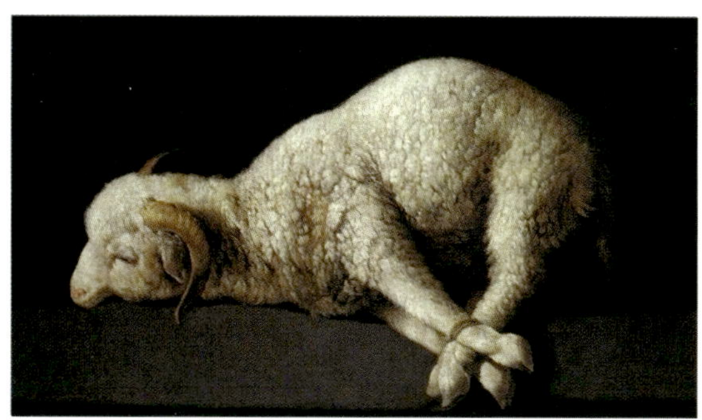

When the background is no longer a background

The goal that should be pursued is the elimination of the background as such. A still life should have no background, because it is impersonal, marginal, and lacks expressive charge. When the objects of a still life present themselves within a vague, neutral, or dark space, that space should be approached as such and not as a background. It must say something (as much as the figure); it should evoke depth, denseness and lightness, presence or absence. Those problems can also be resolved later by applying certain techniques: like formal connections or repetitions, or an overall glaze that ties the entire scene together with a single color.

Esther Olivé de Puig, Still Life, *1996. Private collection. Olivé has painted over a picture to create a breakfast scene that has a unified overall feeling with no background. The first painting, placed upside down to avoid too much confusion, has inspired lines and colors that would not have existed any other way. The first image has not been completely eliminated, it has been integrated to enrich the painting.*

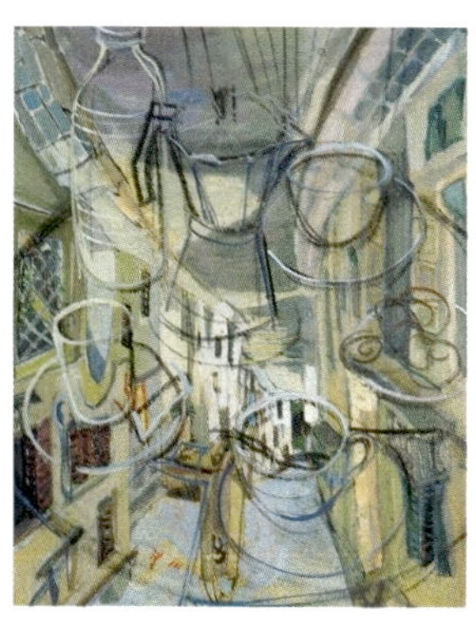

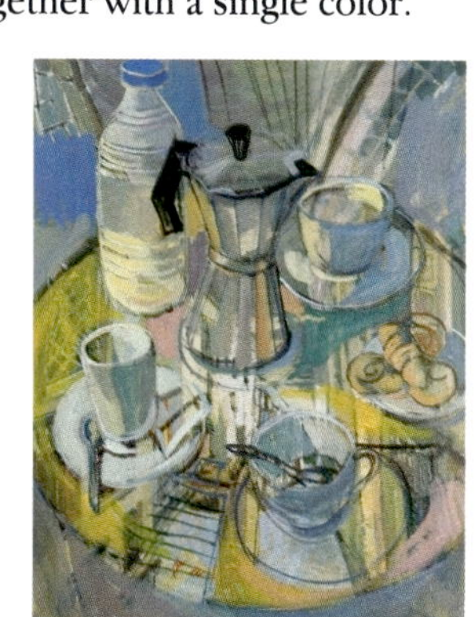

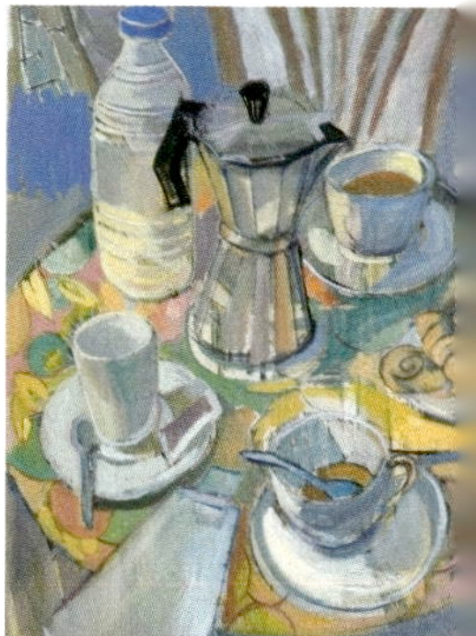

Perspective in still life

Perspective is a technique that is used to explain the concept of depth graphically. Humans have a conical vision system, not a flat one. When we look at a straight road from a car, it looks to us as if the edges were converging in the distance. In reality, though, they always maintain the same distance between themselves. This perception of depth caused by the effect of the vanishing point of parallel lines is called conical perspective.

The same effect occurs when we look at a table, a wall, a suitcase, or any other object that has parallel sides. The edges, which in reality are parallel, slant to converge at a distant point called the vanishing point. All the vanishing points are found on the horizon line, which is always located at eye level. Sometimes the horizon line can be seen clearly (in the ocean or in very flat landscapes), but normally it cannot be seen, only imagined by extending the arm in front of the body at eye level.

Any object that has a circular base must be laid out in perspective with respect to its axes to define the elliptical forms.

To draw the corner of this bathroom, it is necessary to find the converging lines of the space and to fit every element into them.

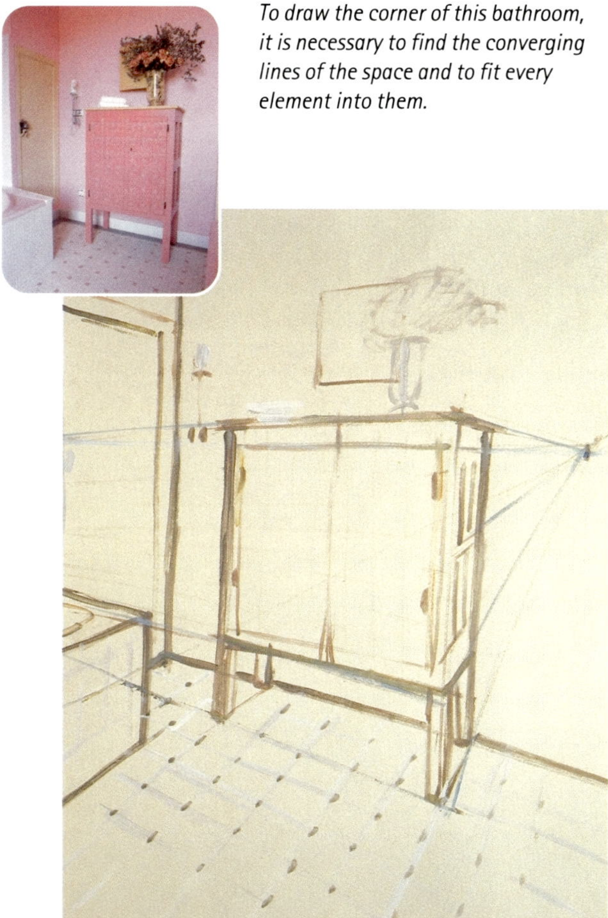

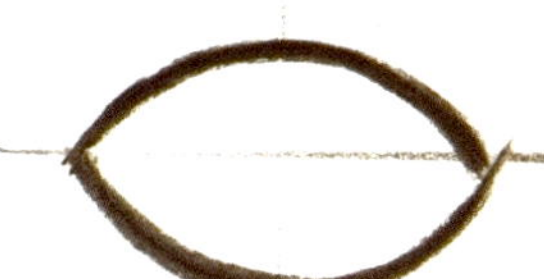

Incorrect drawing of an elliptical figure.

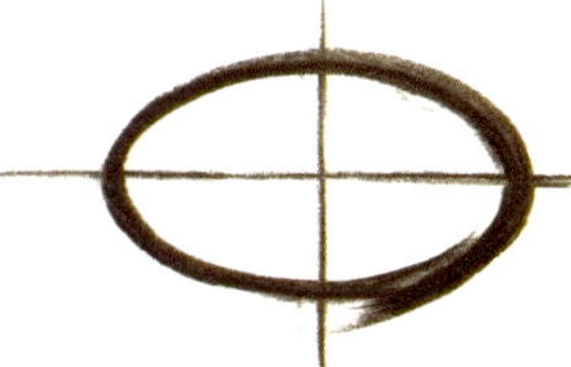

Correct drawing of an elliptical figure.

Circles in perspective look like ellipses. They have a large axis and a short axis. The proportion between the axes makes them look more or less opened, independent of their size. As the axes become more similar in size, the elliptical shape gets rounder until it becomes a circle. As the axes become increasingly different in size, the ellipsis looks flatter, until it finally turns into a line.

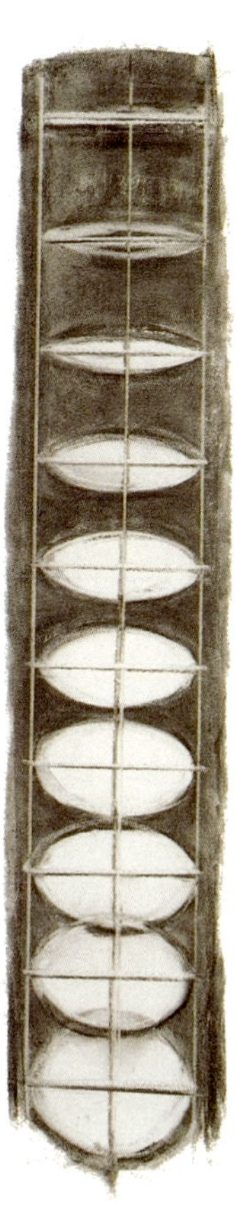

Point of view

Choosing the point of view to observe the scene is as important as selecting the model, the composition, and the lighting of the scene. Every position that the artist adopts in reference to the model results in a different expressive effect and also in a different treatment of the image. The feeling can also be varied in terms of height. An angled view from above implies dominance; a frontal, piercing approach produces a feeling of awe and reverence.

In terms of distance, the traditional approach is to find one that is neither too close nor too far so the scene is neither cut off nor lost in the picture plane, but this does not constitute a rule. The artist may be interested in transmitting a strong feeling of closeness, as if it were the zoom in a camera, to create an intimate atmosphere, or a very distant view—as if it were a landscape. The latter method was frequently used by Dalí to create a disturbing perception of depth that is grandiose and desolate.

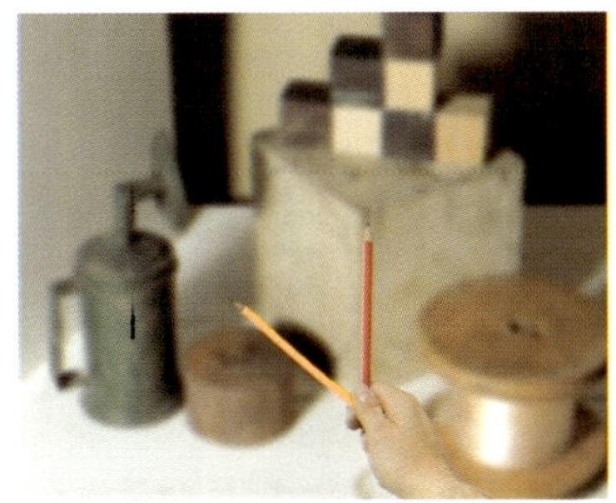

The angle of a line can be found using two pencils or brushes and closing one eye.

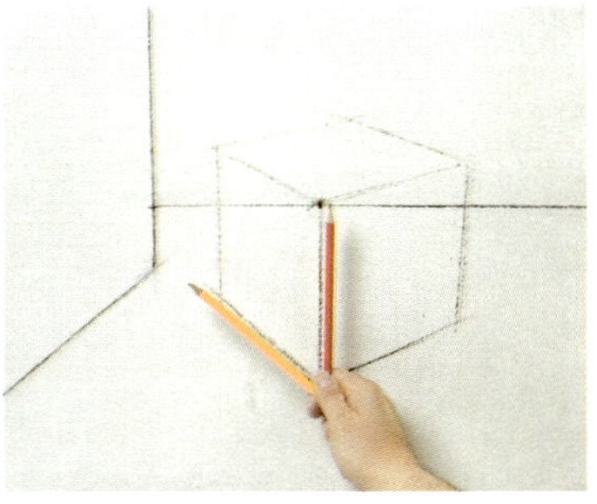

Without changing the position of the pencils and without opening one eye, the angle of the real object is transferred to the paper.

OBLIQUE AND ELLIPTICAL PLANES

Knowing how the vanishing lines are laid out in a perspective drawing is important because they are the ones that ultimately define the space. In practice, we use measuring methods to figure out the angles of those oblique planes.

The axes of elliptical planes are always parallel to the margins of the paper or the canvas unless the ellipsis is tilted within a tilted plane. In this case, we must resolve the plane first and then insert the axes and diagonals within that plane to draw the desired elliptical shape proportionately.

Each point of view creates a different picture of the subject on all levels, expressive and formal.

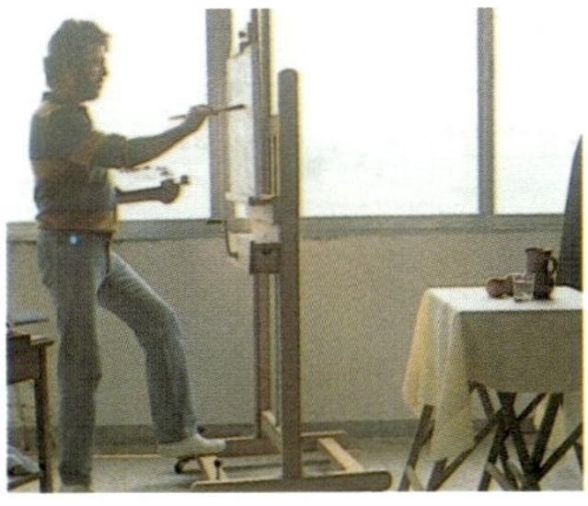

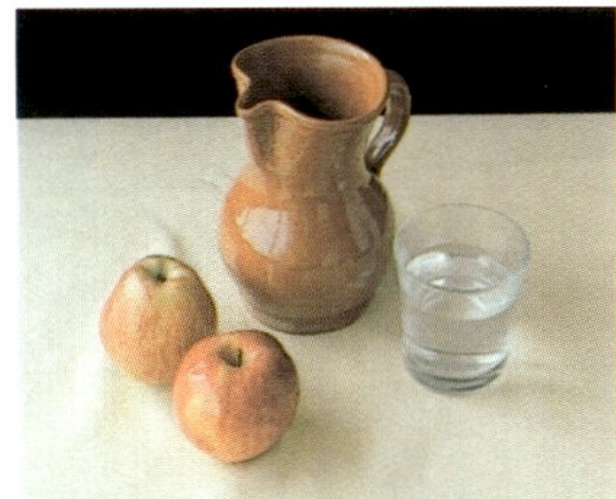

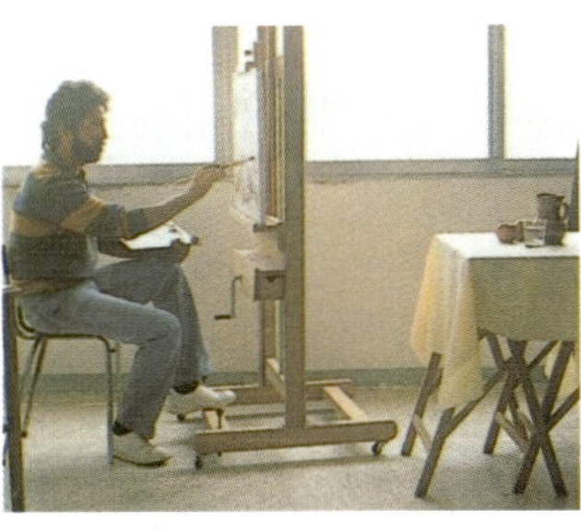

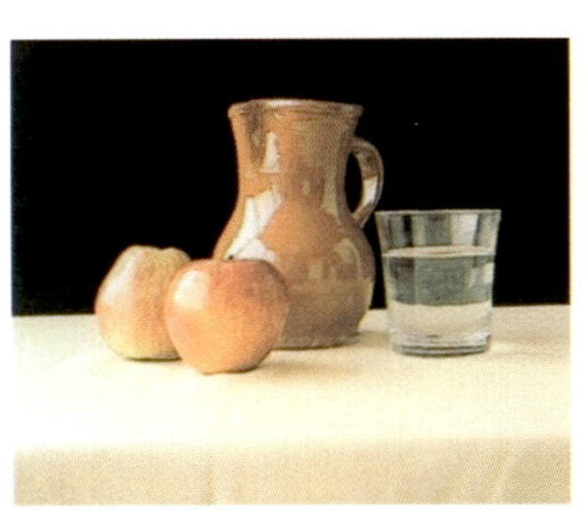

A tilted plate is an ellipse within an oblique plane. For all the ellipses in oblique planes, tilted or not, you must first draw the axes and the diagonals, which will serve as guides for drawing the ellipses.

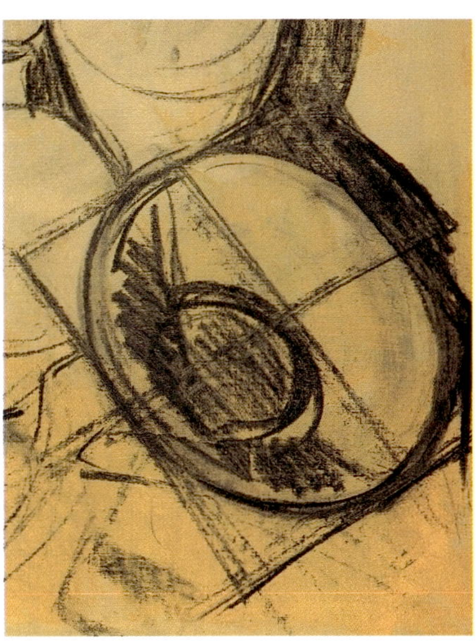

The composition creates unity

According to Plato, making a composition means "finding unity within variety or variety within unity." This definition is very appropriate for understanding the true meaning of composition. Making a composition does not mean making all the parts the same or blending them in a common overview. Instead, it means making them relevant according to a plan, to an overall idea that creates a relationship among them, a coherence that unites them.

The closest thing to visual composition is musical composition. In a symphony, all the instruments have a particular role. Some play longer than others, but all are together following the score, forming a musical piece the composer created. In a painting, each brushstroke, line, color, and texture act as those musical instruments. Still life is the ideal genre for exploring the compositional possibilities to the fullest extent, because the artist can move the models, his or her point of view, and the framing as he or she pleases, searching for the composition that best adapts to the expressive intention of the artist.

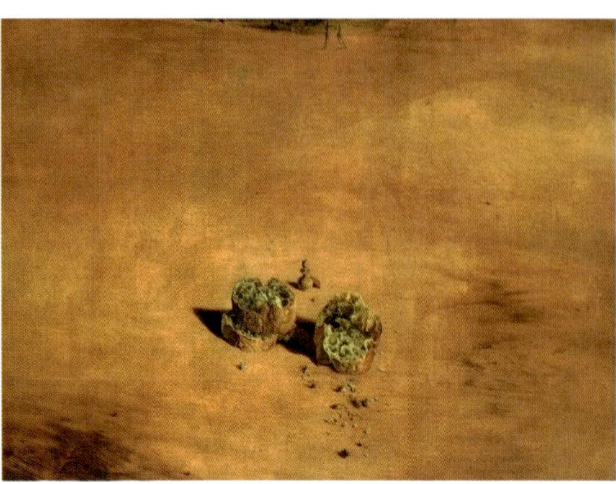

Salvador Dalí, Two Pieces of Bread Expressing the Feeling of Love, *1949. Fundación Gala-Salvador-Dalí, Figueres (Spain). This surrealist composition reminds us of a chamber music trio or quartet. There are fewer instruments, of which two are the main protagonists: two pieces of bread that establish a visual dialogue over the tablecloth-beach, as if it were a vocal duo.*

BREAKING THE MOLD

Some traditional compositional structures should not be discarded given their proven effectiveness, for example, all those that promote simplicity (central, pyramidal, or symmetrical). However, it is very interesting to experiment with new compositional possibilities. One of them is framing that captures a fragment of the scene. To do this, a small opening can be cut out of a piece of cardboard or construction paper through which the artist can view the model and select and decide on the portion that he or she wishes to develop. Many compositional possibilities can be discovered this way.

Arturo Solari, Variations of a Theme, *1999. Private collection. In this triptych, Solari has developed some very personal approaches. His view of the model implies more reflection. The slight angle changes and the repetition of some of the points of the still life indicate a poetic desire to return to the same theme but changing its perception. Nothing is completely known; everything becomes new at every glance, ready to be discovered.*

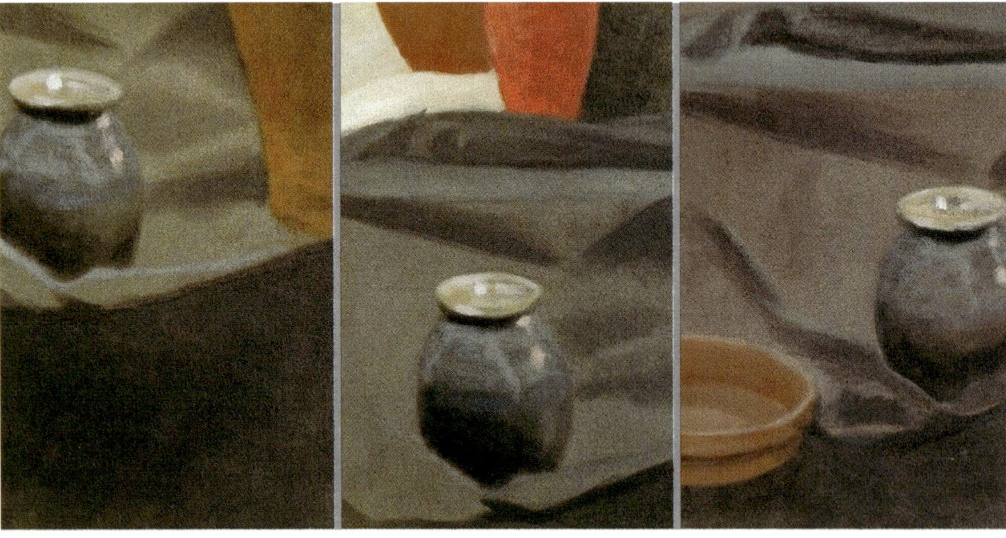

Traditional compositional structures for still life

In practice, compositions are nothing more than a puzzle. All the pieces end up fitting together if they are placed in their respective places. However, if we do not know how to assemble them, the final image will fail to come together. The image is not usually defined from the beginning. Instead, it forms slowly during the process, thickening the paint in one area, darkening another, highlighting an element, changing the color of a different one, searching for the harmony and tension that bring an image to life.

These changes, which can be more or less evident, are like a dance of masses. Mass or weight is in a composition like the value of intensity that the element acquires. It can be expressed in the size, the light value, or the power of its colors. A centered composition shows all the masses gathered in the middle, while an asymmetrical one will respond to the principle of balance: the larger the mass, the shorter the distance from its center, and vice versa.

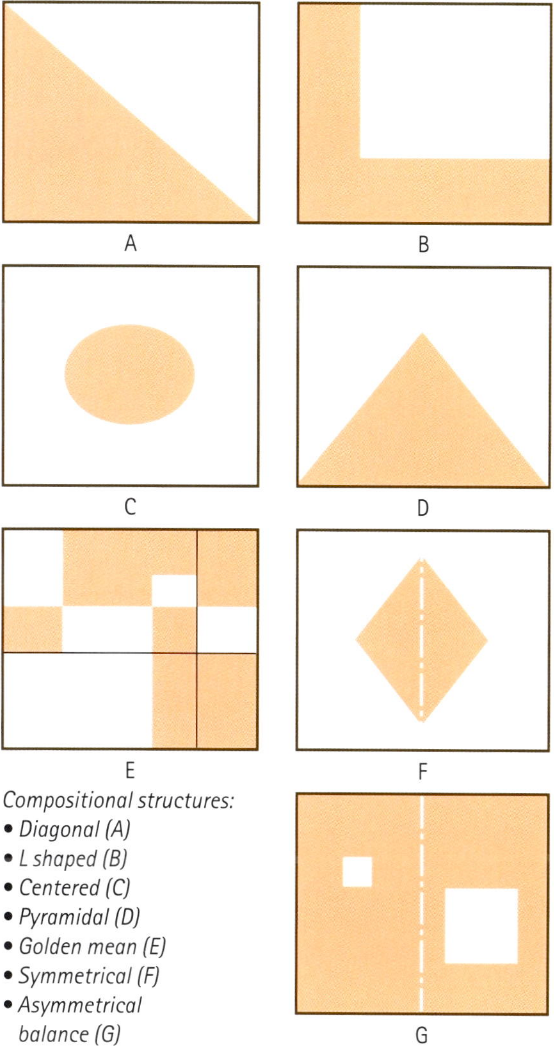

Compositional structures:
- *Diagonal (A)*
- *L shaped (B)*
- *Centered (C)*
- *Pyramidal (D)*
- *Golden mean (E)*
- *Symmetrical (F)*
- *Asymmetrical balance (G)*

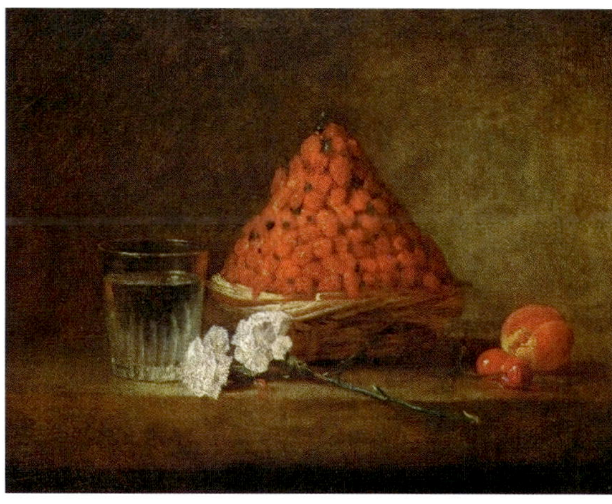

Jean-Baptiste Siméon Chardin, The Basket of Wild Strawberries, *c. 1761. Private collection. This is a clear example of a pyramidal composition.*

Antonio de Pereda, Vanitas, *c. 1640–1650. Museo de Zaragoza (Spain). This* vanitas *by Pereda uses the compositional structure of the golden mean. By dividing the sides of the rectangle by the golden mean, the resulting points are where the skulls or the border of the pedestal should be located.*

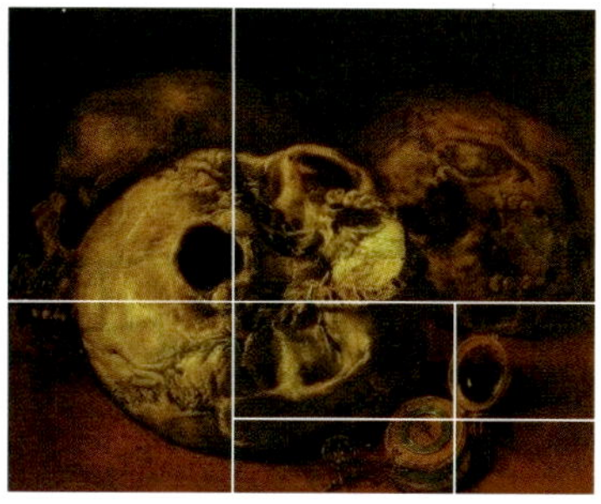

THE GOLDEN MEAN
The Greeks discovered a proportional relationship, which they called the "golden mean" because of its perfect harmony. This relationship is found in nature, for example in the proportions of the body, in many plants, and so on. Two dimensions are said to have the golden mean if the ratio of their relationship is 1 to 1.618. That is, if one measures 1 inch (or 1 cm), the other should be 1.618 inches (or 1.618 cm). To find out what the golden mean (the smaller segment) of a measurement is, we multiply by 0.618, and to find out what measurement of a segment the golden mean is (its corresponding larger segment), we also multiply by 1.618.

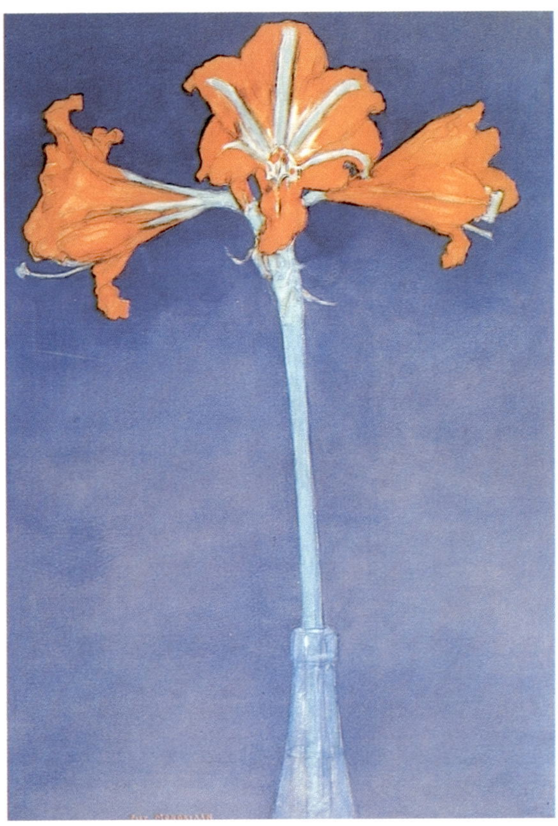

Piet Mondrian, Red Narcissus with Blue Background, *1907. Museum of Modern Art, New York (United States). This symmetrical and balanced composition conveys a feeling of serenity, peace, and poetry. Placing the flower on the upper part of the painting creates a subtle feeling of tension that forces the viewer to consider the void in the space as a value in itself.*

How to read an image

In the process of perceiving, we intuitively seek a sense of balance first. When there is a difference in the distribution of mass, we tend to look for a counterbalance that compensates for the mass. A stable and balanced composition will give the spectator a feeling of serenity. The calming effect will be even greater if the structure contains verticals and horizontals. However, if the artist wishes to provoke tension, he or she must look for instability by placing the main elements in areas of visual tension, working with round or diagonal structures, being careful not to exceed certain reasonable limits to avoid ambiguity and confusion.

Second, we should be aware that the viewer is always drawn to the lower left corner of the painting. This is due to the left-to-right Western style of reading. If we place some elements in other angles, we will create confusion. Finally, it is important to consider the perceptive rule of grouping objects. The eye looks for relationships among similar objects (with proximity, color, dimension, form, or texture). The greater the affinity, the greater the normalcy and vice versa.

John F. Peto, Palette, Mug, and Pipes, *c. 1890. Meredith Long Valley, Houston (United States). The diagonal composition of this image and the play of shadows create a dynamic effect.*

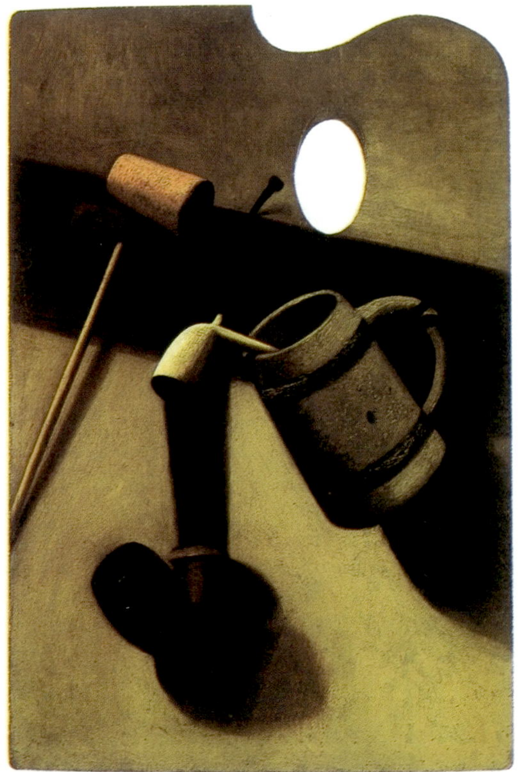

Knowing how to compose is knowing how to express

The composition dictates the arrangement of the shapes, colors, spaces, and so on to create a particular feeling, the same way that words can convey a different message depending on their order. The success of a composition is in achieving the desired expressive effect. Although the number of effects that we can achieve according to a particular composition is endless, we will see the most common ones and their opposite effects. Many more could be added to this list.

- Balance or instability.
- Order or chaos.
- Uniformity or fragmentation.
- Simplicity or lavishness.
- Calm or movement.
- Realism or distortion.
- Definition or insinuation.
- Neutrality or focus.
- Opacity or transparency.
- Weakness or energy.

The media

The following pages will cover the theory related to the practical and technical aspects of still life. We have already seen the first three elements of the visual language—color, form, and space—related to the image. Now we will review the last two, texture and technique, related to the physical aspect of the painting.

It is not enough to know the proper elements of the formal language and how to arrange them. It is also necessary to know what media are available to make them become a reality, because without these media we would not be able to materialize the ideas.

To enjoy a musical composition, we need the sheet music and the musicians to play it, but without instruments it would be impossible. The different type of media would be for the visual artist what instruments are for the musician. Each instrument makes a different type of sound, and its particular characteristics make it ideal for a specific piece of music. A xylophone would not be suitable for playing a piece written for piano, and the sound of the cymbals could never be produced with a flute. The same is true for the art of painting. It would be quite difficult to make fine lines with heavy oil paint; pencils would work better. The clean and transparent effect of watercolors could never be achieved with charcoal pencils.

If the media are the instruments, the technique and the texture represent the way they are played: the speed, the intensity, the quality that can be achieved, the emotional charge. . . . Knowing how to choose the appropriate instruments for each composition is as important as knowing how to play them to convey the message.

◆

If the media are the instruments, the technique and the texture represent the way to play them: the speed, the intensity, the quality that can be achieved, the emotional charge. . . .

◆

Many musicians prefer a particular instrument because they can establish a personal connection with its sound. He or she identifies with it, and that is why it is easier to communicate with it than any other particular instrument or family of instruments (air, strings, percussion). The same is true in the field of visual arts; we can find the dry techniques ideal for communicating, or oil. . . .

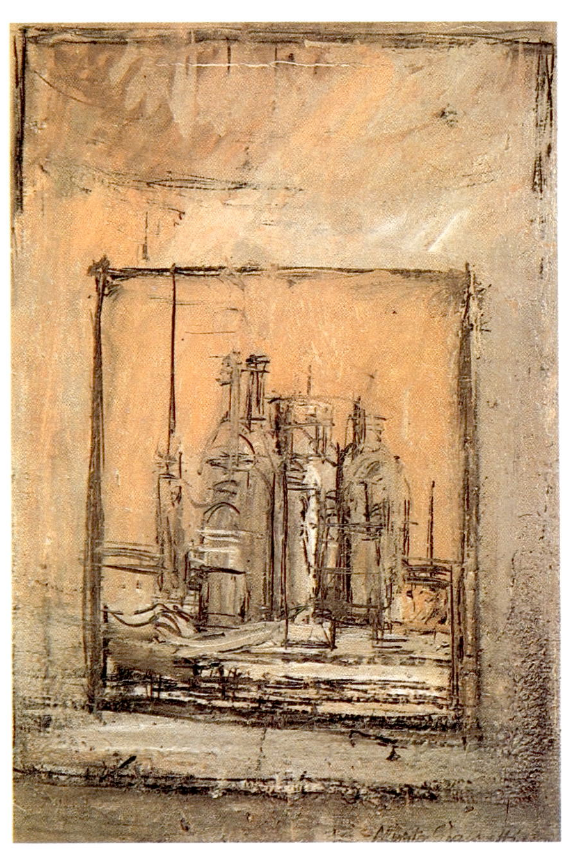

Alberto Giacometti, Still Life. *Private collection. Giacometti focused his investigation on the exploration of space and the human figure, their limits, their placement, the concept of full and empty. To express this spatial experience of humans, which has to do with their transpersonal and spiritual dimension, he stylized the figures and objects to the maximum with a vibrant and energetic stroke, as if the air penetrated the bodies, fusing the tangible with the intangible. Oil paints allowed him to work by blending and crossing through lines, sometimes painting and other times scratching with the handle of the brush to create less tangible lines.*

Still life and dry techniques: pencil, charcoal, pastels, and crayons

Dry techniques include the media that are normally used without any solvent (water, mineral spirits) except when a very special effect is desired. The tools can be made from the raw material itself (graphite, organic charcoal, pigment) or from the material plus a binder (wax, gum . . .). The most usual ones are pencil, charcoal, pastels, and crayons.

The most common supports for dry techniques are paper, cardboard, and, in some cases, wood. They should always be placed on a hard surface because pressure needs to be applied.

Each technique can be used directly on the support or applied with other tools to create special effects: rags, erasers, diffused, water, or mineral spirits for watercolor pencils or crayons.

The pencil is a stick of graphite encased in wood. It is available in many hardnesses. The hardest graphite pencils (identified with the letter H) make hard lines and are ideal for applying very light grays. Soft pencils (B) create darker and more malleable lines. The fingers or a blending stick can be used to soften the lines as well as erasers for creating highlights and for negative drawing. Pure graphite sticks, without the wood, are a variety of pencil that are used for making thick lines and for modeling. Graphite is also available in powder form, which is applied with a cotton ball. A fixative is not required but is highly recommended.

Pastels are made of pigment compressed with tragacanth gum. Light tones usually have white in them, producing the distinct "pastel tones," and the dark ones have black. Their hardness will depend on the amount of binder in them. They can be worked with a blending stick, with the fingers, with cotton balls, or directly with more marked lines, especially with the harder pastels. The lines are rough and dry and the areas of colors soft and atmospheric. They can be erased to create light effects, although this is not very common because pastels are already very luminous. They produce realistic finishes, and normally lightly textured color papers are used with them. They must be sprayed with a fixative.

Charcoal is nothing more than a piece of charred wood, willow, or vine. It is the oldest technique known. It is available in bars of different hardness and thickness and as a compressed pigment with a binder. A special eraser, softer and more malleable, can be used to erase it, or a rag, which is an indispensable tool for this procedure. Charcoal is used with textured paper, and it has to be sprayed with a fixative.

Crayons are a dry and oily medium and can also be considered wet due to their versatility. Their composition is of pigment, wax, and resin, and it is available in bars. This medium is very expressive, the lines are coarse but oily, and they can be blended with mineral spirits or a blending stick if the paint has softened with the heat, which produces very special textures.

There is another type of oil-based bar that is very similar to crayons: oil stick, which make it possible to use this material as a dry technique very similar to charcoal or pastels. It does not need to be sprayed with a fixative.

Still life and wet techniques: watercolors, acrylics, and oils

Wet techniques are the ones that involve the use of solvents. There are two groups among them: water based and oil based. The first group includes inks, watercolors, acrylics, tempera, and frescos, which are used diluted with water. The second group comprises the media that use turpentine and mineral spirits as solvents, oils, colored pencils, synthetic varnish, and crayons (although the latter are usually worked as a dry medium).

Wet techniques are also very versatile. The mixture can be very thick or very thin and can dry quickly or slowly, which can help create very realistic finishes and at the same time very spontaneous lines and areas of color.

They are applied on hard or soft supports, the most common one being canvas. Normally, these supports require priming to minimize excessive absorption and to protect the fiber of the paper, fabric, or wood. The most common working tools are brushes, spatulas, rags, and sponges.

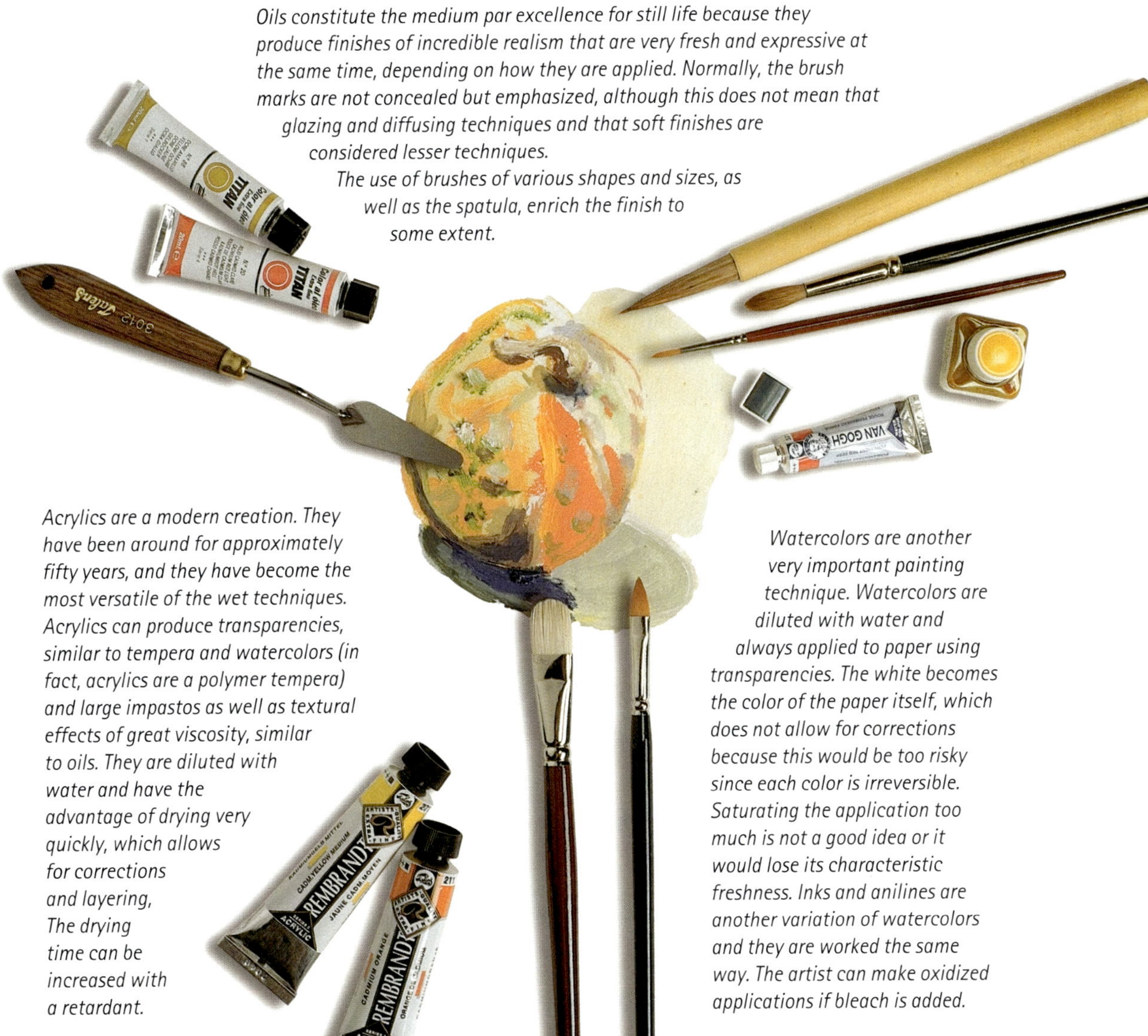

Oils constitute the medium par excellence for still life because they produce finishes of incredible realism that are very fresh and expressive at the same time, depending on how they are applied. Normally, the brush marks are not concealed but emphasized, although this does not mean that glazing and diffusing techniques and that soft finishes are considered lesser techniques. The use of brushes of various shapes and sizes, as well as the spatula, enrich the finish to some extent.

Acrylics are a modern creation. They have been around for approximately fifty years, and they have become the most versatile of the wet techniques. Acrylics can produce transparencies, similar to tempera and watercolors (in fact, acrylics are a polymer tempera) and large impastos as well as textural effects of great viscosity, similar to oils. They are diluted with water and have the advantage of drying very quickly, which allows for corrections and layering, The drying time can be increased with a retardant.

Watercolors are another very important painting technique. Watercolors are diluted with water and always applied to paper using transparencies. The white becomes the color of the paper itself, which does not allow for corrections because this would be too risky since each color is irreversible. Saturating the application too much is not a good idea or it would lose its characteristic freshness. Inks and anilines are another variation of watercolors and they are worked the same way. The artist can make oxidized applications if bleach is added.

The hand of the artist

When still life appeared, painters were very interested in the realistic representation of the model. The painting was supposed to reproduce the object faithfully to make it desirable or worthy of contemplation, that is why oils and pastels were used less frequently. With the arrival of impressionism and the cultural success of photography, though, artists wanted to leave a record of the technique used for creating an image, to affirm that it was the product of an individual, a personal and unique effort, the fruit of his or her labor.

This craftlike approach to painting and drawing is something very valuable, especially in still life, due to the human and intimate characteristics of this genre and for its incredible simplicity and natural look.

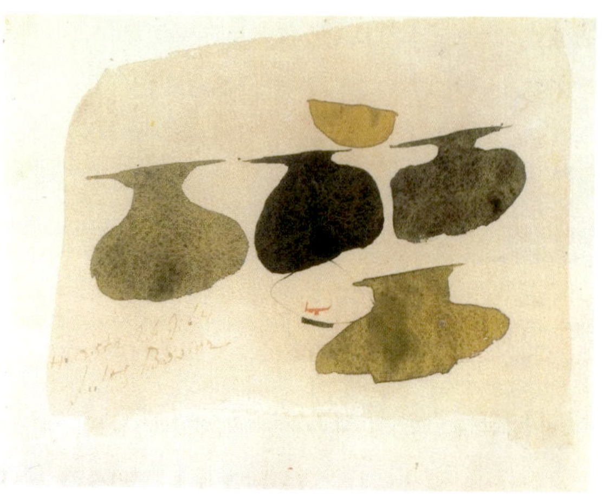

Julius Bissier, H.O.Sta. 26.9.64, *1964. Kunstsammlung Nordrhein-Westfalen, Düsseldorf (Germany). All the poetry of this small watercolor by Julius Bissier is based on a slow and delicate process, resulting from the use of a water medium to create transparencies and sponge effects and the use of fine and delicate lines.*

José María Sicilia, Bricolage 2, ocre, *1984. Private collection. The large 117 × 78 inch (3 × 2 m) canvas that Sicilia painted with oils and a large amount of paint, heavy brushstrokes, dripping, and puddles of paint is a very representative icon of Spanish painting of the decade of the eighties: wild, expressive, and generous, where the pleasure of painting is the true motivation of the artist.*

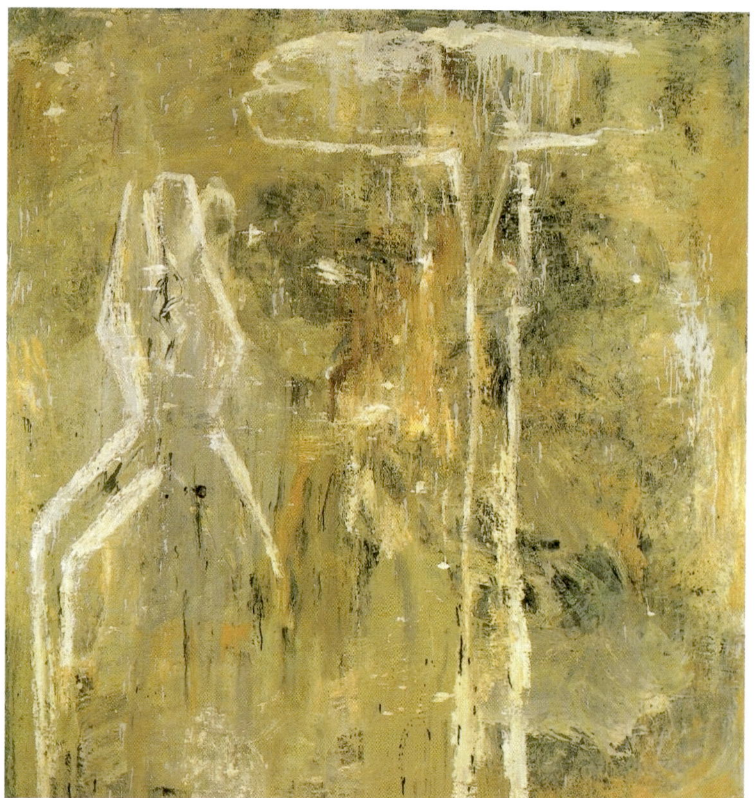

The concept of the technique

In painting, when we talk about technique, we refer to the way the painting was made, to craft. This "how" is as important as "what" because it makes us acknowledge the artist's hand, his or her personality, experiences, and particular sensibility. It is not the same to work slowly as quickly, gently as aggressively, to do it with thin brushes as with large spatulas. This constitutes the "how," what defines how a painting is made and what gives it a personal and poetic character.

As we will see later, the process goes through a series of decisions with respect to the media, tools, attitudes, even the painting position of the artist, because it is not the same to paint seated at a table as standing in front of the easel or with the canvas on the floor. The painting can be approached in different ways physically. Therefore, the results change greatly.

The drawing: tools, form, speed, and intensity

The speed with which lines and color are applied determines a specific effect. If it is very slowly, the imprecision is very noticeable, even the tremor of the hand, showing the insecurities. Morandi exploited this characteristic deliberately to transmit the vulnerability of humankind. If the speed is very fast, the lines will have little precision. If it is more energetic, the lines will transmit strength and speed.

The intensity factor refers to the energetic charge of the line or color. If a dry technique is involved, the pressure of the line will be the defining factor. If it is a wet technique, it will be related to the amount of paint. If the speed and intensity factors are combined, the effect will be increased; for example, a very intense (charged) brushstroke applied very quickly will produce spattering and will exaggerate the strength of its effect.

The form factor is the way the hand moves over the canvas: shaking, modeling the tool, creating streaky, broken, sinuous, and very straight lines. The tool is what is chosen to create this process: brush, rag, the hands, scraper, spatula . . . each one will produce different effects.

THREE DIFFERENT VERSIONS OF A FRUIT BOWL

Raoul Dufy approached the theme with a low-intensity, quick stroke—the paint is diluted. He used thin and soft brushes to create sinuous and sensual forms. Muxart exploited impastos to give the fruit bowls concentrated energy. He used slow speed and very high, almost physical intensity. The shapes are very harsh, created with hard brushes and spatulas. Finally, Schnabel applied the paint on a very large, very crude, and absorbent canvas, at a medium speed, using large brushes to create the feeling of imprecision.

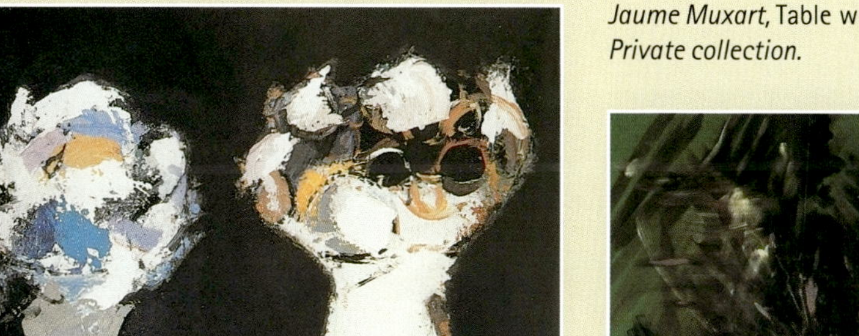

Jaume Muxart, Table with Fruit. *Private collection.*

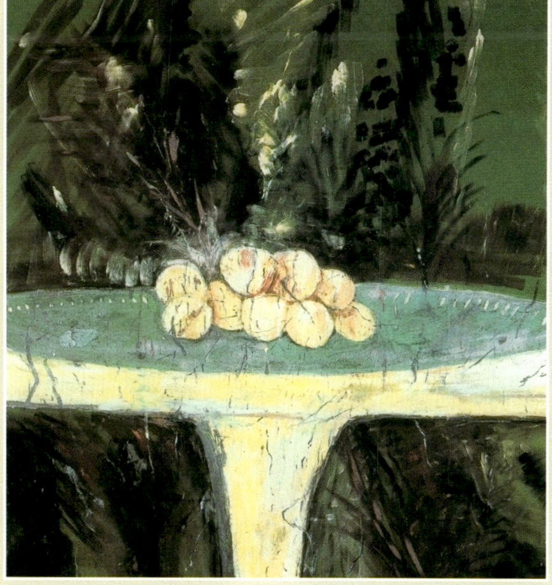

Julian Schnabel, A Few Peaches *(summer poem by Sebastián), 1984. Musée National d'Art Moderne, Paris (France).*

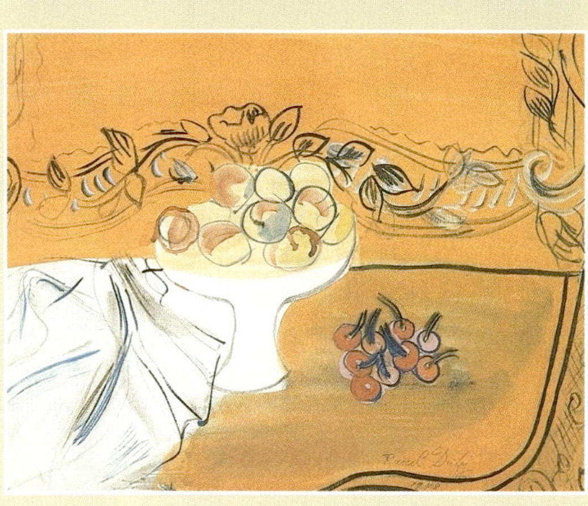

Raoul Duffy, Fruit Bowl with Peaches on Top of a Console. *Musée National d'Art Moderne, Paris (France).*

Contrast: constructive and expressive tool

In visual art, contrast is a powerful tool of expression, a way to intensify the meaning of the image, helping convey the message much faster. Contrast helps emphasize the differences. A form may appear large if seen by itself, but it will look gigantic if surrounded by very small shapes.

The main function of contrast is to enhance the perception of the image, because it will be the counternote, the tension that the painting needs to capture the attention and the interest of the spectator very powerfully. Any visual creation is based on contrast: full-empty, light-darkness, saturated-neutralized color, big-small, position and orientation changes, and so on. Without it the work is boring and lacks interest. When a still life looks to us lost or inexpressive, we should ask ourselves where the tension factor is. Normally, it will need more texture or color contrast, of chiaroscuro or composition.

Francisco de Goya, Still Life with Ribs, Meat, and Lamb's Head, *c. 1808–1812. Musée du Louvre, Paris (France). Goya painted this still life during the same period he was working on the horrors of war. Nothing is further from the classic still life with food, because it contains an incredible dramatic charge. The contrast of light created by the chiaroscuro and the central density provoke a presence of the model that is almost physical, which is troubling.*

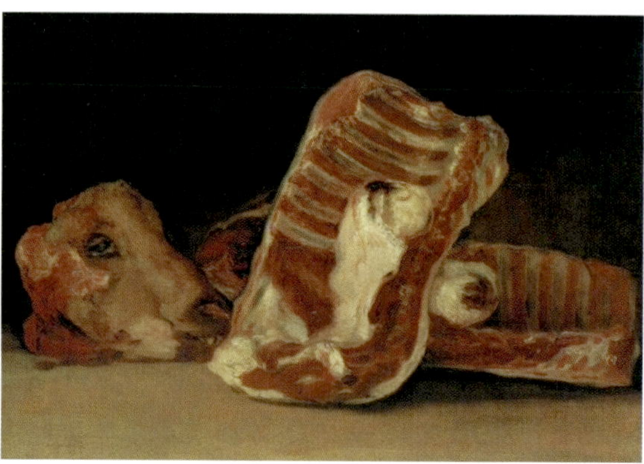

TRANSMITTING EXPERIENCE

When a still life is born as the consequence of personal experience, it transmits a greater energy of force. The life of an artist flows through his or her work. Every work, no matter how small, takes on meaning.

Pablo Picasso, The Enameled Pot, *1945. Musée National d'Art Moderne, Paris (France). This was one of Picasso's favorite paintings. He wrote to a friend, "Notice how even pots can scream." A quiet scheme of colors, except for the pot, a sculptural treatment of the volumes, and a false perspective make us establish certain connections with Zurbarán three centuries later.*

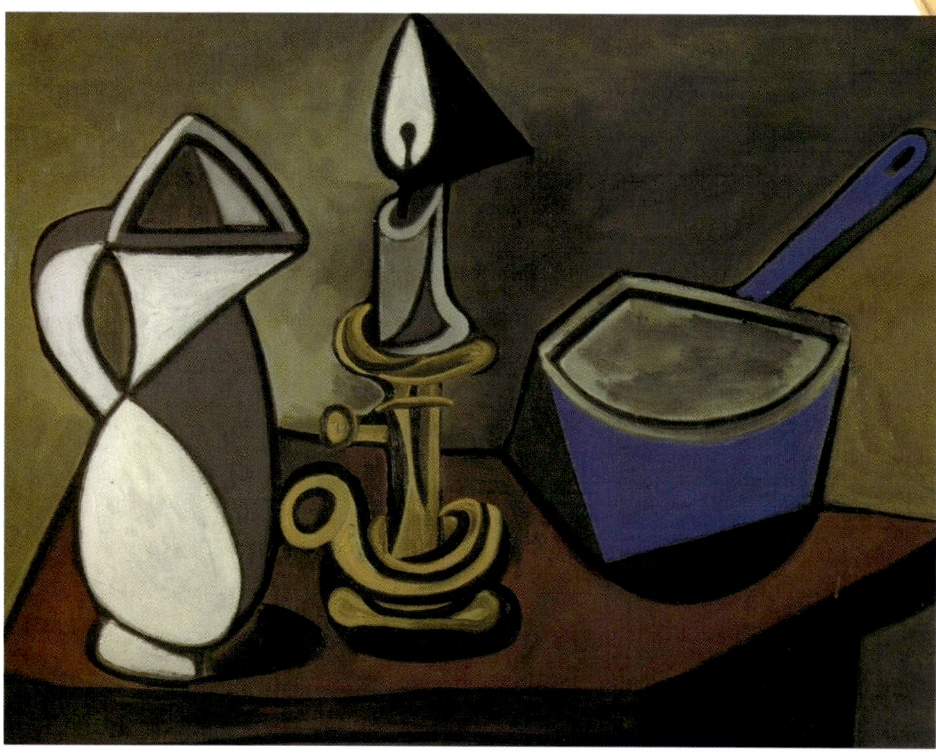

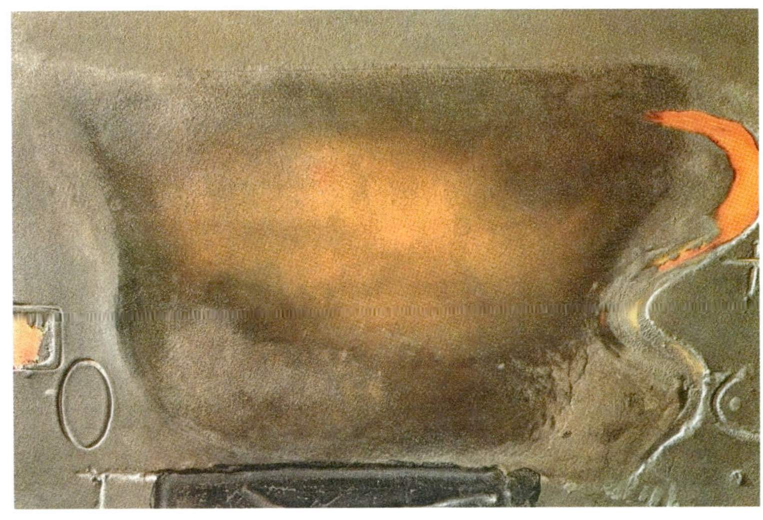

Antoni Tàpies, The Cup, *1979. Private collection. With Tàpies, form is subordinate to matter; form emerges from it. Working on the material (scratching, displacing, printing, and so on) gives way to the shape. There is a very rich language, an array of procedures explored by this researcher, who elevates art to the level of reality.*

The concept of texture

The definition of texture by the Italian artist and teacher Bruno Munari is very clear and suggestive, "Texture is the sensibility that a surface provides." This sensitive character is fundamental because it evokes tactile experiences, which psychologists indicate are stronger and more significant than visual or auditory ones. They penetrate our subconscious strongly, and they awaken a great number of emotions.

Texture has the great characteristic of uniformity. It extends across the surface, it does not consist of forms but of effects that are reminders of the characteristics of the material:
heavy-light,
rough-smooth,
soft-hard,
mobile-rigid,
flat-wrinkly,
cool-warm,
dry-wet,
regular-irregular,
consistent-inconsistent,
liquid-solid . . .

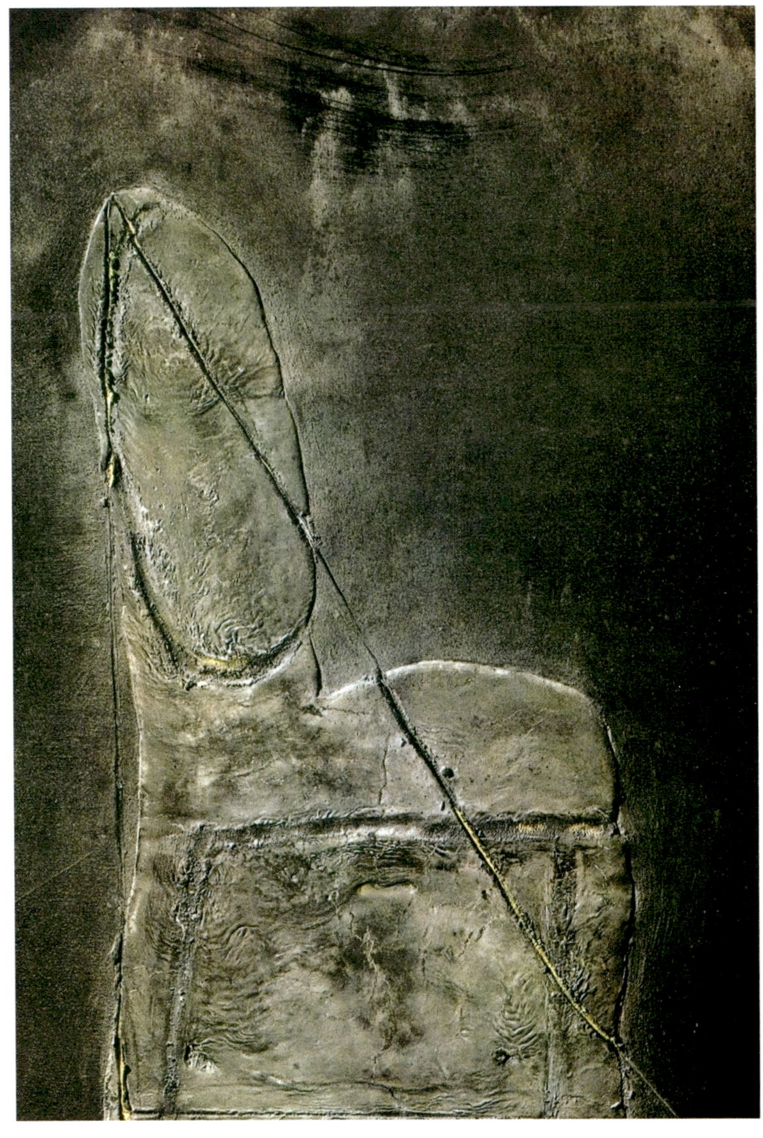

Antonio Tàpies, In the Shape of a Chair, *1966. Private collection. A statement by Tàpies will help us understand his work and the importance of texture in the visual process of communication: "I remember having thought of and produced work in which I wanted to suggest the presence, for example, of a reptile and I did it without drawing it, giving the surface a scaly look."*

Scraping, dying, blending, gluing, impasto . . . texturing

Texture can be classified into two large groups: natural and artificial textures. The first ones are those of nature without any manipulation. The second are man-made, from the handle of a knife to a metal screen, or fabric. We as artists can incorporate all those materials in our compositions by gluing them, printing them, or by being inspired by them.

In the first group, we find the outer skin of things (peels, parchment, shells . . .), their imperfections (worn-out areas, dents, tears . . .), and the efforts of growing and degeneration (wrinkles, dried-out areas . . .).

In the second, we can use textures (screens, grids, fabrics . . .), mechanically altered surfaces (wrinkled papers, cut-out cardboard, torn fabric . . .), textures on commercial materials (tires, plastics, metals . . .), and discards (cans, cardboard . . .).

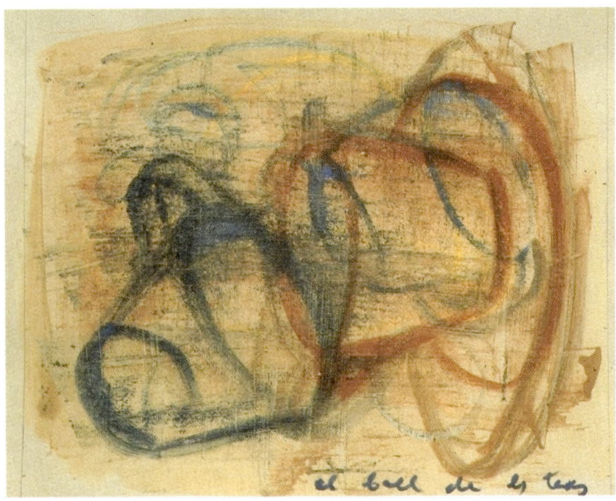

Gemma Guasch, The Dancing Cups, *1999.*
Private collection.
We can paint wet on wet, diluting the image, blending, printing, rubbing on textured surfaces (frottage), spraying, spattering, dripping, scratching, gluing (collage), dragging . . .

In this poetic still life, Guasch has experimented with rubbing to insinuate a dance of lines and colors.

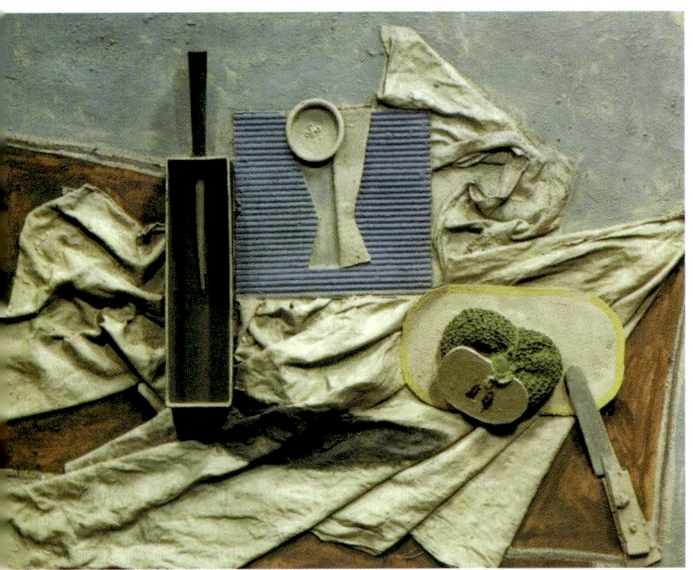

Pablo Picasso, Still Life with Apple, *1937.*
Private collection.
During the cubist and Dada periods, many artists developed collage as a way of expressing themselves by incorporating nonartistic materials that were raised to that category in the painting. Collage is halfway between traditional painting and sculpture. This still life by Picasso is a clear example of that phenomenon.

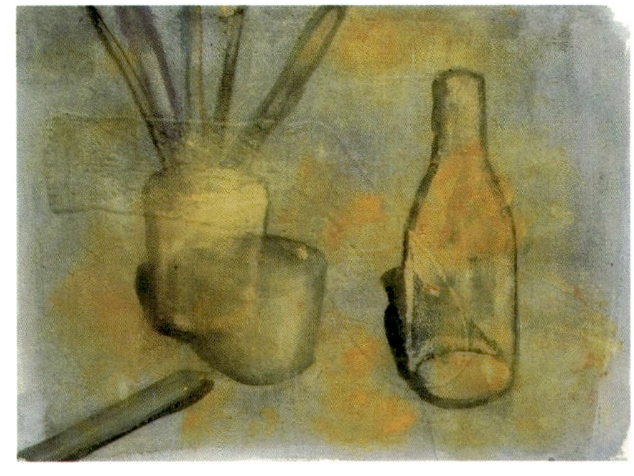

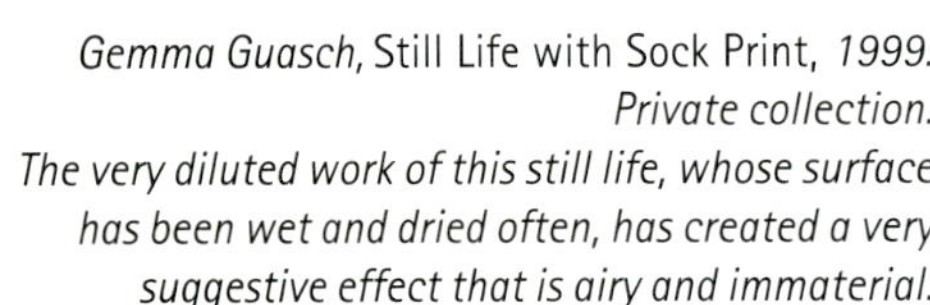

Gemma Guasch, Still Life with Sock Print, *1999.*
Private collection.
The very diluted work of this still life, whose surface has been wet and dried often, has created a very suggestive effect that is airy and immaterial.

Techniques and processes applied to still life

In the following pages, we will develop several still life projects, explaining them step-by-step. Ten different subjects with very diverse techniques, approaches, and styles will be presented. Following these examples will provide the reader with a good hands-on overview of still life.

Until now we have studied the theory of making a still life, its history, language, a general overview of the media, and so on. However, we have not looked at the actual practice of this genre. In the following pages, we will approach still life through specific and practical exercises. Each one of the paintings that we will analyze summarizes in some way a classic subject matter: objects, flowers, fruit, jewelry, containers, clothing, and glass. These are all recurring themes that have been chosen as specific examples, always focusing on the affinity between the theme and the technique: pencil for detailed drawings of jewelry, charcoal for geometric volumes, oils for traditional containers and plates, collage for the daring scene in a garage, and others.

In the following pages, we will approach still life through specific and practical exercises.

If we observe carefully, we will discover that all of them have two things in common. The first thing is that they all follow the same process, the painting is always developed from the general to the specific. The second point in common is the importance of the line. The artist's hand and the mark left by the brush, pencil, or even the fingers is what constitutes the painting. A simple line can describe the fold of a blouse or the volume of a lemon.

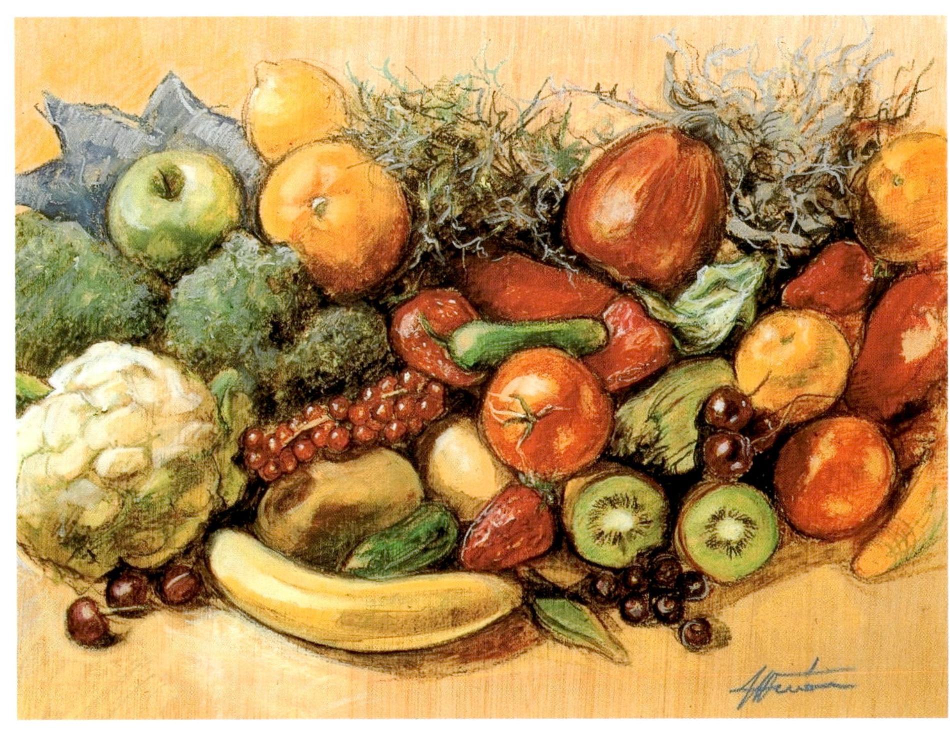

There is always an ideal technique for each theme. Experimenting with all of them gives us a good base to decide which one is the most appropriate for expressing our intentions. In this still life with fruit and vegetables, crayons offer a rich color and an energetic and vital line.

Modeling with charcoal

To model a form, that is, to give volume to it, we have two options. We can work with chiaroscuro, the most traditional approach, which began with the Renaissance period and reached its peak with baroque's mannerist movement. The second option, initiated by the impressionists, consists of the use of color contrast. It is put into practice by using the characteristic light values of each color, without neutralizations, and using blue for shadows.

Charcoal is the ideal technique for initiation in chiaroscuro because of its great plasticity. It is appropriate for delicate areas of diffused color and for hard lines, and it is also suitable for a wide range of grays.

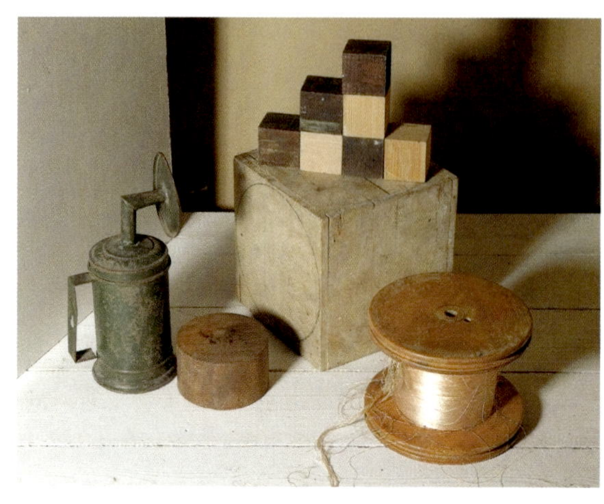

The models that we have chosen for this project, cubes and cylinders, are easy to draw because of their geometric structures. Artificial lighting produces long, diverging shadows. This harsh type of lighting exaggerates the effect of depth and drama.

MATERIALS

- White Ingres paper
- Charcoal sticks
- Rag
- Erasers (hard and soft)

1

1 The first step is to lay out the image. The lines of the three main planes of the composition and of the cube are established, calculating their sizes on paper very precisely, so all the pieces can be blocked in.

2

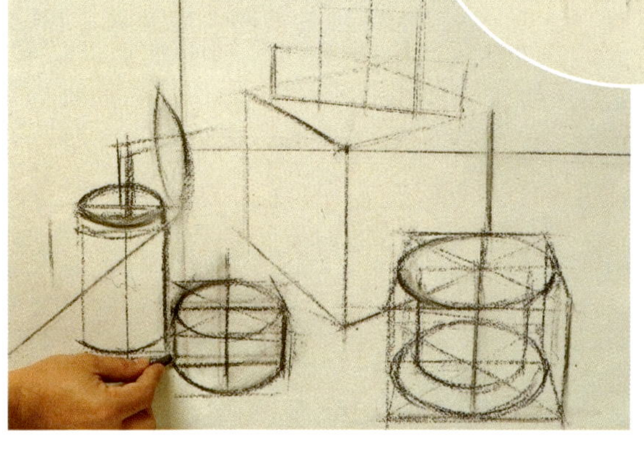

2 Next, the rest of the elements are indicated by calculating their exact placement on the plane (height and width) and the distance between them. To help us with the task, a pencil is used as indicated in the previous chapter devoted to perspective. The elliptical forms are handled the same way.

3

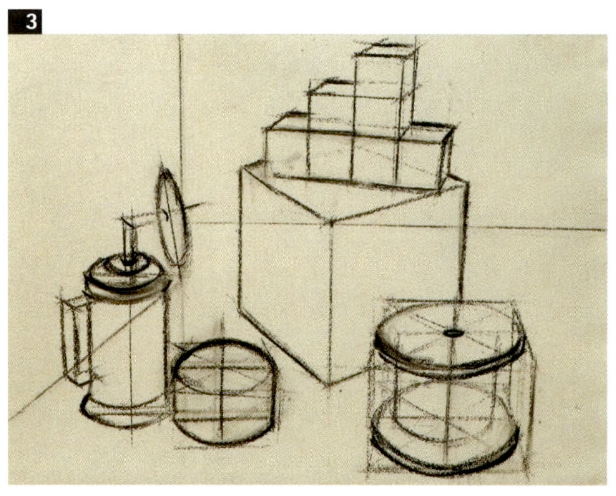

3 Here we see the completed blocking in; the sides of the cubes, the handle of the lamps, and their widths have been drawn. It is a good idea to draw these secondary elements later, after confirming that the important volumes are in their places and that they have the correct proportions.

TECHNIQUES USED

◆ Blocking in with perspective and geometry ◆
◆ Blending ◆
◆ Drawing with charcoal and eraser ◆
◆ Monochromatic harmony ◆

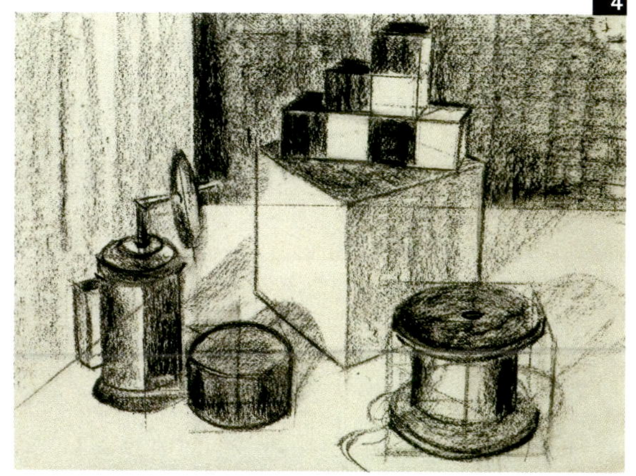

Monochromatic chiaroscuro

Monochromatic chiaroscuro is developed in a scale that ranges from the darkest tone of the chosen color to the lightest. There is no other color involved other than the chosen one and black and white, if any. In this still life, we will work with a scale of pure grays. To create the brightest light tones, we have decided not to use white chalk but the white of the paper, producing the most intense lights by erasing or with reserves. To create the deepest black, the paper, previously covered with color and blended, will be intensely rubbed with charcoal, saturating the black color to the fullest.

4 The first applications indicate the overall value of light and shadow, background and figure, of the entire scene. Working on the values of the background and the figure at the same pace is important because they will look light or dark depending on the color behind or beside them.

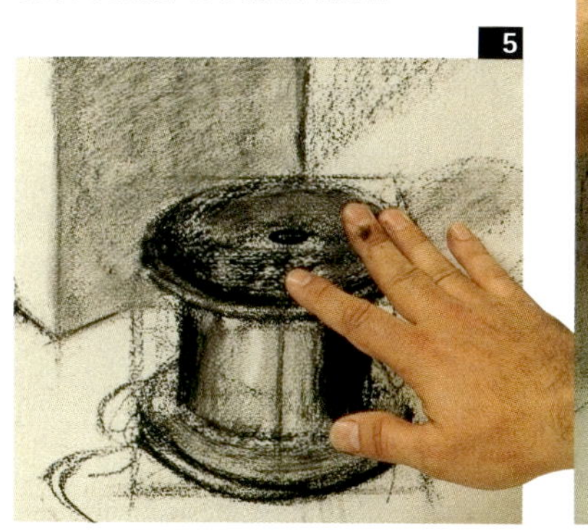

5 The charcoal is spread on the paper with the finger or a blending stick, creating an even tone that covers the surface. If the desired result is a very dark gray or an absolute black, the application of charcoal can be repeated as many times as necessary.

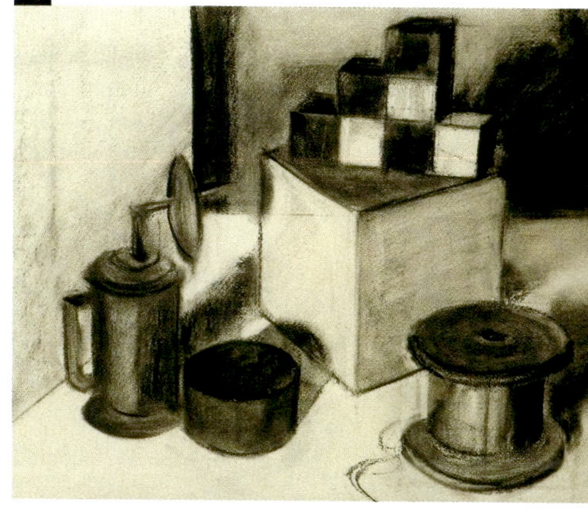

6 A rag is used to eliminate excess charcoal and to lighten the grays.

7 The value of the entire composition has already been established. All that is left is to draw a few details.

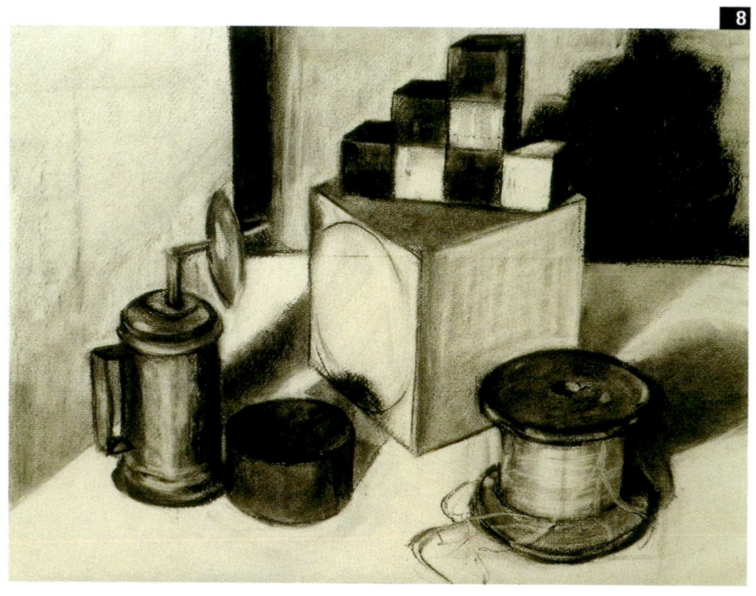

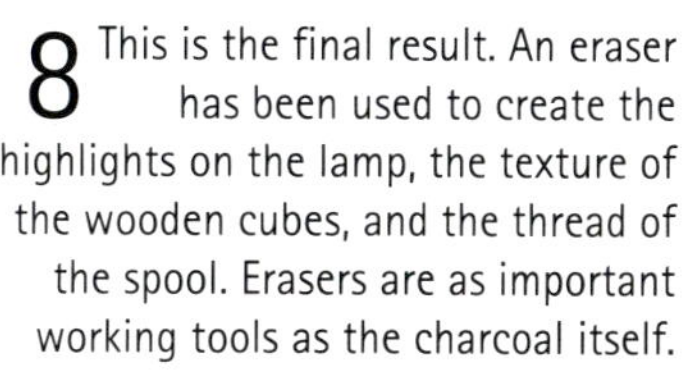

8 This is the final result. An eraser has been used to create the highlights on the lamp, the texture of the wooden cubes, and the thread of the spool. Erasers are as important working tools as the charcoal itself.

Representing and interpreting the same theme

This second phase of the process is another approach that the author of this still life will take to show other very different ways of working with charcoal. By popular belief, charcoal has been associated with academic work. However, many artists use it for representations that are more expressionistic due to the technical possibilities offered by charcoal, with which energetic lines and very dramatic but fresh chiaroscuros can be created.

9 The final stage of the previous work has been partially erased with a rag. The new base is blurred but suggestive, especially the result of the dynamic gesture of the erasing.

10 A new still life is being built over the previous one, which has been partially eliminated. Now the development is more interpretative and subjective. Each line suggests the following step, without a previously established structure.

11 This is the final step. Contrasting effects have been used: soft-hard, textured-smooth, graded-uniform, light-dark, to produce a creative and unique still life.

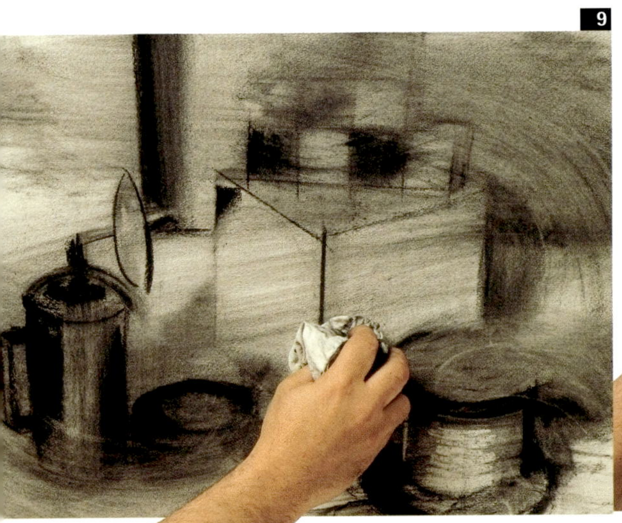

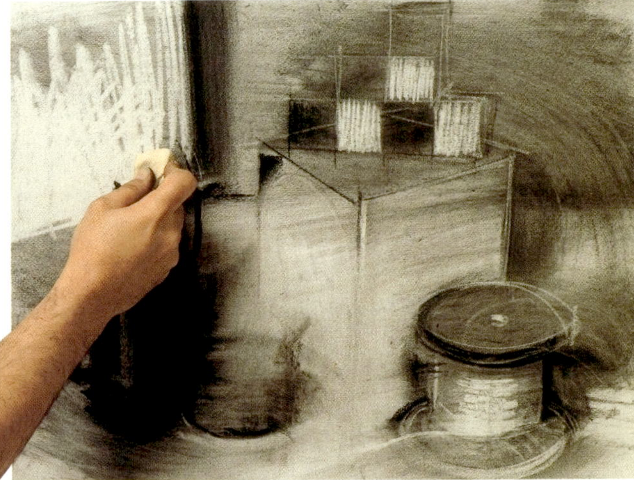

PRESERVING THE DRAWING
Charcoal, as well as pastels and chalk, need a final spraying of fixative because the products lack an agglutinant in their composition. Normally, special fixatives are used that can be sprayed from a distance of about 8 inches (20 cm) from the drawing. Do not stop over any one particular area of the drawing for an extended period of time. You should go back and forth repeatedly over the entire area, pausing between layers to prevent staining.

A sketch in the kitchen

Next we will see a still life theme that will remind us of many others in our daily lives that normally go unnoticed. The same way seventeenth- and eighteenth-century still life scenes represented the interiors of kitchens with their pots and pans and their hearths, this one also shows a modern-day kitchen with its utensils and its hearth (the microwave oven). When Zurbarán or Chardin painted those kitchen scenes, they did them in their own kitchens, with all the amenities of their times. In that sense, we can affirm that this is the most authentic contemporary still life.

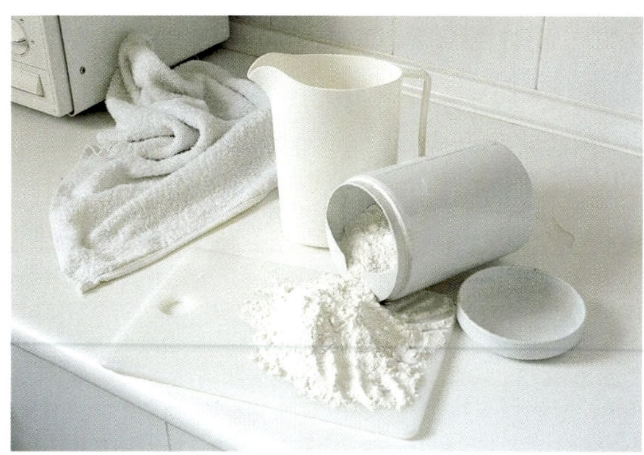

This is the scene that we have chosen for a sketch with pastels. A diagonal composition offers the dynamic layout for which we were looking.

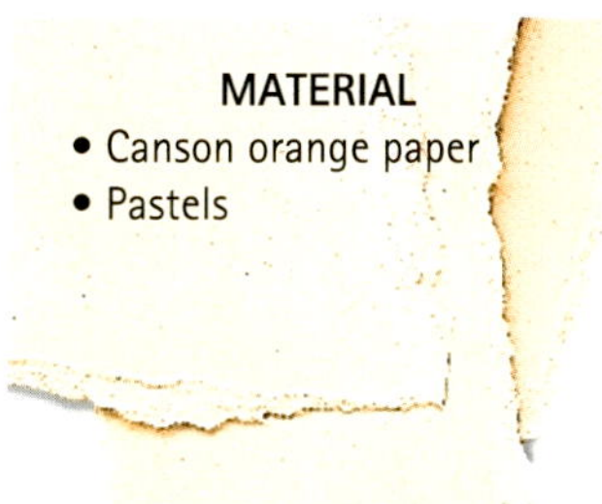

MATERIAL
- Canson orange paper
- Pastels

1 We have chosen a very bright orange paper for its color, because the excess of white would create a monochromatic scheme that would not render very attractive results to convey the ingeniousness and spontaneity of the theme. The image is laid out with a preliminary drawing done with pastel in a quick and loose style.

1

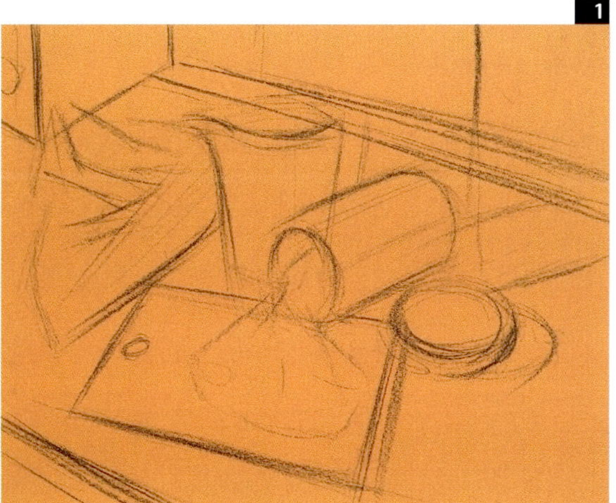

2

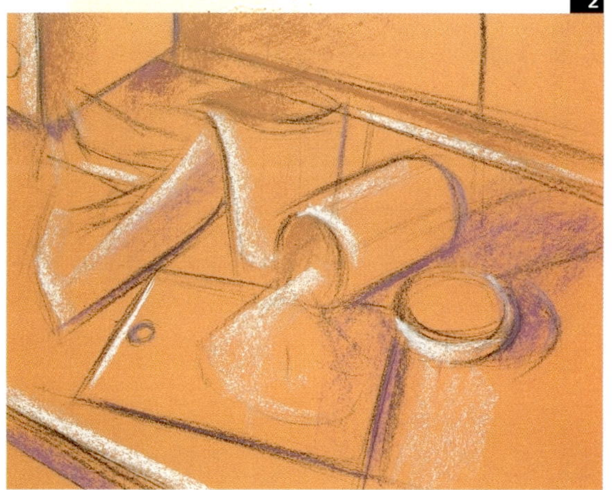

2 After establishing the shapes, light and shadows are beginning to emerge. For this task, we will only use two colors: white for the areas of light and violet for the shadows. The orange of the background acts as an intermediate color.

3 The first creative decisions of this study take place at this stage of the process, and that is planning the color layout: the jar will be green, the rag violet, and the pitcher orange.

TECHNIQUES USED

◆ Preliminary drawing ◆
◆ Line value ◆
◆ Three-color harmony with secondary colors (orange, green, and violet) ◆

3

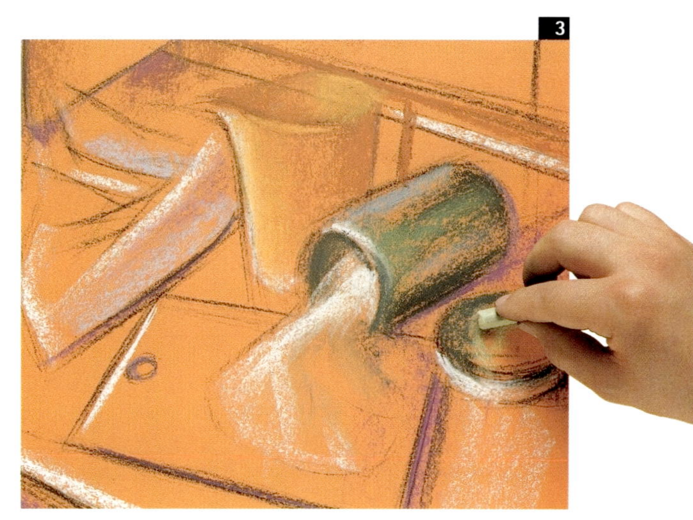

The importance of the line in a sketch

A sketch is nothing more than a drawing or a painting but without a preliminary layout, with no other purpose than to capture and summarize a moment very quickly. A sketch does not usually have a lot of detail. It looks as if it were not finished or as if the artist could continue the drawing or the painting at any given time but decides not to do so because he or she wants to maintain the original freshness and spontaneity. The line is vital in a sketch. Sometimes, varying the pressure or direction of one single line describes an entire shape, and quickly applied cross-hatching can describe a dark area.

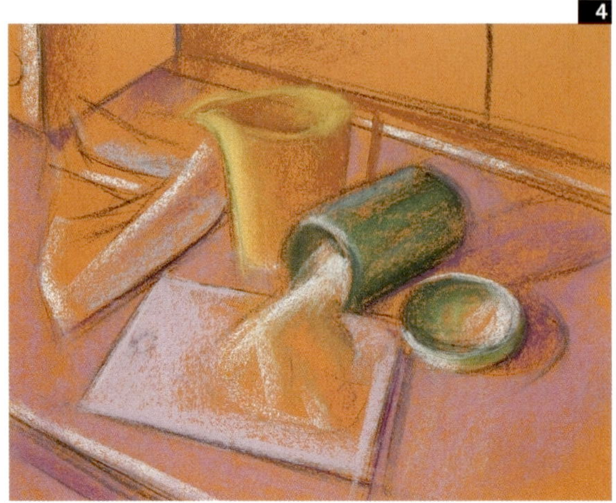

4

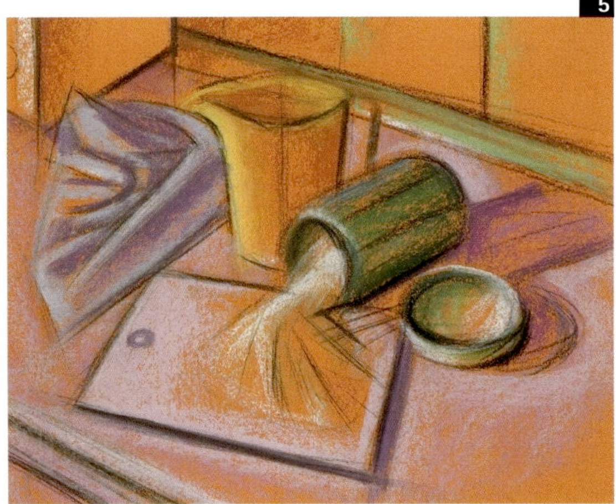

5

4 Color is extended over the areas that were not still very defined, and the volumes begin to take shape.

5 By using the same tonal values for the background as for the figures, the resulting still life is one that emphasizes the scene rather than the individual objects. Space and form interact, and each one plays its role. There are no first or second planes, the image is seen as a whole.

6 We see how colors are distributed over the entire plane. The green of the jar is repeated on the wall, the violet of the rag appears in the shadow of the jar, and the orange of the jar is in the flour. Most importantly, the orange background is repeated everywhere, creating color unity.

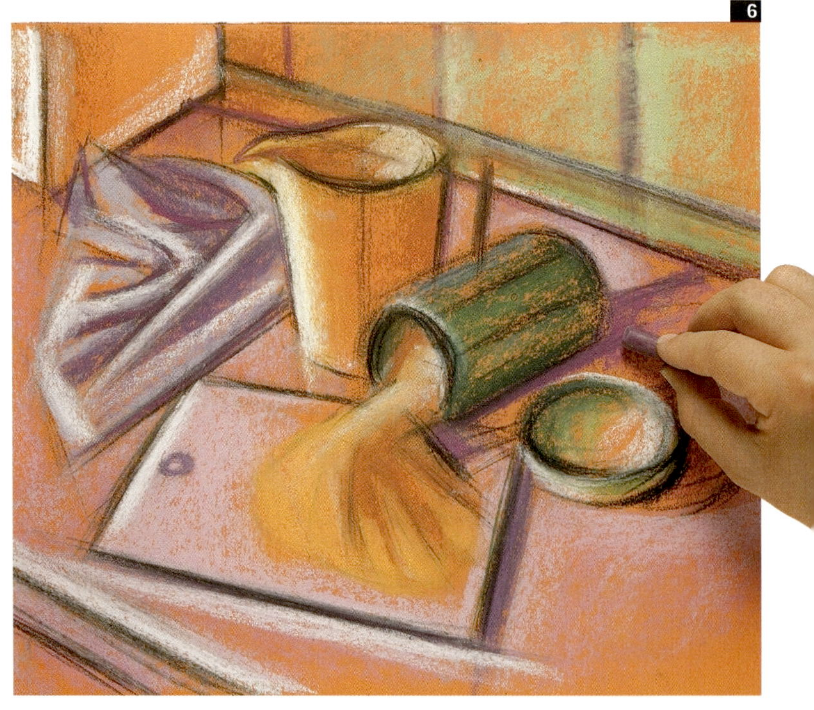

6

LETTING THE BACKGROUND BREATHE

When the work is done on a colored background, very interesting results can be achieved by letting that color show through the ones we are adding. Letting the background breathe gives the composition some life and avoids resulting in an image that is dense or static looking. For a sketch, this is a very important decision because it creates an image that is free and fresh.

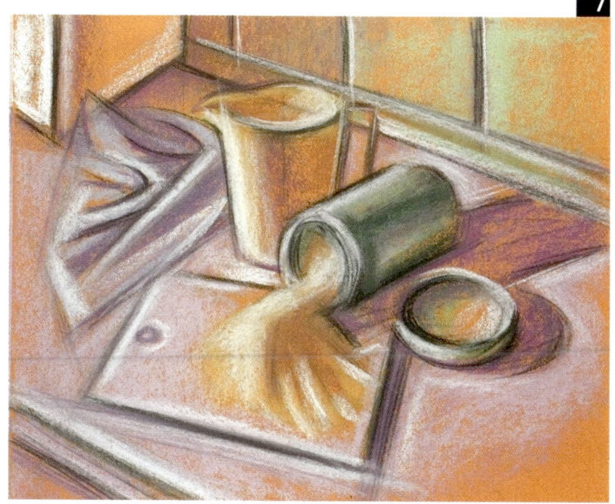

The level of completion

When does a sketch cease to be a sketch? When the finished product is too elaborate. This refers to the level of information conveyed: texture, color, form, space, details. . . . The closer to photographic realism, the further away the idea of a sketch. The more details conveyed, the further it gets from a sketch.

A sketch should preserve the feeling of immediacy and spontaneity. Normally, a sketch involves a reality that is not manipulated, that is presented as is. Doing a sketch is like conducting a photographic documentary. It means capturing the scene but taking artistic license to improvise and to make changes, allowing and integrating trial and error and corrections.

7 The strong presence of white in the model has been recaptured. This color always represents cleanliness and light. Adding white to the elements produces special, plasticlike luminosity, like in the real model.

8 Here is the finished sketch. Keeping in mind that this is a sketch, its level of completion is quite advanced. The process could have been stopped two steps back, but we wanted to push the limit to combine spontaneity and a finished look. The colors have not been blended, so the grain of the paper could be left exposed. This way color and texture are emphasized.

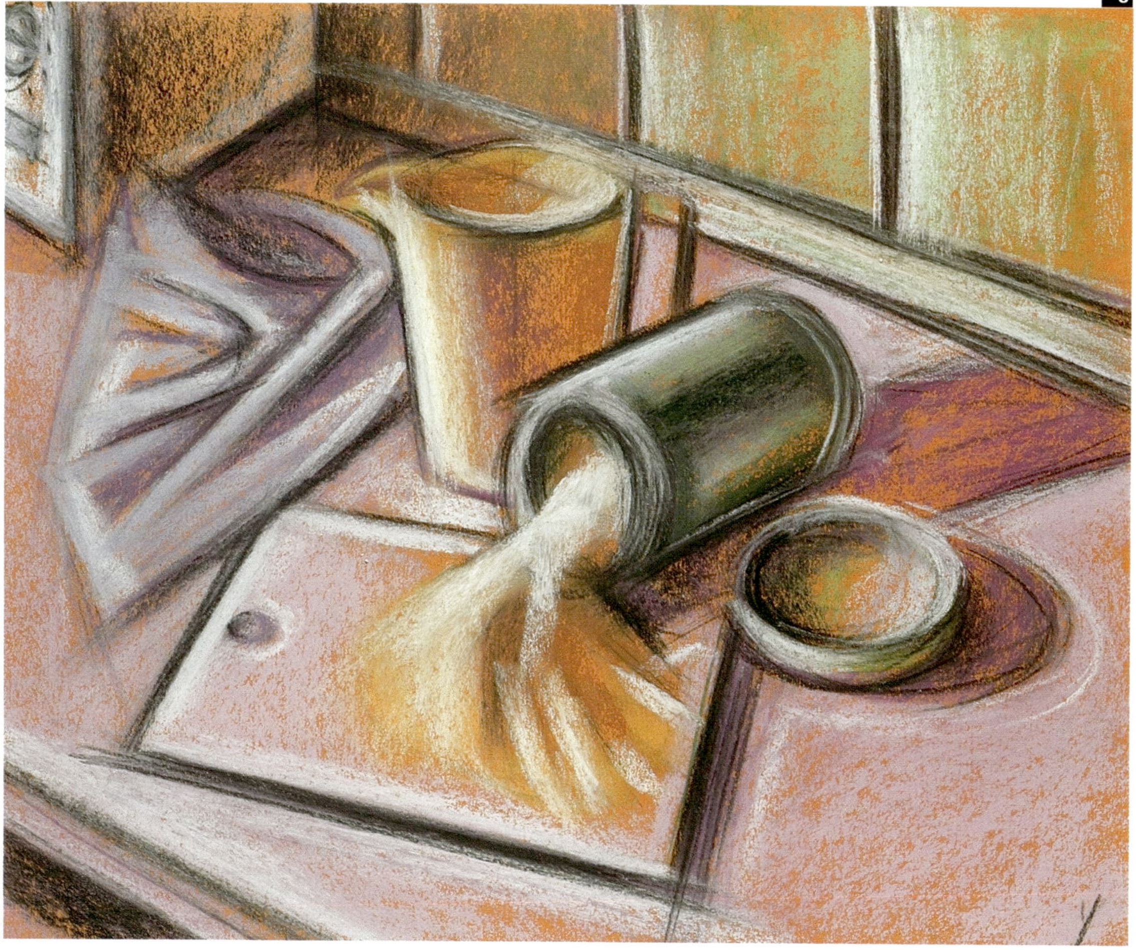

The softness of pastels

Pastels are an ideal medium for very realistic drawings. Since this is a soft material, it can produce very delicate gradations by blending the colors. The final effect is very special, velvety, and soft. It is used very often for portraits because it produces very realistic, fleshlike effects.

In still life, taking advantage of the softness of pastels may be very interesting if the chosen theme has a poetic, delicate, and atmospheric feeling. This is the case of this simple composition, which follows a very oriental aesthetic that values simplicity and space.

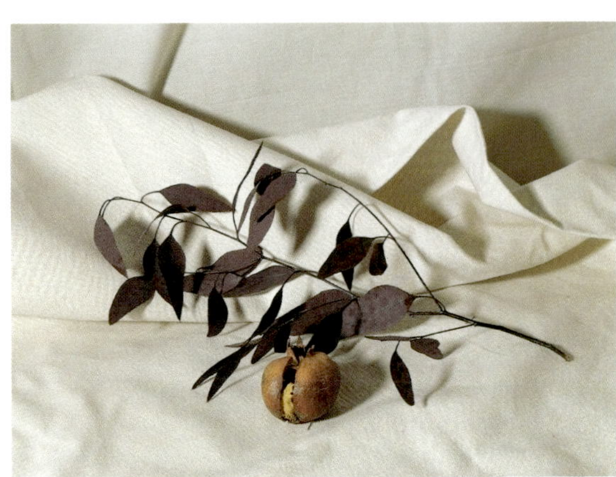

A composition of contemplative character that attempts to represent a peaceful feeling must utilize a horizontal plane as a structural axis. The slight inclinations of the branches and folds of the fabric provide a certain, although very slight, amount of movement. The leaves appear as if floating in the air because of the delicate branches.

1

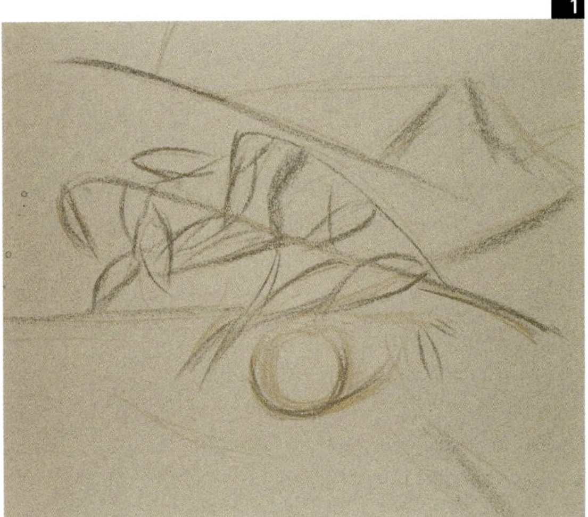

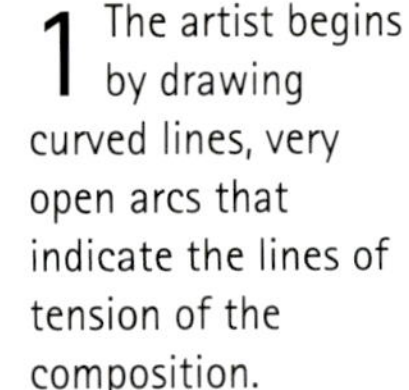

1 The artist begins by drawing curved lines, very open arcs that indicate the lines of tension of the composition.

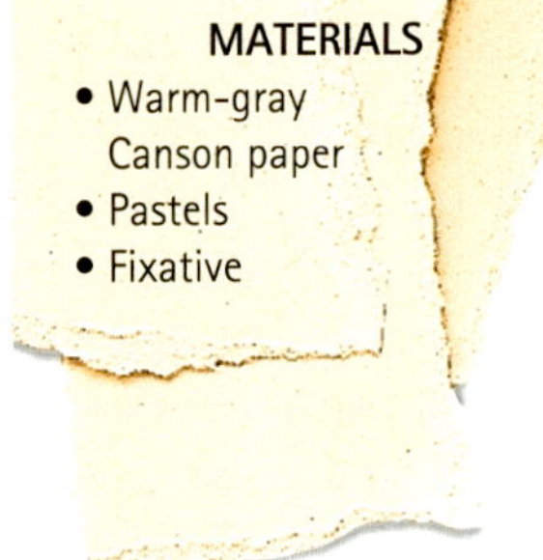

MATERIALS

- Warm-gray Canson paper
- Pastels
- Fixative

2

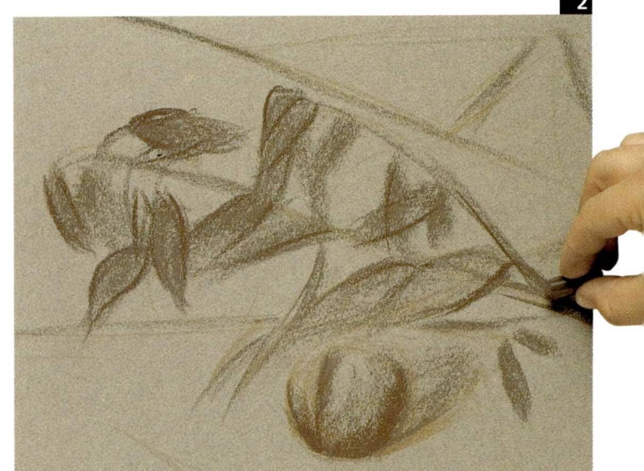

2 The first blocks of color establish the mass of the still life. Since this is more of a play of density and suppleness and not as much about color and volume, it is important to focus on that to establish a strong foundation for the still life.

3 The second application will be indications of color. The different areas of the drawing have been established very generally, although this is still just an approximation.

3

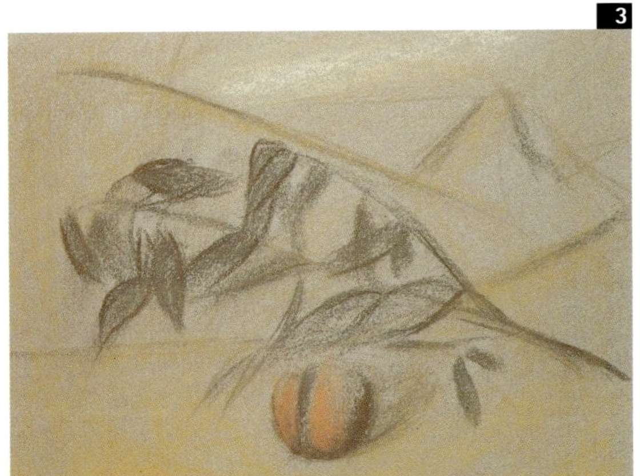

TECHNIQUES USED

◆ Preliminary drawing ◆
◆ Lines ◆
◆ Blending ◆
◆ Dominant color scheme (earth tones) ◆

4 Working on a gray tone paper means using white or light colors to paint the areas of light. This has advantages because we eliminate the need for reserves and the contrast of light and dark can be dealt with directly. Here are the first areas of light.

5 As the representing of the light areas progresses, establishing the shaded areas becomes necessary since one does not exist without the other and the effect of light is produced by both. Notice how when the first shadows are represented, the model begins to stand out against the background and to acquire its own presence.

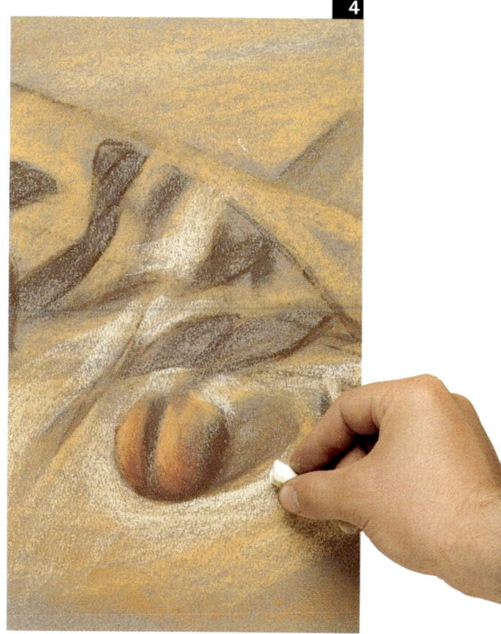
4

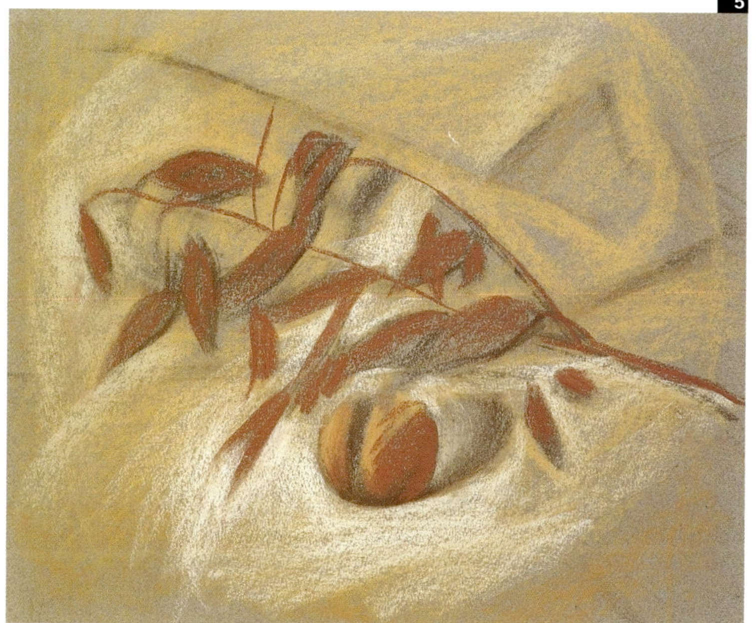
5

TO BLEND OR TO EMPHASIZE THE LINE?
With pastels, blending looks so attractive that it is easy to abuse. If this is practically the only technique used, the final image may look soft, which is normally referred to as "the buttery" effect. It is so soft that it looks like it is going to melt. To avoid this unwanted effect, combine the softness of the blending with the energy and natural feeling of the line.

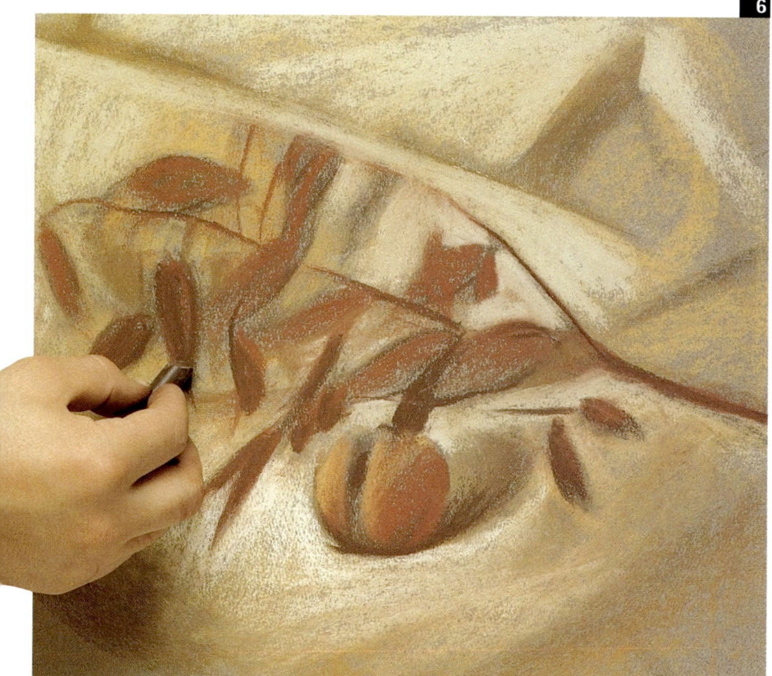
6

6 We can begin to see the light spreading through the entire image. This will be the base for subsequent steps.

Creating an atmospheric effect by blending

When we talk about atmosphere in painting, we refer to the weather or to the artistic environment created in a painting. In art, the atmosphere is created with color because the effect produced this way is more spatial and environmental than the line. Applying color covers the surface and creates density, like fog or clouds in a landscape. It provides texture, gives the air body, makes it artistically visible and dense. That result constitutes the atmosphere of the painting. Leonardo da Vinci was one of the first to talk about this atmospheric effect in landscapes. However, it can be applied to any genre. The way to create an atmospheric effect in a painting with pastels is by diffusion, by softly blending the colors, by creating a heavy atmosphere that floods the scene to produce an intimate and warm feeling, like in this still life.

7

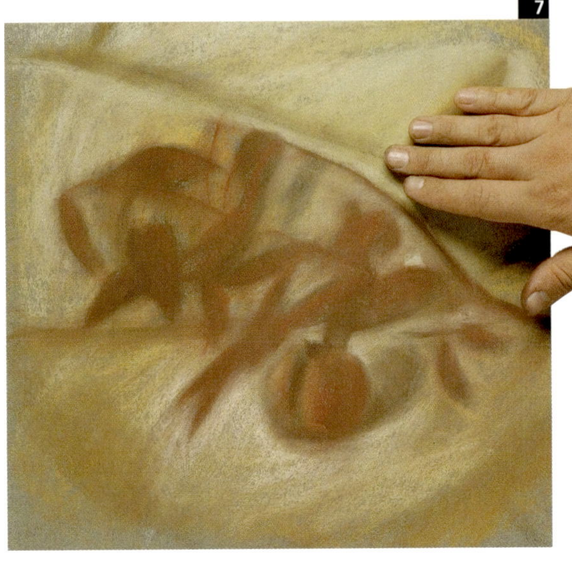

7 If the artist wishes to create a dense finish, with a heavy atmospheric effect, the colors should be half-diffused to continue over that base that is more opaque later. In this case, the fingers have been used, but a blending stick is also a suitable tool.

8 To prevent the painting from getting ruined with subsequent applications, it should be sprayed with fixative. Now the base is solid and the colors and light can continue to be adjusted without fear of losing control of the material.

8

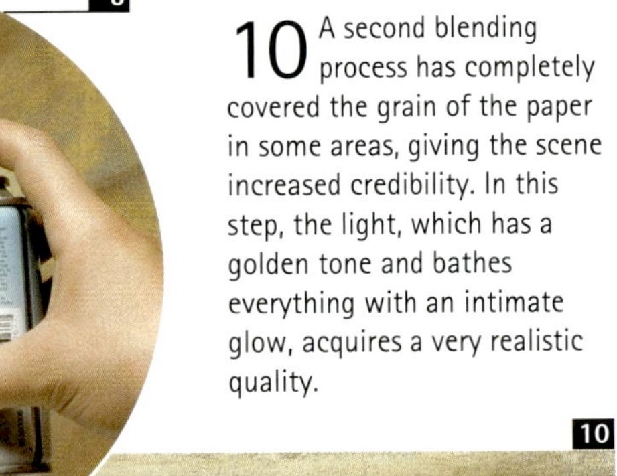

9 Now, we only need to reestablish the crispness of the image by strengthening the light and shadows according to our final goal. From this moment on, everything stands out more vividly because it has a stronger base that calls for more vigorous applications.

10 A second blending process has completely covered the grain of the paper in some areas, giving the scene increased credibility. In this step, the light, which has a golden tone and bathes everything with an intimate glow, acquires a very realistic quality.

9

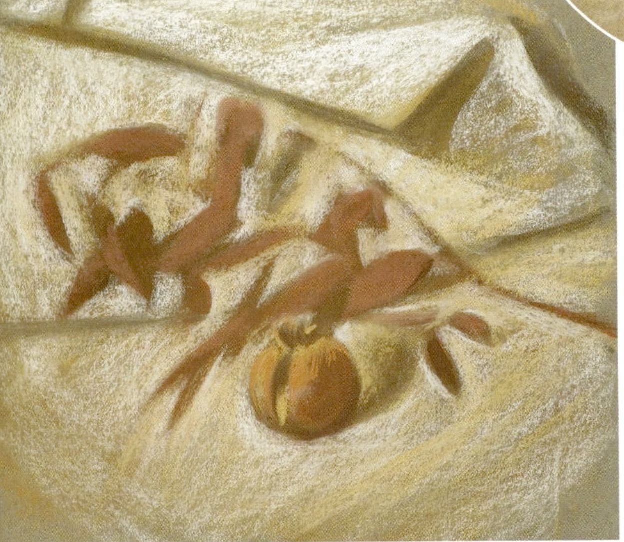

10

PASTELS AND MIXING COLORS

With this medium, color mixing always takes place on the paper, on the drawing itself, never someplace else. Pastels do not require a palette; that is why there is a great variety of colors available, because it is very laborious, and sometimes impossible, to produce a specific color by mixing primary or other colors on the paper itself. Besides, it ends up being very dirty as a result of the excess accumulated pigment. Have a large variety of colors available if working with this medium.

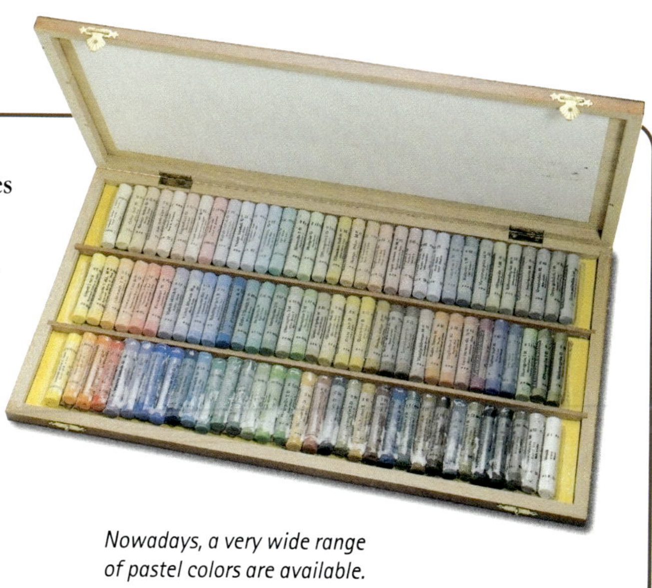

Nowadays, a very wide range of pastel colors are available.

11 The still life has been completed. The shadows have been emphasized with the final touches. This way, we have been able to make the branches and the pomegranate stand out again against the background, making them more palpable and realistic.

11

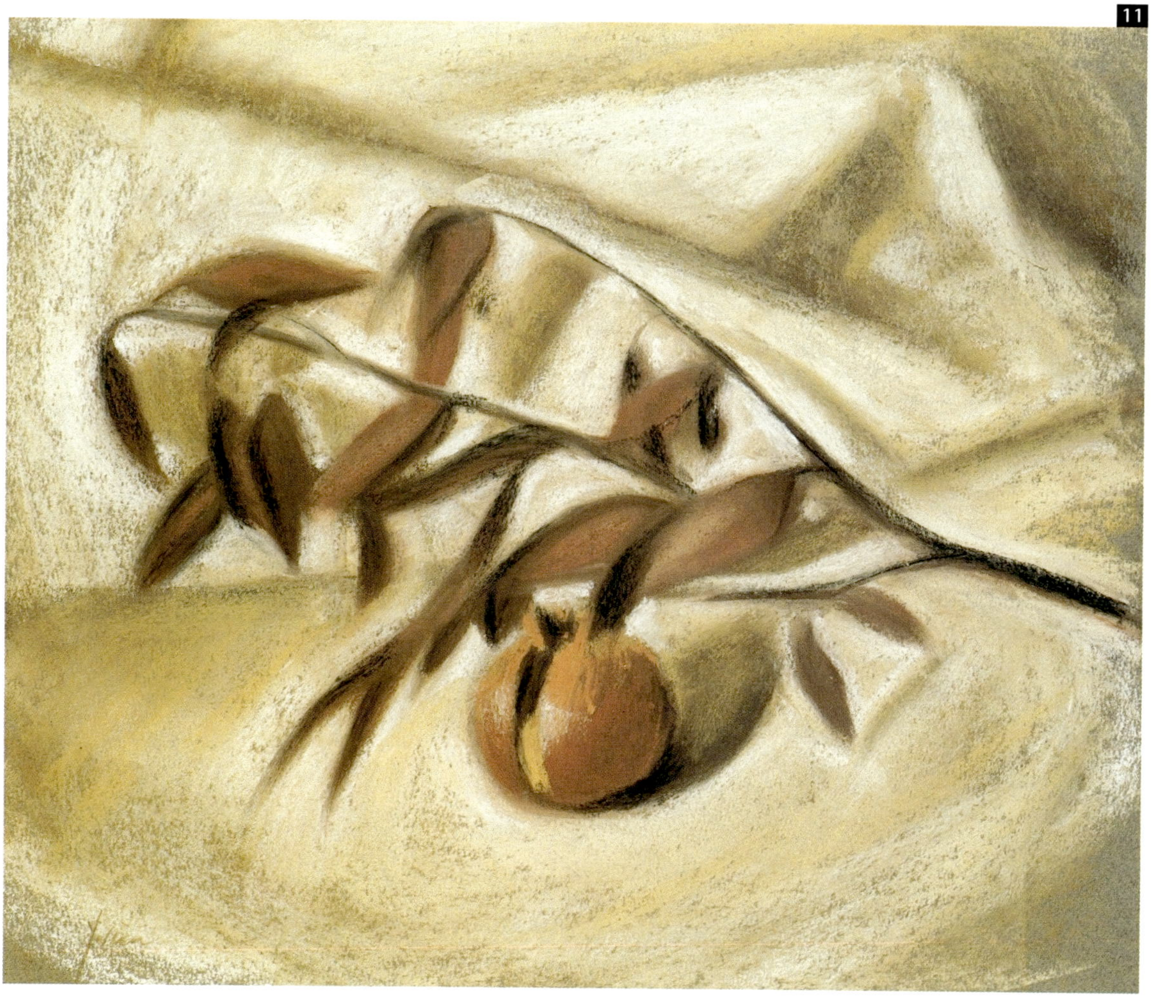

The expressiveness of vegetables as subjects

Fruits, vegetables, and flowers are traditionally the most colorful and vital components of a still life because they are natural elements. The same is not true of game animals, though, which remind us of the sad end of life in the wild. A still life with fresh food is a representation of an instant, of the moment. Fruits spoil and vegetables are not edible after a few days. The goal of still life in depicting these themes is to stop time and to enjoy the feast offered by nature.

For this still life, we have chosen a composition full of vegetables. It is a representation of edible things, another classic theme of this genre that has an exuberant composition.

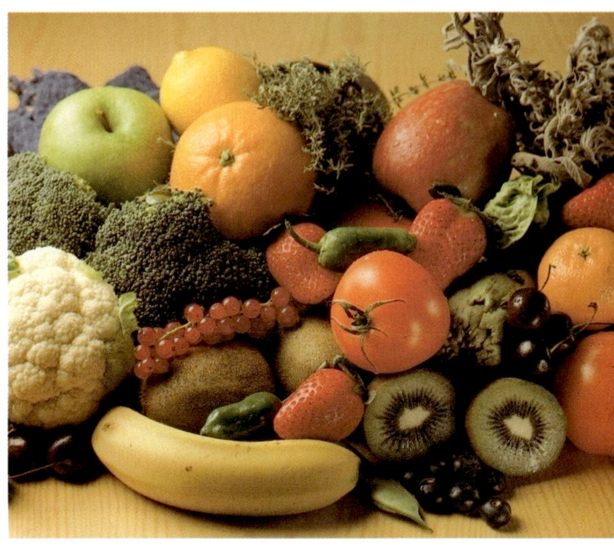

1 The layout is executed with chalk of a neutral color, without pressing too hard so it can be corrected if needed. The corrections are made with a rag wetted with mineral spirits, never with an eraser because this would just cake up the line but would never eliminate the oil of the crayon.

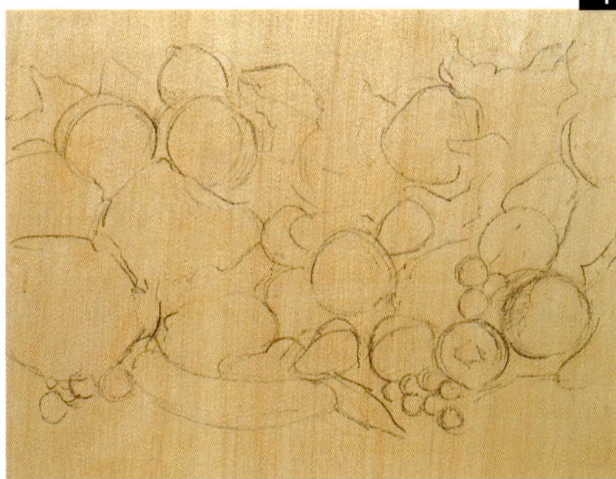

A still life representation with so many components requires patience and an observant eye so each texture and color contributes its full potential.

MATERIALS

- Prepared wood surface
- Crayons
- Mineral spirits
- Round bristle brush

2 Density is indicated with cross-hatching. Still, the crayon should not be pressed too hard because this is a planning phase.

3 The composition is already completed. All the elements are in place, well proportioned, and the volumes are sketched in. The painting is ready for color.

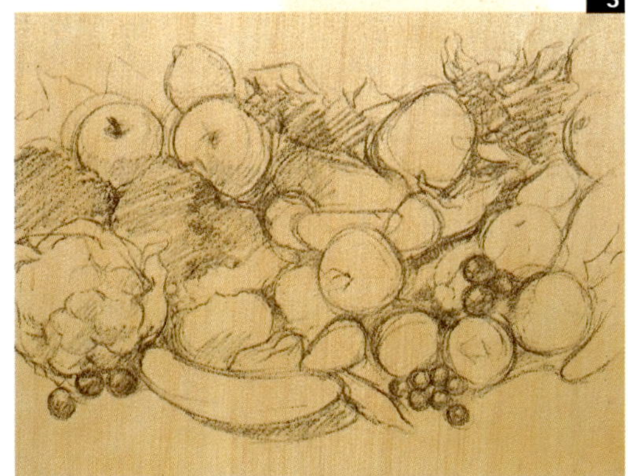

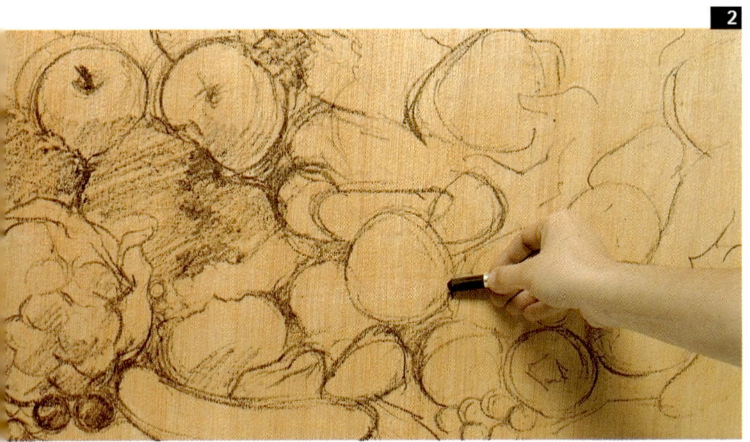

TECHNIQUES USED

- Layout with curves
- Chromatic chiaroscuro
- Dry and diluted crayons
- Full-color harmony

THE VIBRANT COLORS OF CRAYONS
As with pastels, crayons are not mixed on the palette but on the painting itself, which acts as palette. A wide range of tones are available on the market, but the difference with pastels is in the color. Pastels always have a dull color, whitish, normally considered "pastel-like." Crayons, on the other hand, offer a vibrant, active, and direct color. This is their great expressive advantage.

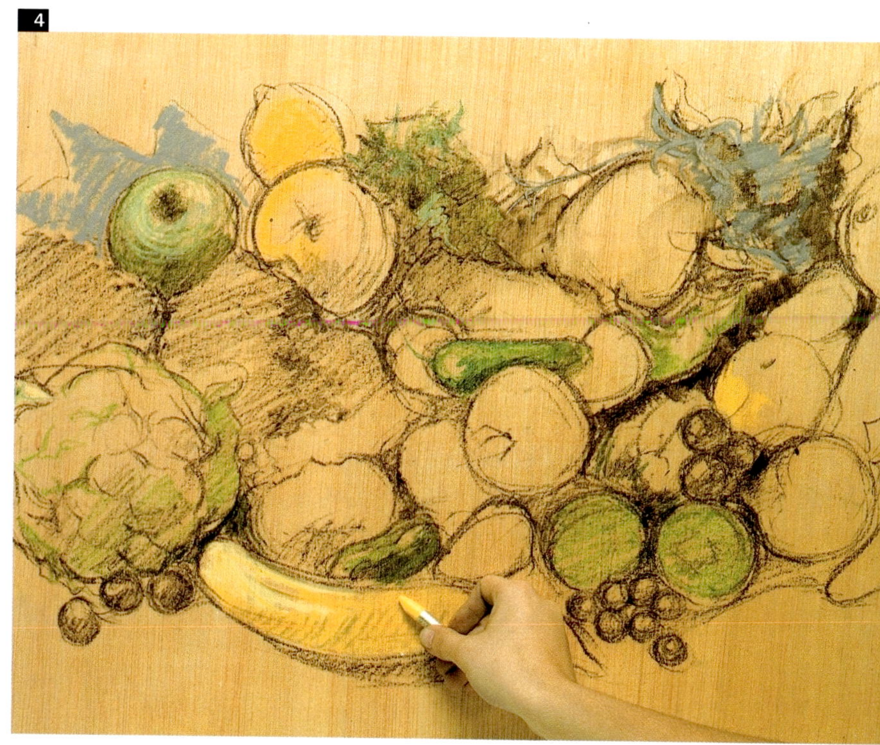

4 The first applications of color are concentrated in one particular area or object, on the overall tone of each element, although the direction of the line and reserves are used to form the volumes gradually. It is a time-consuming task but very much needed if we want to represent what we see.

PREPARING THE SUPPORT
The work will be developed on wood to take advantage of its durability and beautiful texture. Since at some point of the process the crayons will be diluted with mineral spirits, the support must be treated with varnish to cover the grain and allow the brush to spread the crayons without difficulty.

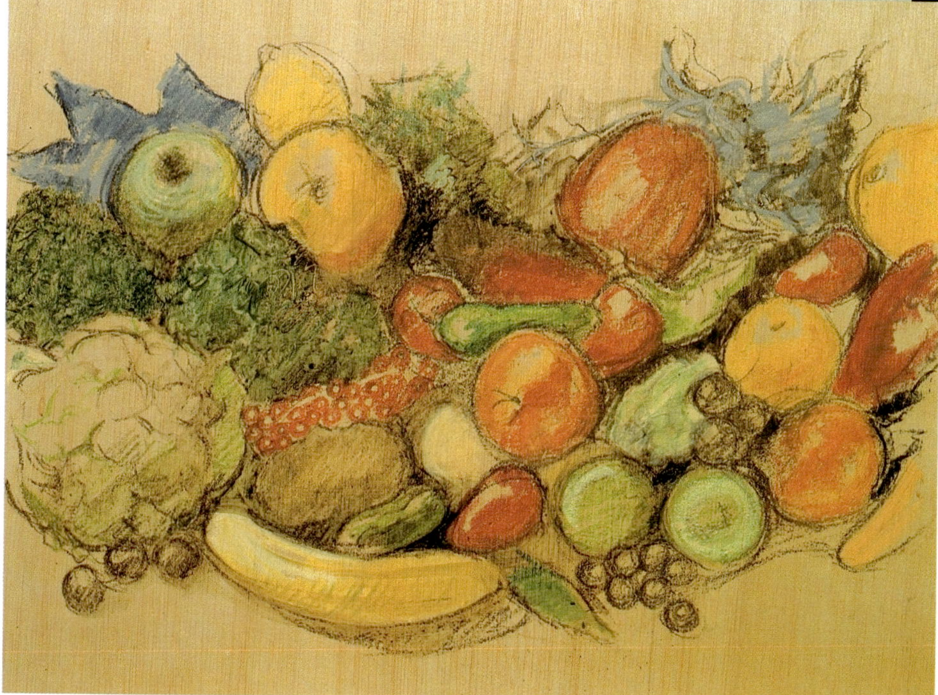

5 Every element of this still life has now been defined with its dominant color, and its volume is developed with a few touches of light and shadow. In some cases, the direction of the line resolves the volume with exquisite precision. This is the case of the banana and the orange.

Modeling with color

Chromatic modeling requires a minimum knowledge of color so that values of light and shadow of the same color do not cancel out each other. It is often the case that when one color is lightened it turns whitish or milky, and when it is darkened it becomes dirty instead of dark. Therefore, it is advisable to experiment with each color separately. For example, lemon yellow does not get darker the same way yellow ocher does, even though they are both yellow. Black is not a good mixing color for lemon yellow, because it turns it green, and neither is violet because it draws all its energy, but orange is good. On the other hand, orange is not a good mixture for yellow ocher because it changes its hue and not the value so much. However, natural umber and dark violet are good if we wish to neutralize the color and make it cooler.

The presence of blue in the shadows is a good general rule. You should keep in mind that there is always a certain degree of risk when using blue because it tints the color as well as darkens it, changing its hue.

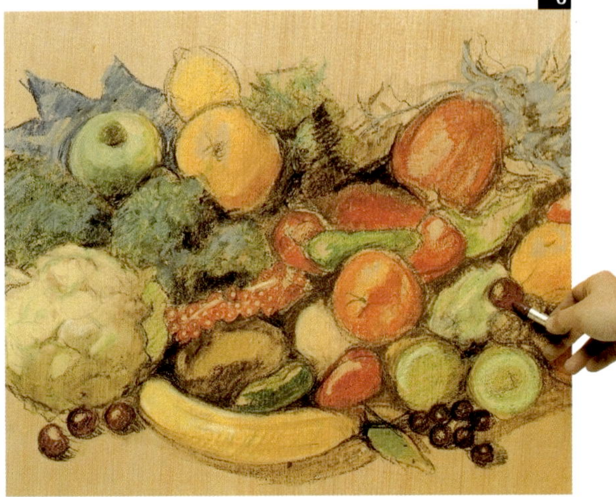

6 This step illustrates how the cherries, the cauliflower, the potato, and so on. have been modeled. Little by little, the volume of each piece is completed.

7 The crayons are diluted by applying mineral spirits with a brush wherever a different, more fluid type of color is needed. We will have to wait until this area has dried before we continue drawing over it with the crayons.

MIXING COLORS WITH THE EYE
When the colors are mixed on the canvas and not on the palette, we can rely on our eyes for the job. This technique was experimented with at great length by impressionists and artists working in pointillism. It consists of placing the colors on the drawing without mixing them and then letting the eye do the job.

8 This step shows all the color and volumetric features of the still life. In this sense, the work is completed; only the details of the texture and touching up a few highlights remain.

The versatility of crayons

Crayons are a very unique medium. They can be used as a dry medium and also as a wet medium. When they are worked as a dry medium, undiluted, they resemble pastels, although it can be said that they have a more expressive color and presence. If they are used as a wet medium, their colors look very similar to oils. They require a temperature-controlled environment. They can be very unpleasant to work with in the summer, especially if the artist wants to avoid blending because the sticks get extremely soft.

A particular way to work with crayons is through impastos. The sticks can be melted with a torch or on the stove, and the melted wax can be applied on the support with a spatula or with a scraper as if they were oil paints. Crayons dry much faster than oils, and they can be corrected if the area of application is carefully reheated.

9

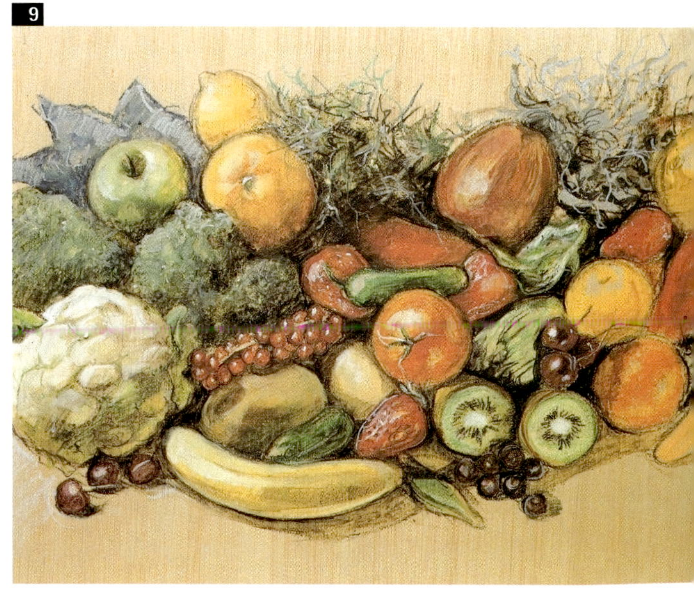

9 In this final phase, the line acquires great importance because it defines all the outlines and textures, like that of the kiwi, tomato, artichoke, and especially the herbs in the background. This type of work has been logically left for the end.

10 Finally, we can enjoy this magnificent still life, which is fresh and very detailed at the same time. The final step of lightening the bottom left corner has resulted in breaking up the possible monotony of the background.

10

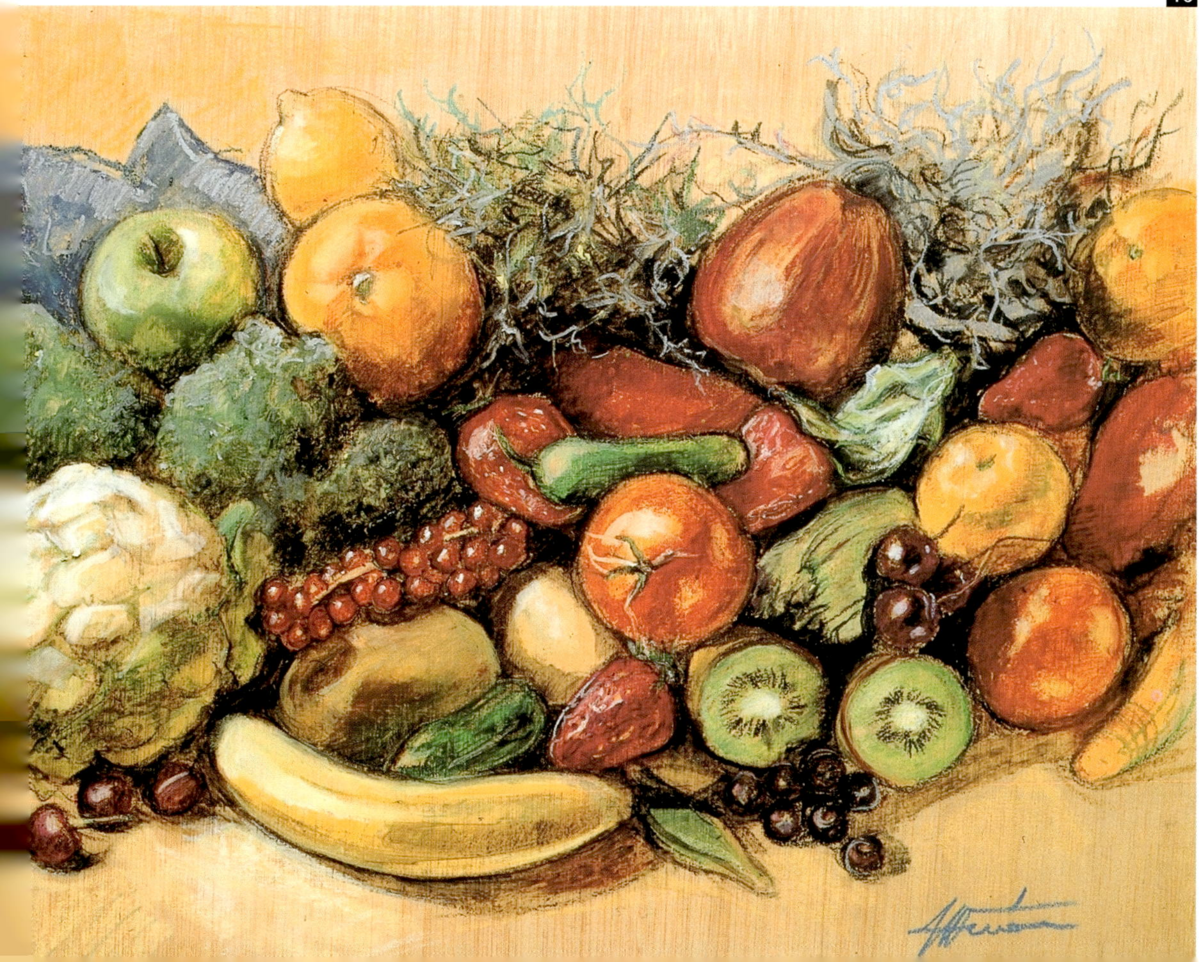

Representing jewelry

Jewelry pieces are often part of still life paintings and portraits. They are almost always an element that accompanies the main subject. However, they are not easy to represent because they do not allow for a big margin for error, especially if they must be drawn exactly, showing the kind of material that they are made of and the light effects. Painting and drawing jewelry requires detailed and careful work. At the same time, though, it must flow freely to avoid taking on an impersonal look that is so common in many commercial catalogs. Realism and effectiveness must go hand in hand. The best way to embrace these two concepts is to approach the representation with the same attitude you would any other theme.

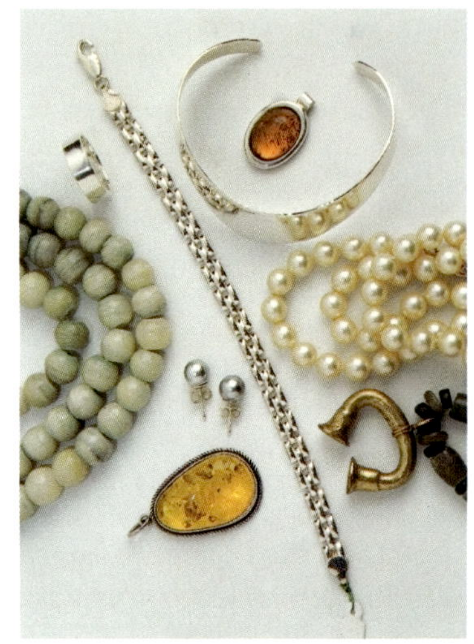

A jewelry piece is a very personal item. For the most part, it defines the person that wears it; that is why jewelry is often depicted in portraits and still life. This still life theme shows only the jewelry of a person, as the only motif being represented.

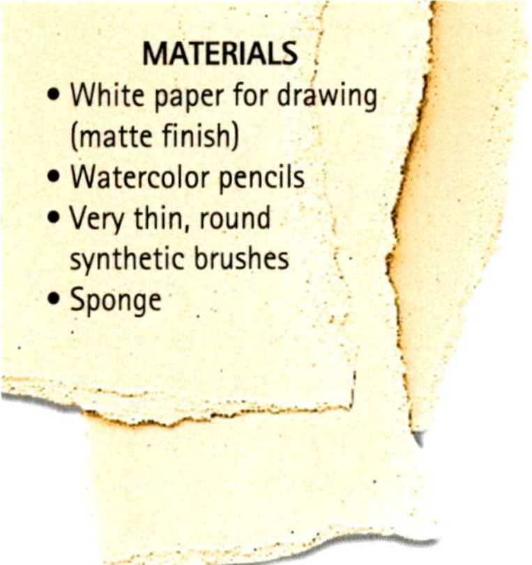

MATERIALS

- White paper for drawing (matte finish)
- Watercolor pencils
- Very thin, round synthetic brushes
- Sponge

TECHNIQUES USED

◆ Geometric blocking in ◆
◆ Detailed drawing ◆
◆ Painting with watercolors ◆
◆ Color harmony with dominant color (gold) ◆

1

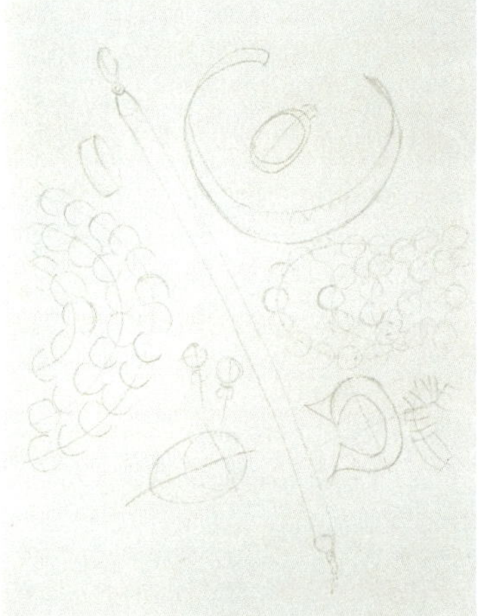

2

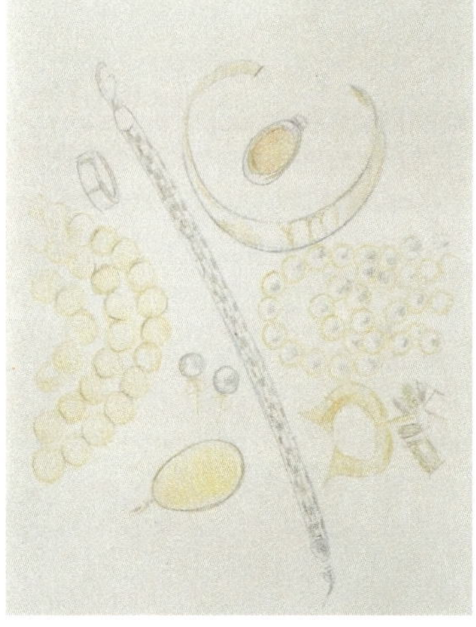

1 Blocking in the still life elements consists of identifying the placement of each piece of jewelry, sometimes with lines, other times with shapes. This can be executed with a normal lead (HB) pencil so as not to leave marks on the paper when erasing.

2 The first tones are lightly painted over the piece. If the lines of the sketch are too visible, erase them a little before applying the color. To begin with, the color pencils should not be pressed too much on the paper because they cover the grain very quickly and then it is impossible to draw over them.

3

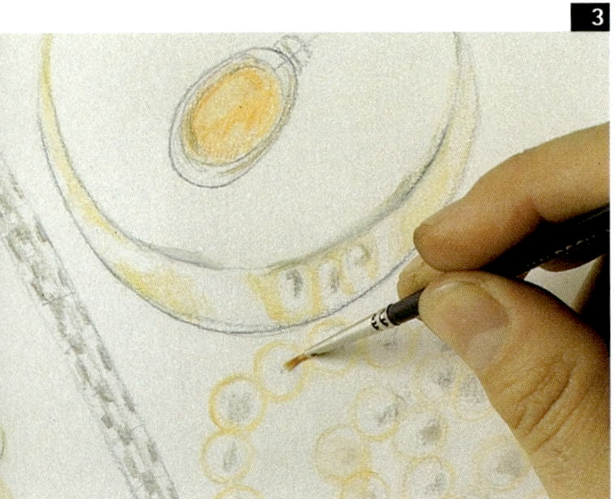

4

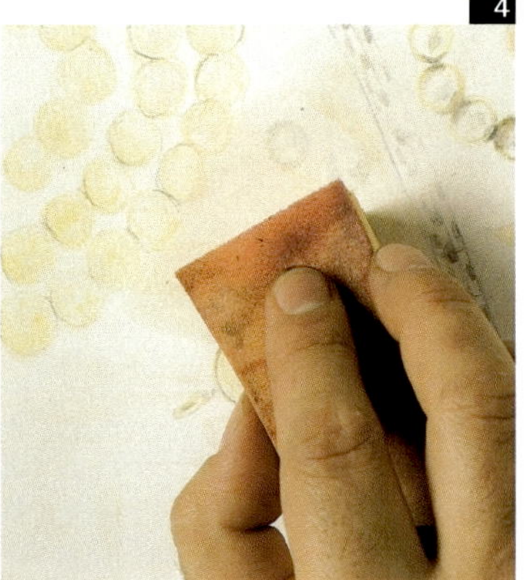

3 The color is applied with a soft watercolor brush. It is important to keep the white reserves in mind.

4 A damp sponge can also be used to create watercolor-like effects, taking care not to overdo it because the paper would soften and buckle.

Working with color pencils

Color pencils are normally associated with children's school projects. However, they can create very interesting artistic effects if one knows how to take advantage of this expressive medium. Due to their structure and because they are a dry medium, they are especially suitable for drawing lines, producing the best results when they are used to create expressive lines. The areas of color are produced with cross-hatching, that is, by grouping many lines together. The combination of speed, form, and pressure applied to the paper can make a drawing either a weak and stereotypical image or a true work of art.

With the arrival of watercolor pencils, there is more versatility because the areas of color that can be created when water is applied are very suggestive, establishing a very appealing dialogue between the line, hatching, and watercolors.

RESERVES
White colored pencils have a very low covering power, therefore it is better to reserve the white of the paper, as is done with watercolors. If the work is executed with watercolor pencils, gouache or white tempera can be used, but only for the final touches of white, without overdoing it.

5 The drawing and the shape of the jewelry pieces continue to be defined using more pressure and intensity over the first areas of watercolor.

6 The development of the drawing is slow due to the number of pieces and their complexity. Each representation requires a lengthy period of observation.

7 Little by little, the drawing acquires more contrast. If we want to correct something, we can use an eraser. However, doing so does not always work because sometimes there are so many pencil lines that erasing them without damaging the paper is difficult.

5

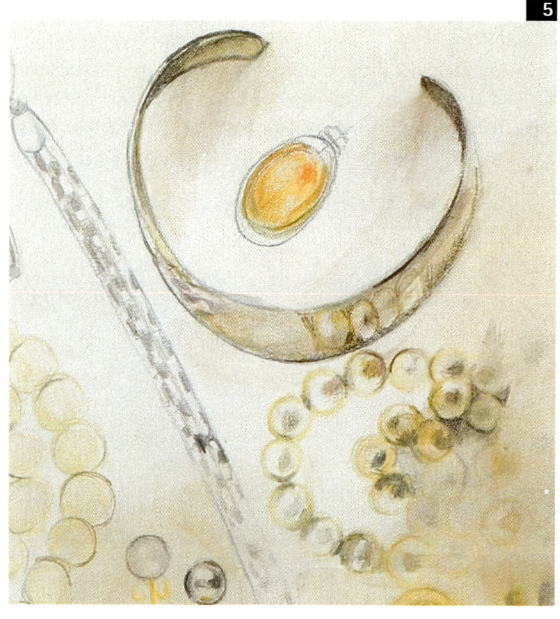

6

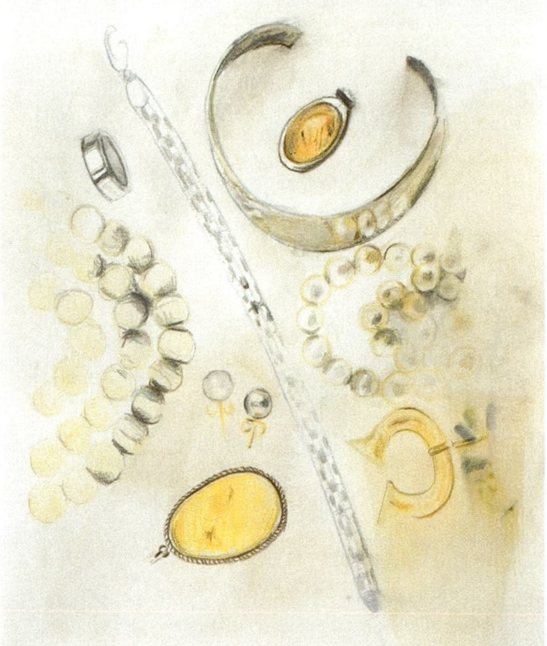

7

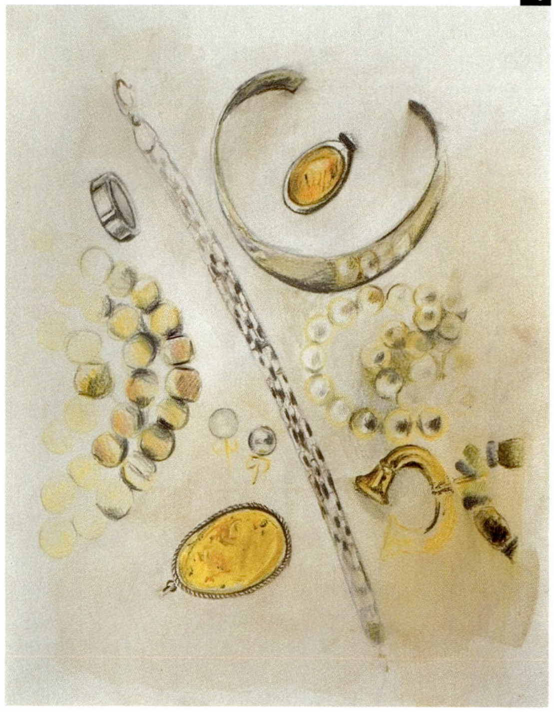

Highlights and reflections

The shapes that appear on the surface of the jewelry are the reflections of everything that is around them. A highlight is nothing more than the reflection of a light source. The graphic description of the reflections and highlights are the result of careful observation of the lines and colors that have been created by the effect of the light on the surface of the object.

On polished surfaces, the edges are harsh and the contrast strong to convey the feeling of reflection. Matte surfaces, on the other hand, present soft outlines and the contrasts show diffused areas of color. This is a vital aspect of pearls. If we look carefully, we will notice that they are spheres modeled with a few reflections and satinlike highlights surrounded with a halo of light.

8

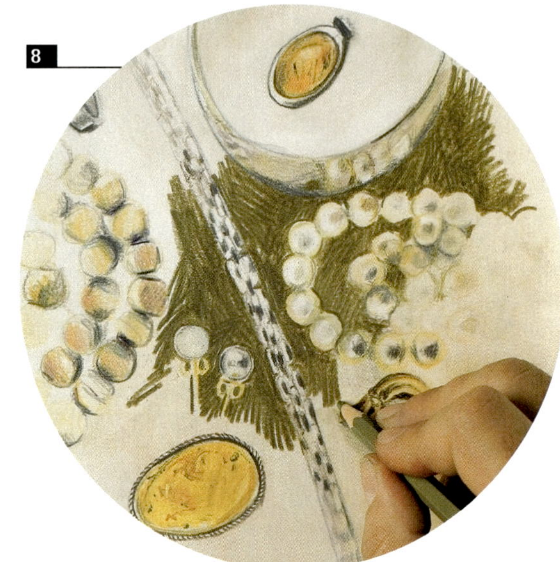

9

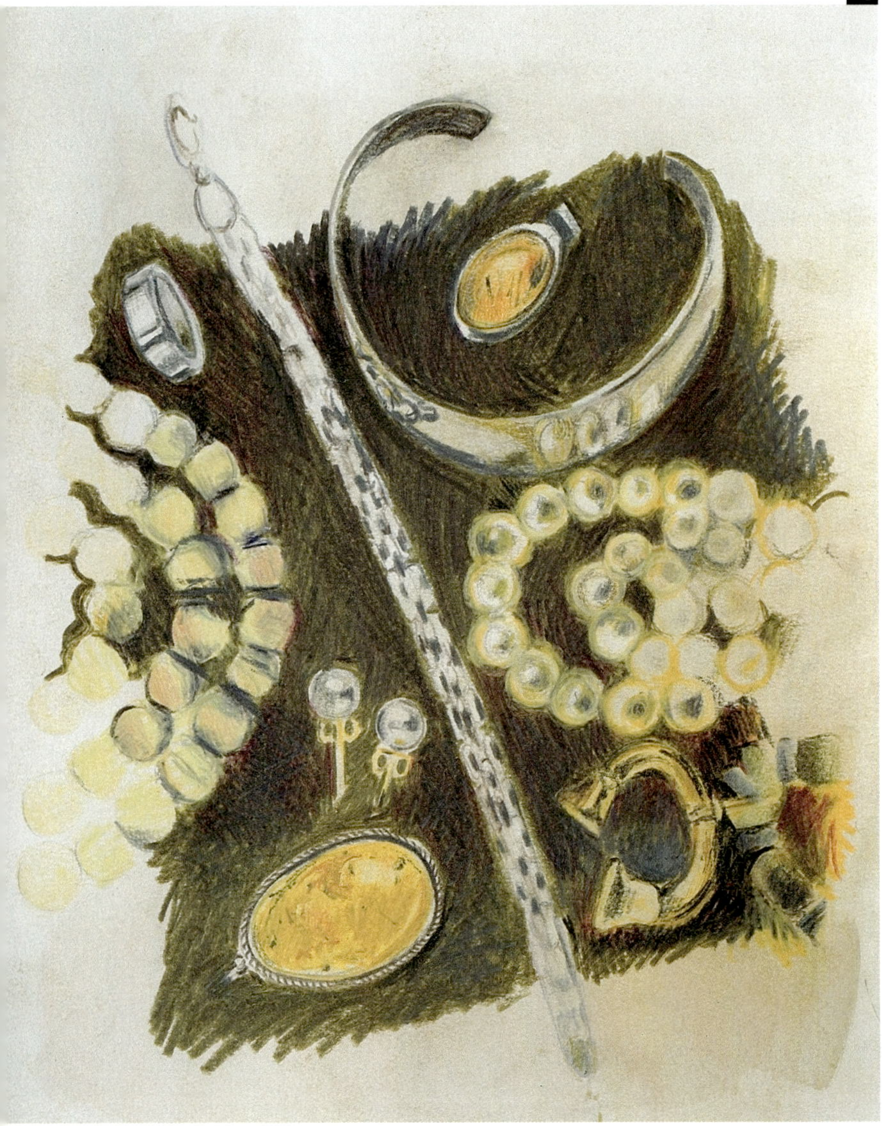

8 To emphasize jewelry, we must darken the background, otherwise the light of the piece and of the background are the same. It can be covered lightly with a pencil and then brushed with a sponge or with a brush, or drawn with rich hatching. Here, we have chosen the hatching approach to provide a more graphic effect.

9 Here is the final result of this interesting still life. A few details have been completed with extreme precision, and others have been left unfinished to remind us that this is a drawing, not a copy of a photograph, and to convey the feeling of freshness and spontaneity.

EXPRESSIVE STATEMENT

By applying different amounts of pressure with the pencils, we create a variety of intensities, enriching the group of objects. The natural tendency is not to press with the pencil to avoid damaging the paper. Toward the end of the process, though, it is necessary to do so if we wish to make an expressive statement.

Watercolors and flowers

Floral arrangements are a classic theme in the still life genre. They are executed in such way that the vital character of the flower is emphasized. Flowers represent life: form, color, scent . . . and a still life with flowers should be able to convey those sensations. The most commonly used media for representing flowers are oils, pastels, and watercolors. The advantage of watercolors with respect to other media is their freshness. Watercolors require very little material to produce light colors, but they are very bright. The white of the paper enhances any color applied over it, producing an intense effect of light and life.

The forms are usually modeled by superimposing transparent areas of color, as if they were pieces of colored glass. They can also be applied through blending and gradation, but never with impastos.

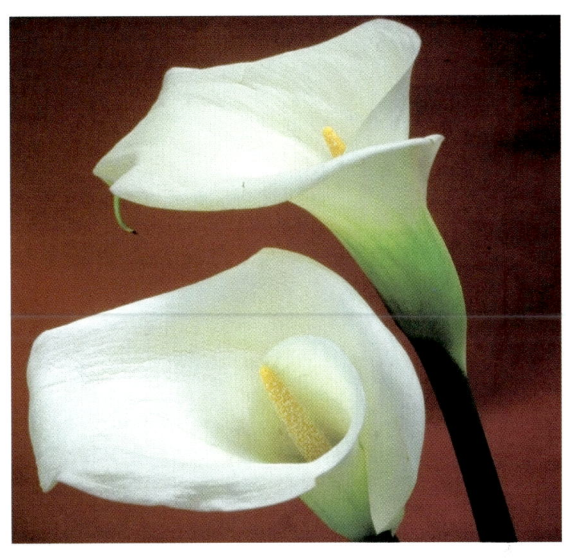

This simple model encompasses the poetic feeling of flowers. There is no need for a big bouquet to fascinate our senses; a single flower can be as beautiful as an entire garden. A still life with flowers is the bridge between a traditional still life and a landscape.

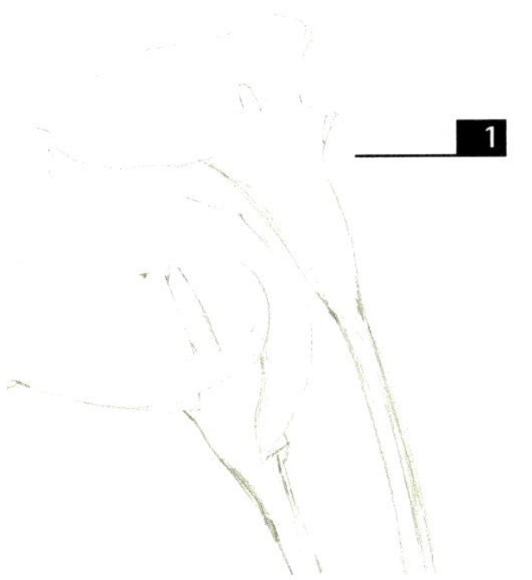

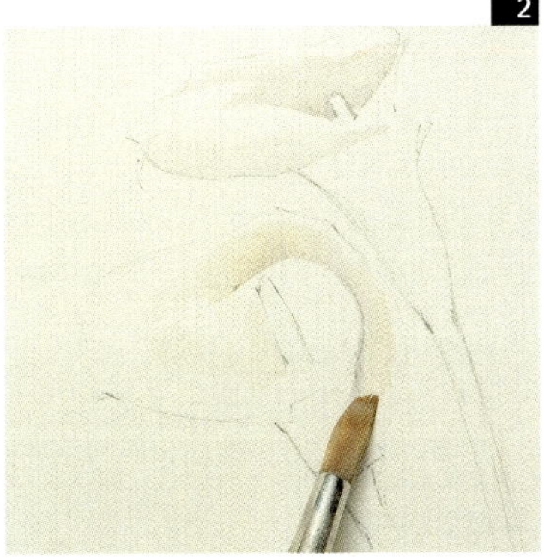

MATERIALS

- Paper for watercolors
- Watercolors
- Synthetic or ox hair round brushes
- Masking tape

1 The preliminary drawing is laid out lightly with a soft-lead pencil that can be erased without leaving any traces. These first lines are hardly visible because watercolors are transparent and they will not conceal them.

2 The first applications of watercolor are hardly visible; they look like water tinted with color.

3 The modeling of the forms must be carefully planned from the beginning because each color is irreversible and is established as a dark value.

4 Color is beginning to acquire some presence, but there is no contrast yet. The irises are still visually attached to the background.

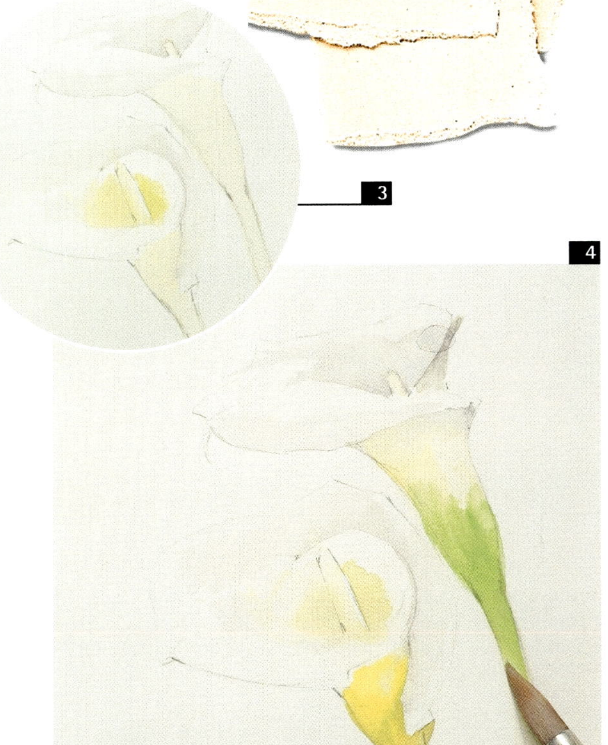

TECHNIQUES USED

◆ Preliminary drawing ◆
◆ Coloring ◆
◆ Harmony with complementary colors (green and red) ◆

Watercolors, a risky technique

Watercolors are considered one of the most difficult media to master. This is mainly because they are not easy to correct. No mistake can be erased or concealed without looking forced. To erase the mistakes, we must first wet them and let them soften a little before we begin to erase with a sponge or rag. This method is not always successful. Besides, it ends up staining the paper and taking away some of its freshness. If we choose to cover the mistake, new layers of darker color are applied. Normally, though, watercolors are not applied in dark tones because doing so goes against their expressive nature. It is better to use very little color to avoid adding too much of one over another and making it look dense and heavy.

5 The first dark tones of very intense color make their appearance. The decisions become more important as we progress because the level of color saturation is higher and going back is not possible.

6 This is a decisive step because the color chosen for the background is very bright. It has been tested on the side before applying it to adjust the hue and the value. It should be applied quickly and decisively. A heavily charged brush and a quick stroke will leave less of a trace and vice versa.

7 The image already has all of its elements. The background and the figure stand out against each other very visibly. The carmine color makes the greens vibrate, and the white looks very luminous.

8 Once the background is completed, the figure is modeled. The shadows do not appear as dark now because the background is darker.

8

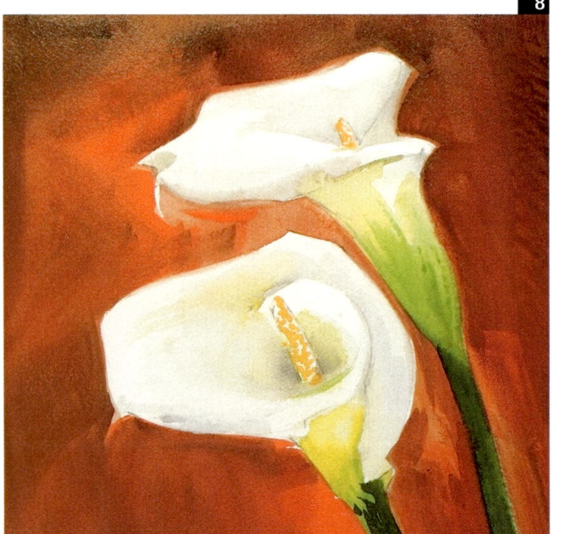

MODELING AND RESERVES
With watercolors, modeling is done with gradations or by superimposing layers of color. In the first case, the colors should be worked quickly and wet on wet before the first brushstrokes begin to leave traces on the edges of the images. In the second case, the process is similar to overlapping colored glass. Here, it is important to control the direction and the number of lines and areas of color because the image tends to darken very quickly and the colors begin to change.

9 Certain details of the color and the forms have been adjusted. The yellows are darker, and the stems appear more robust.

10 This is the completed watercolor. To detach the image from the background a bit further, a faint shadow has been added around the petal. The light and color contrast is superb.

THE ENERGY OF COMPLEMENTARY COLORS
A very strong vibration is created when two complementary colors are placed next to each other without mixing. This can be observed in nature: poppies in a field (red and green) or wheat fields under a bright blue sky (orange and blue).

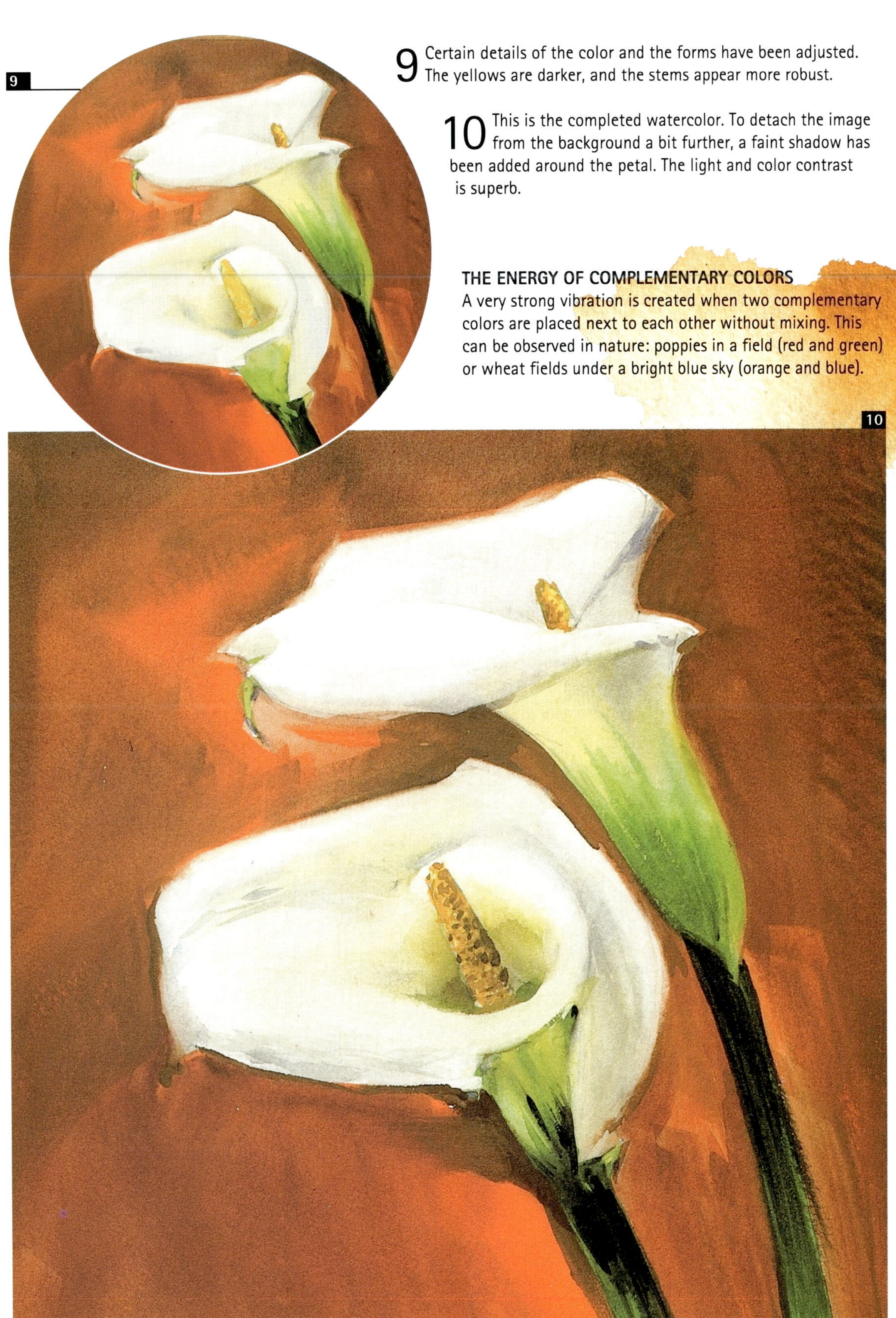

Modeling with oil paints

Oil paints are the ideal medium for visually modeling volumes due to their elasticity and their slow drying time. To model with oils, we must begin with very diluted general tones of light and shadow to create a tonal base that dries quickly. Then, more heavily charged brushstrokes are added so they can be mixed on the canvas itself until the colors blend completely with those that are added later. Working the wet and oily medium this way can produce very fine blends and gradations but also expressive impastos that are very useful for defining details, heavier areas, or textures. The painting that we will analyze in these pages is a classic theme in oils.

This theme presents traditional ceramic pieces from Spain: jugs and plates that could have very well been painted by Zurbarán or Velázquez in their time. Nowadays, they are still valid models for teaching still life painting because their volumes and chiaroscuro effects are very interesting.

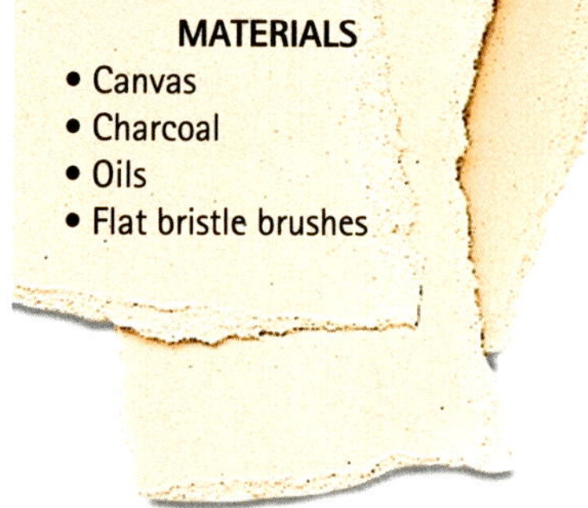
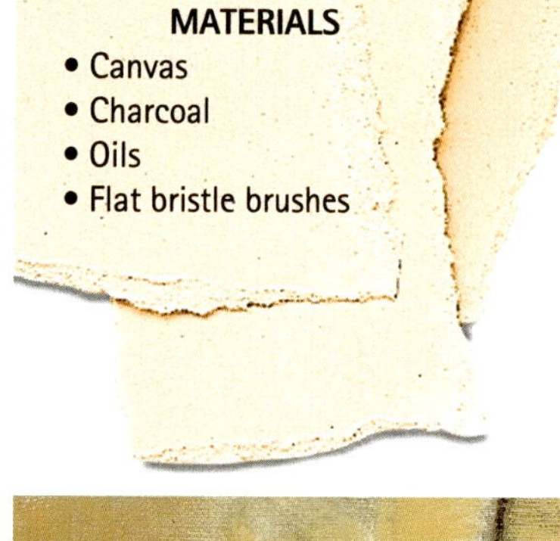

MATERIALS

- Canvas
- Charcoal
- Oils
- Flat bristle brushes

1 The preliminary drawing is done with charcoal by blocking in the figures using spheres and tilted ellipses. The canvas was previously covered with a raw sienna color.

2 Over the drawn base, color is applied with slightly diluted paint, defining the tones of the light in the background, and modeling of the water jugs begins.

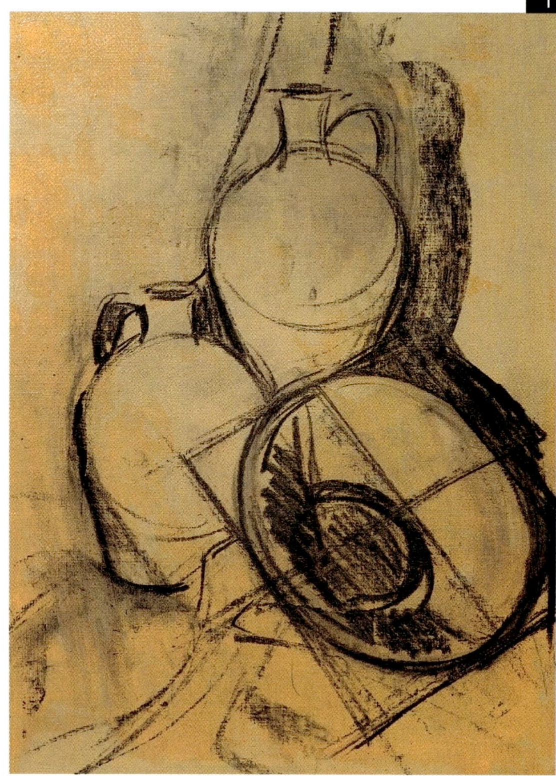

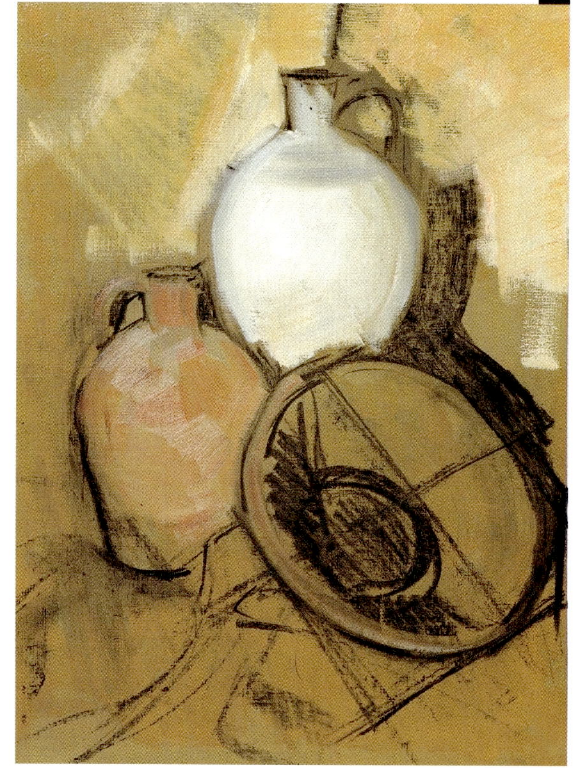

WORKING ON A COLOR BACKGROUND
This fulfills several purposes. The first is the emphasis that light colors acquire over the dark background (when working on white, the brightest light is always the background). The second is to give the composition a sense of coherence, because the color chosen for the background will activate the rest, and will normally show up everywhere. Finally, we can leave some areas unfinished without disrupting the general feeling, because the color of the base is already well integrated with the rest of the colors.

3 The clay plate is painted with raw sienna tinted with red and darkened with shadows, using blue for the shaded areas. One of the jugs is also defined with touches of burnt sienna to make it a little redder, and work is continued on the background.

4 The shapes of the three ceramic pieces are now defined. Notice how the brush gives form to the modeling according to its direction.

3

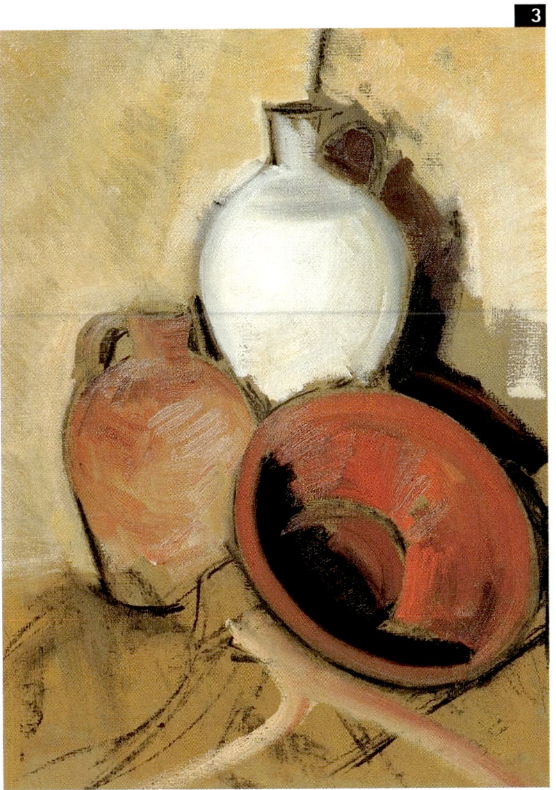

4

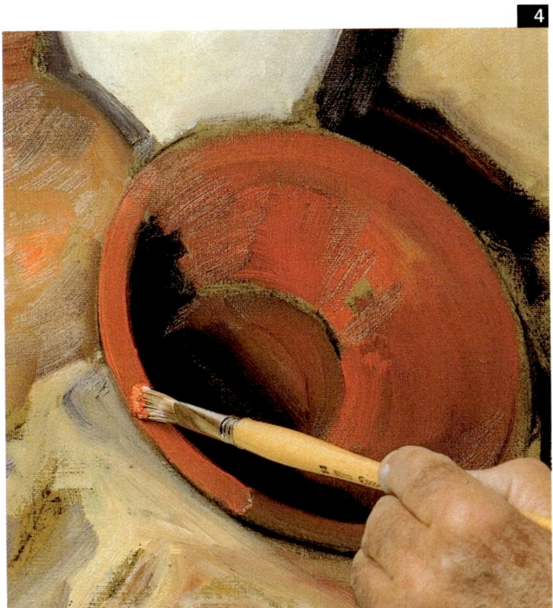

5 The cloth already has some volume. The projected shadows make the pieces stand out against the background as if they were detached from it, creating spatial depth.

5

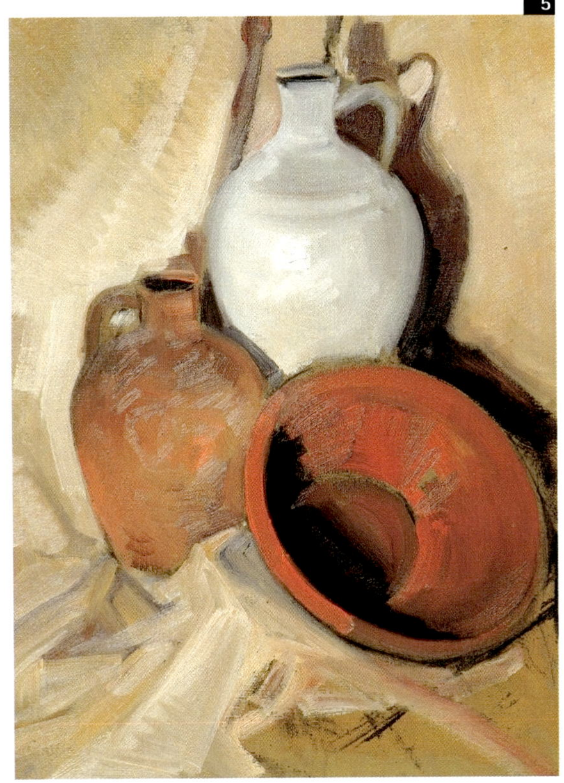

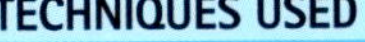

TECHNIQUES USED

◆ Geometric blocking in ◆
◆ Chiaroscuro modeling ◆
◆ Color harmony with dominant color (earth tones) ◆

The plasticity of oils

When we talk about oils, we normally think about the traditional techniques for modeling shapes. However, this medium also allows other procedures, for example, creating saturated effects if the work is executed with a thick paste mixed with a spatula, brush, or the fingers. Oils can also be scraped with a scraper and rubbed with a rag or hard brush. They are suitable as well for diluting with turpentine, which produces a more airy effect than that of watercolors, or for glazing, diluting the paint with varnish and linseed oil. If we wish to create the opposite effect of a glaze, we can add other materials to it, which can be very textured, like marble dust. As we can see, oil paint is a very versatile medium, which is worth exploring in depth to discover all its creative possibilities.

6 The shadow in the background is blended to highlight the shapes even more, and the basic shape of the cloth is now completed. Although the painting needs more contrast, it is very close to its final stage. The highlights on the plate give us a preview of what the rest will look like.

6

7 The direction of the brushstroke and its charge are very important for defining the wrinkles.

8 The contrast is greater now. The shadows have been applied with stronger and more contrasted brushstrokes, adding more blue to enrich the volumes. This blue is perfectly noticeable on the white jug.

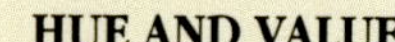

7

8

HUE AND VALUE
Colors interact in a painting. When the value or the hue is altered, it has an effect on the rest of the colors. This is true because a painting is viewed as a whole, not as separate parts. Something like this has occurred in the third step of this still life. When the red of the plate was darkened, the color of the jug to its left looked very light, and the hue had to be changed toward burnt sienna. In the fourth step, the yellow color of the background was completed with raw sienna in the area close to the plate to avoid strong vibration between red and yellow, two very active primary colors.

The final touches

A single, well-placed brushstroke provides the needed tension to a shape, defining a detail or creating a highlight. It must be well thought out but decisive. These interventions constitute the final touches. We often think that executing a painting or giving life to it requires complicated and involved manipulation, but this is not the case. It is a matter of knowing the exact approach, no matter how small. It is the same in the kitchen when we are preparing a dish. Sometimes the final addition of a spice or adjusting the salt is the key to success. Again, as in the kitchen, overdoing these details is not a good idea because they can mask the flavors and aromatic qualities of the dish. In painting, it is not a good idea to abuse them, especially the application of highlights, which is very appealing to the beginner.

BLUE IN SHADOWS

The presence of blue in the shadows is a contribution of impressionist painters. It is a very appropriate way to cool the colors and to create a greater atmospheric feeling. In these volumes, blue has been applied very discreetly and successfully.

9

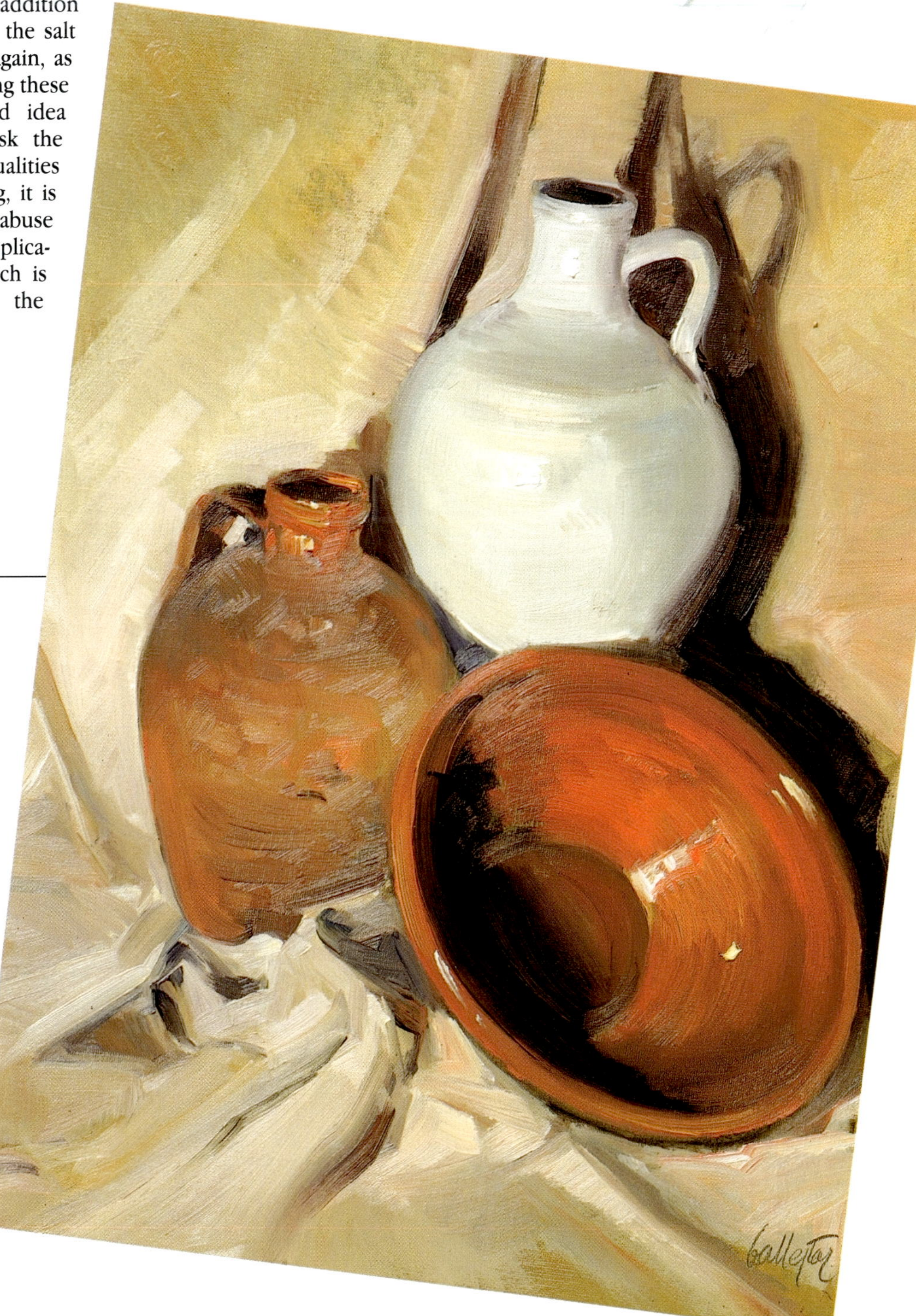

9 This is the finished painting. Light and form have been adjusted using light and color contrasts. The blue-gray colors are the perfect counterpoint to a series of such strong dark earth tones. Notice something important: The final image has great realism and the brush marks and the hand of the artist have not been concealed.

A modern interior: the ironing corner

The scenes of daily life in baroque still life paintings are a graphic documentary of an era and show us the other face of a historic time: ordinary daily life. Modern still life scenes should also depict daily routines but not with the purpose of becoming a graphic record—that is already widely documented these days. Instead, they are a reality, the interaction of the artist with the objects and the setting. In that sense, we will look at a modern still life, an area of the house reserved for ironing, which is the modern version of the sewing or powder rooms of Vermeer de Delft or the writing desks of Chardin.

It is not a still life with objects but with a scene, because there is no figure or background. The painting depicts a situation.

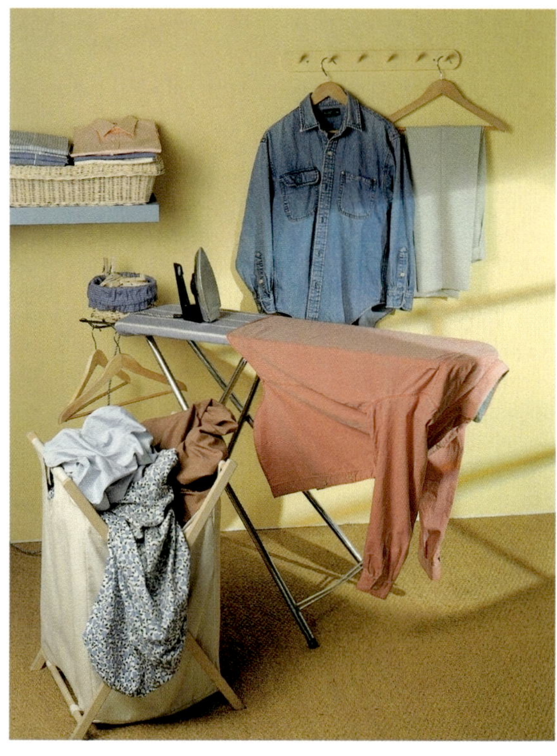

This scene is very familiar and also captivating, because it evokes memories and emotions. A second, more symbolic meaning is more suggestive: The ironing theme can be regarded as an allegory of order. The clothes go from being wrinkled to ironed and organized.

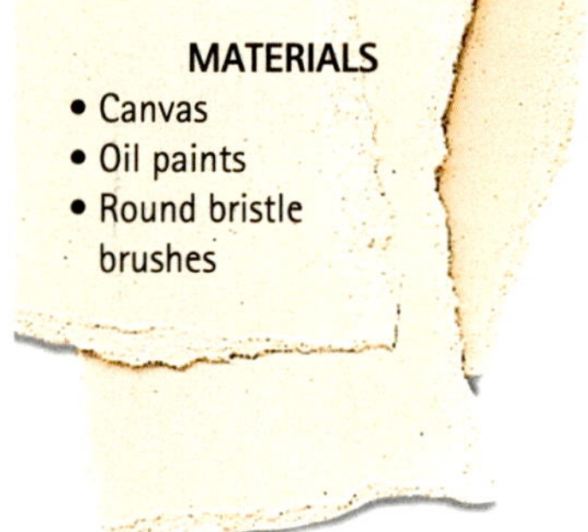

MATERIALS
- Canvas
- Oil paints
- Round bristle brushes

1 To maintain a warm feeling throughout the process, the canvas is prepared with raw sienna. The preliminary drawing is laid out over that base with charcoal.

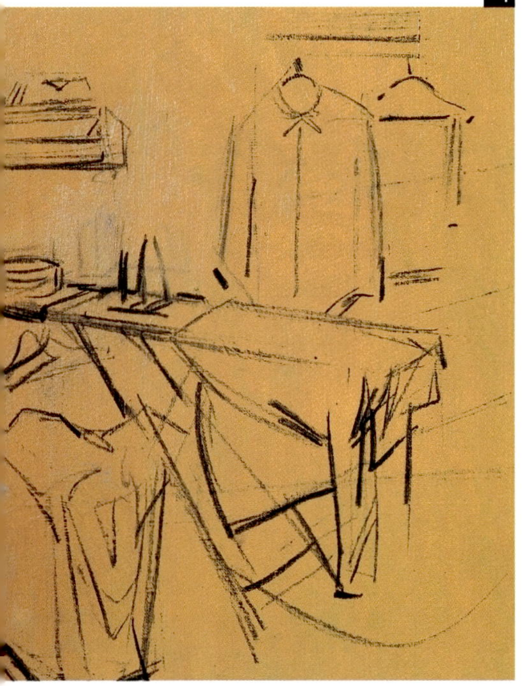

1

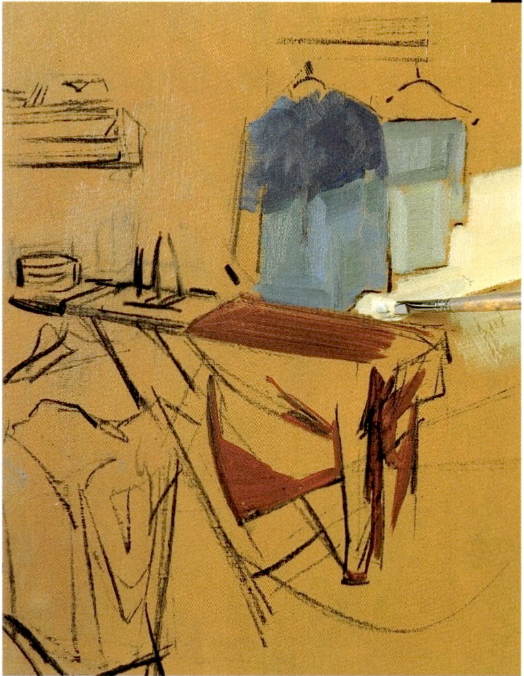

2

2 The main area of interest is the contrast created by the light coming through the window. Even though the tones are muted, that area of greatest illumination contains the three primary colors, yellow, blue, and red, which are the strongest combination of life and color.

OIL PAINTS: THE MEDIUM PAR EXCELLENCE FOR STILL LIFE

It is no coincidence that this genre appeared during the time oil paints were flourishing and in full splendor. Oils are suitable for creating extreme realism and successful *trompe l'oeil* effects as well as fresh sketches. They always produce very warm effects because the painted areas do not appear flat, the colors are very natural, and the texture is velvety. These three factors make this the best medium for still life, the one most commonly used.

3

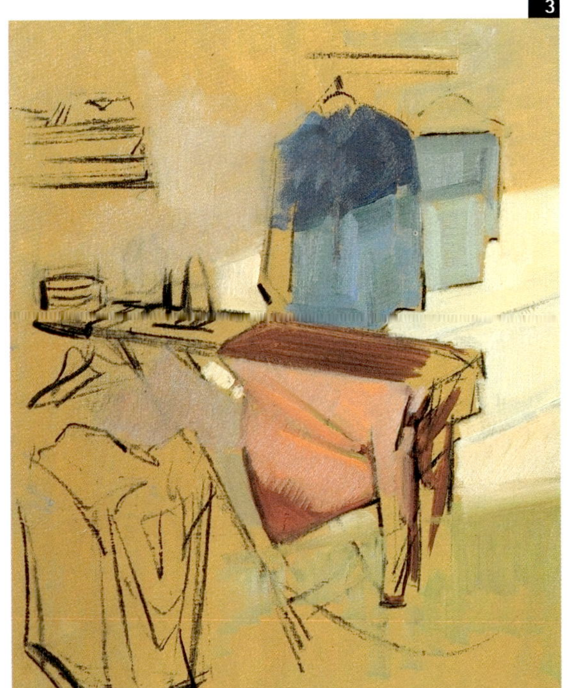

4

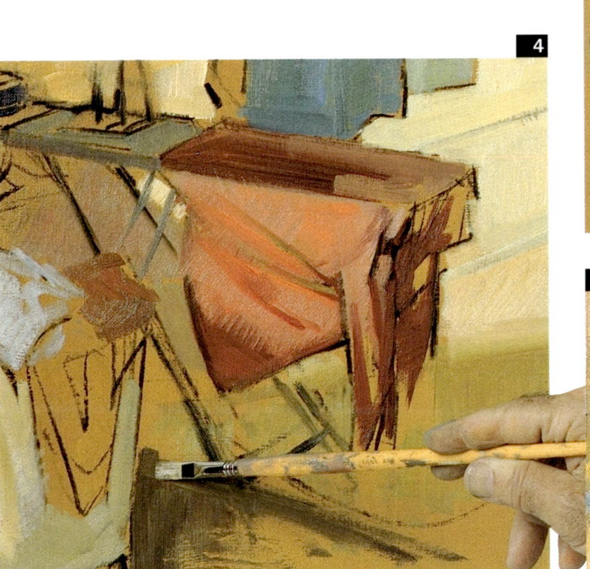

5

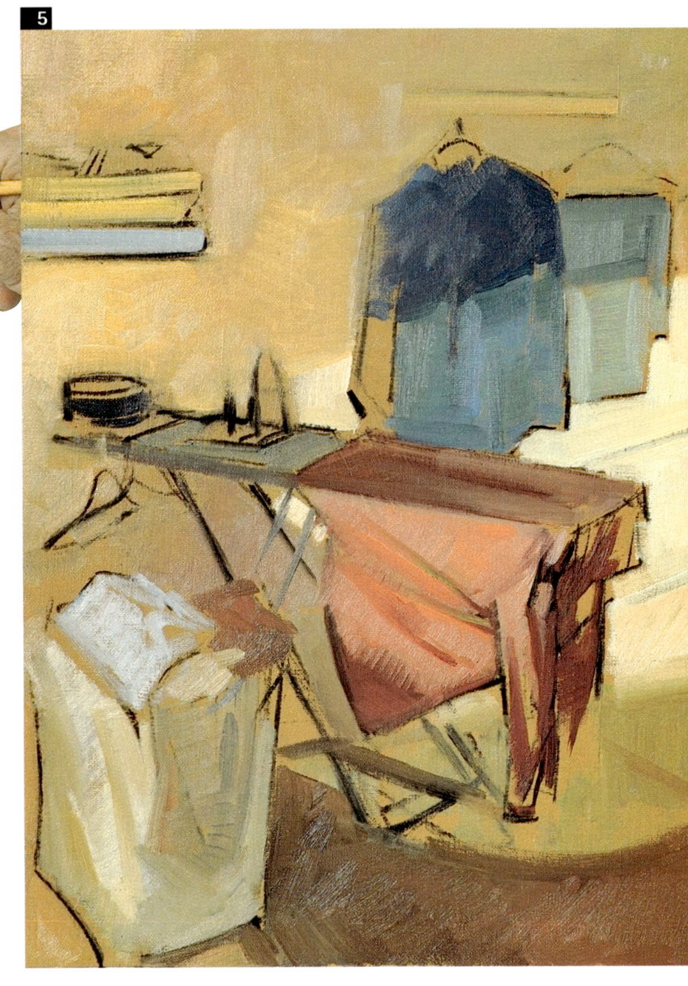

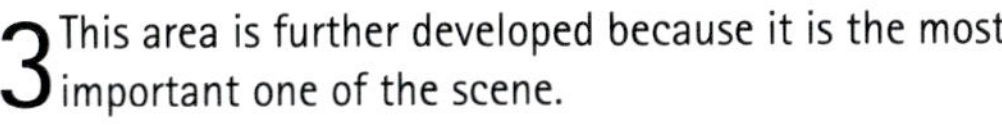

3 This area is further developed because it is the most important one of the scene.

4 The first brushstrokes of color are applied to the rest of the painting. The paint does not cover the initial background in its entirety so as not to lose the dominant color and the overall orange glow.

5 There is nothing more that needs to be painted other than the iron and the sleeves of one of the shirts. Now all the colors interact.

TECHNIQUES USED

◆ Preliminary drawing ◆
◆ Color modeling ◆
◆ Color harmony with the three primaries: yellow, blue, and red ◆

Alterations

Alterations are the changes that are made during the painting process. Since this is a flexible process that is formed as the work progresses, it is normal for the artist to change his or her mind once in a while. A shadow may appear and disappear several times, and the color of an element may change completely. When these alterations remain hidden under layers of paint, it is possible to rediscover them through X rays. This is done in the lab when an old painting needs to be analyzed for restoration. Other times, these changes are not concealed but left visible because they are very interesting artistically.

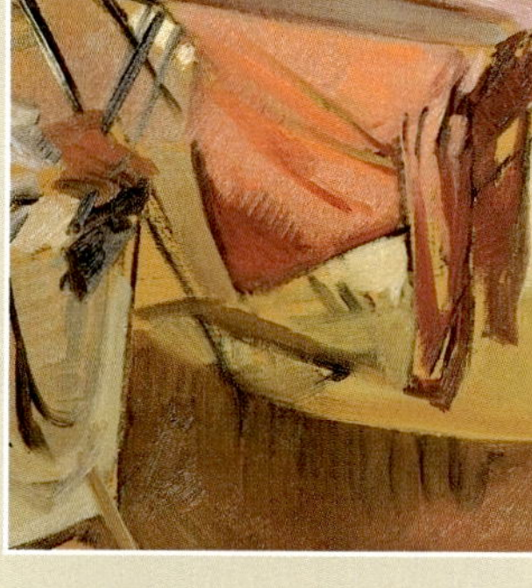

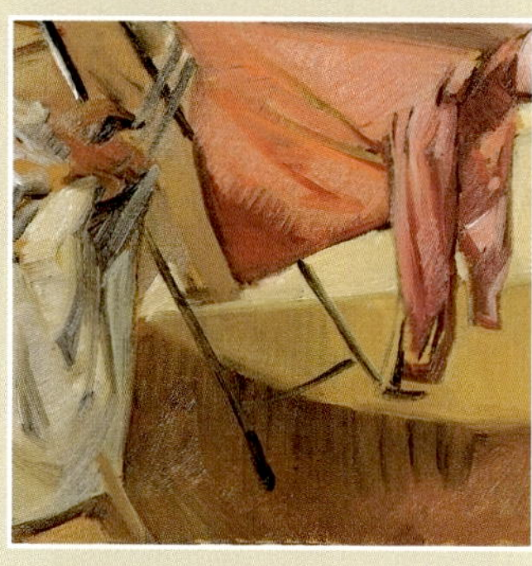

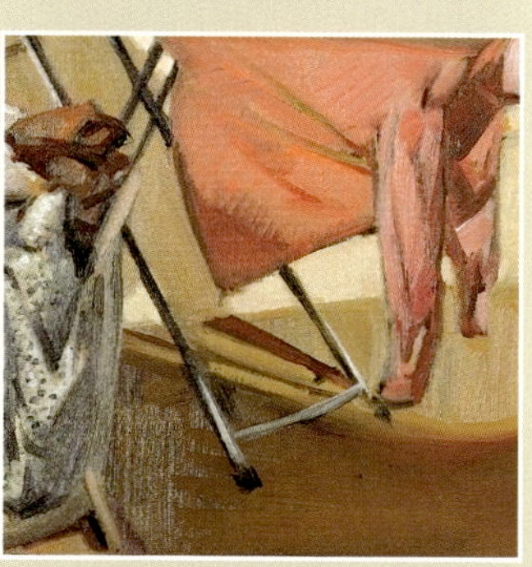

Thanks to photography, we have been able to follow the development of this painting. We can see now the alterations and understand the doubts and changes of mind of the artist.

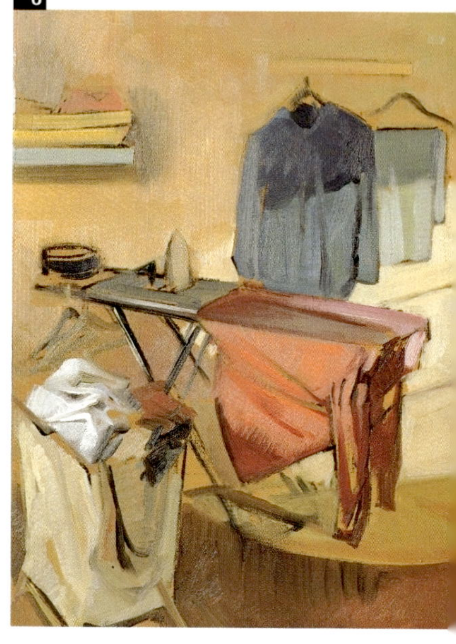

6 The clothing in the hamper begins to take shape. The contours and wrinkles are modeled very decisively, working with chiaroscuro and the direction of the brushstroke throughout the process.

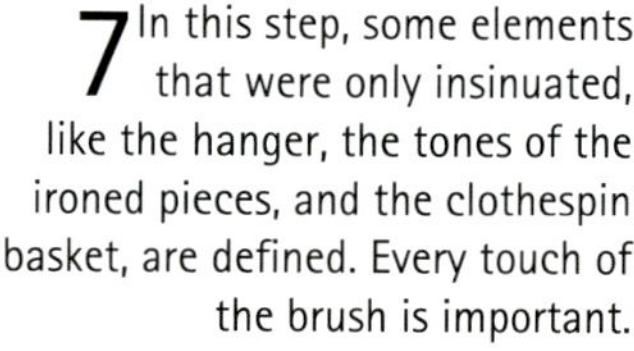

7 In this step, some elements that were only insinuated, like the hanger, the tones of the ironed pieces, and the clothespin basket, are defined. Every touch of the brush is important.

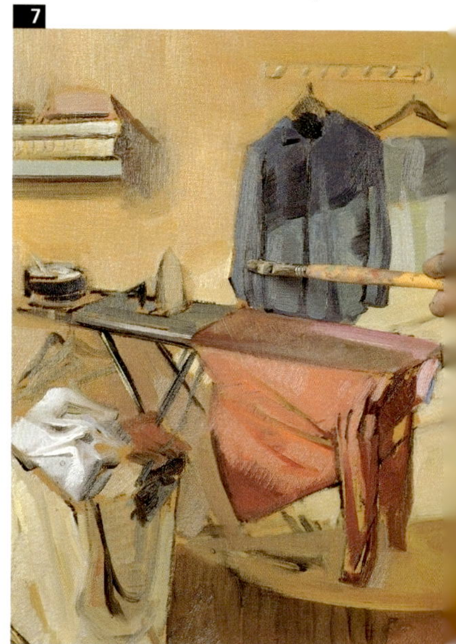

The evolution of the painting

We are going to stop for a moment and analyze the evolution of the painting. We will focus on a fragment of it, the hanging clothes. If we observe carefully, we will discover how the process evolves from general to specific, from the sketch to the finished product.

What is most interesting is that this is only a fragment. This means that every time that the artist has gone back to work on it to get a step further, other areas of the canvas have been addressed as well because the painting is worked as a whole, slowly achieving clarity and adding details. It is similar to when something blurry is viewed at a distance but becomes clearer as it gets closer or when we bring a camera lens into focus.

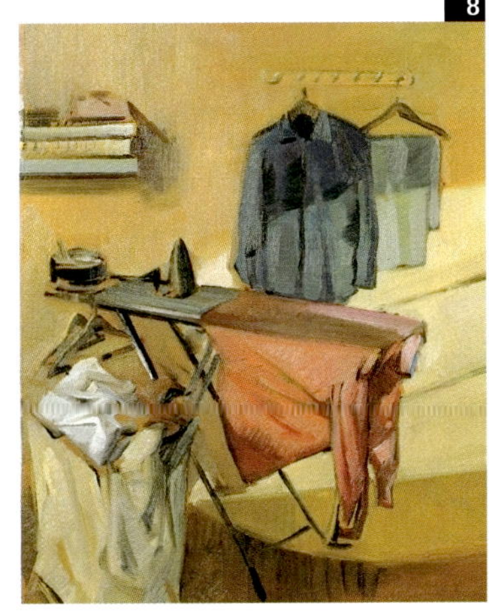

8 In this step, the ironed shirt, the clothes-pin basket, the hamper, the hangers, and the iron are defined. We are getting closer to the end of the process.

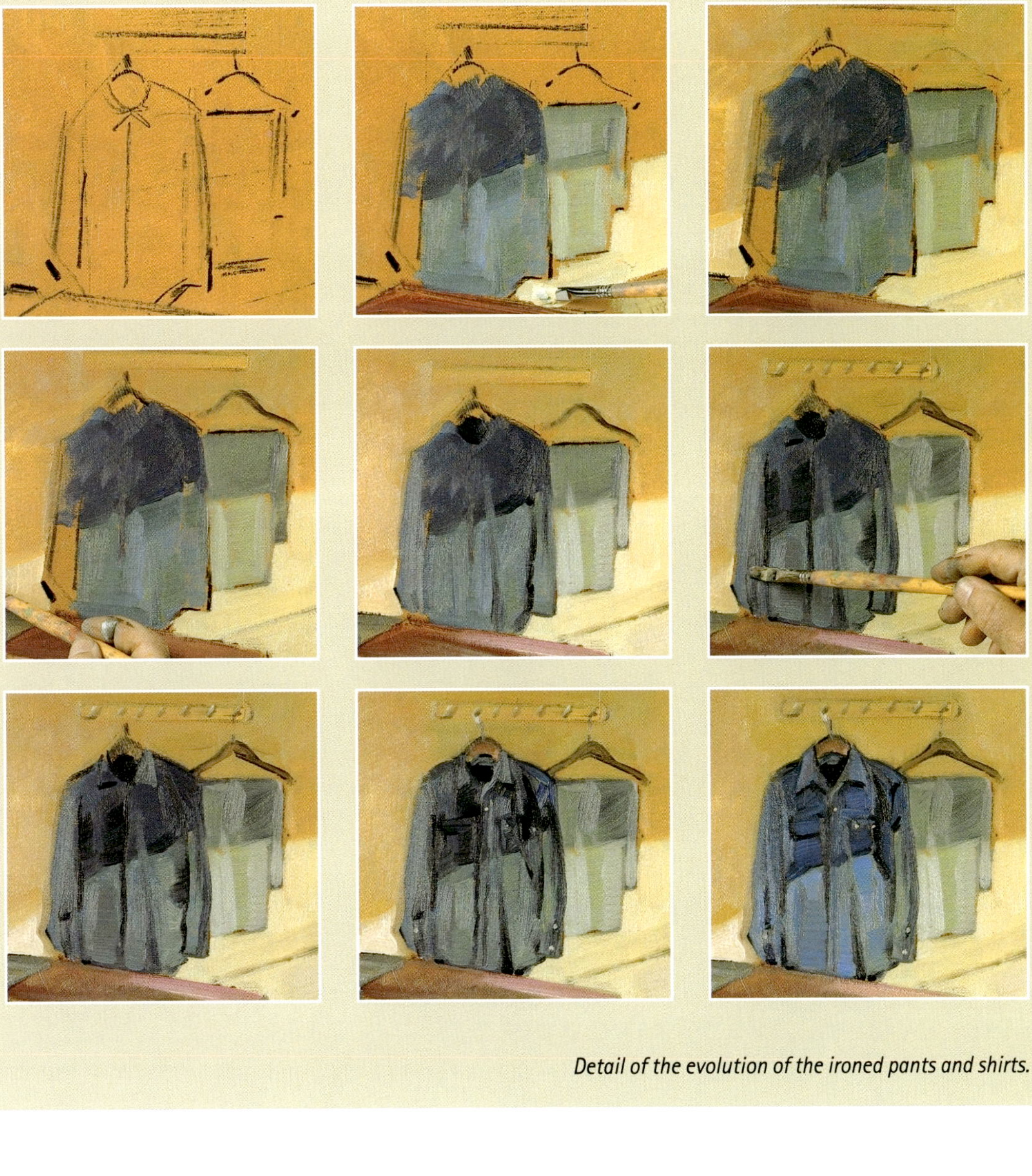

Detail of the evolution of the ironed pants and shirts.

Light and color create the atmosphere

One of the properties of color is its temperature. When we talk about cool and warm colors, we refer to the ability of color to reproduce temperature sensations. A warm color scheme reminds us of warm experiences and a cool scheme of cold sensations. The environment of the painting is dictated by that temperature, which at the same time conveys a luminous sensation. Soft lighting creates an intimate atmosphere, while an intense one depicts openness. Controlling color and light will help us create the proper climate for each still life.

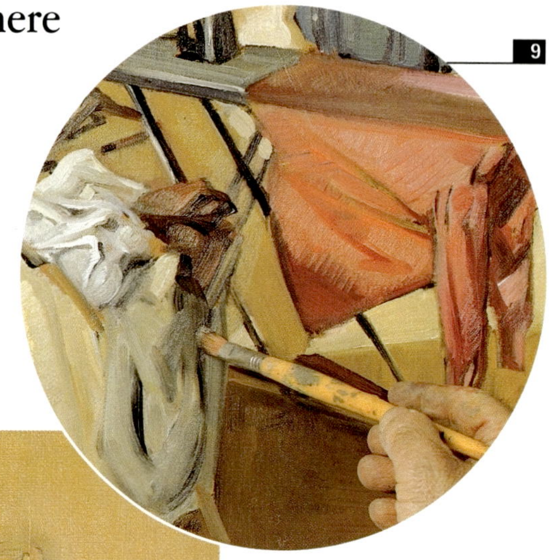

9

10

9 Thanks to the plasticity of oil paints, many color mixtures can be created directly on the canvas.

PRINTS ON FABRIC

To represent the prints on clothing or the designs on walls, the artist can resort to suggestion. One touch of the brush can depict a flower, and a second fine one of the same color can become the leaf.

10 Here is the final image of the painting, a good still life scene with a warm and intimate feeling, vital and dynamic at the same time.

The transparency of glass

Some of the most attractive subject matters for an artist are transparencies.

Observing the play of lights, color, and forms that are generated when light passes through a bottle or glass is fascinating. The effect multiplies with the presence of liquid like water, wine, or liquors. They act as filters for that light, and they produce whimsical forms and sparkles.

For the following still life project, nine glass bottles of different colors and degrees of transparency have been chosen. Acrylic paint is the medium chosen for its execution to show that they can produce either watercolor-like or very dense finishes, if desired, and because their quick drying process makes it possible to layer the colors without mixing them.

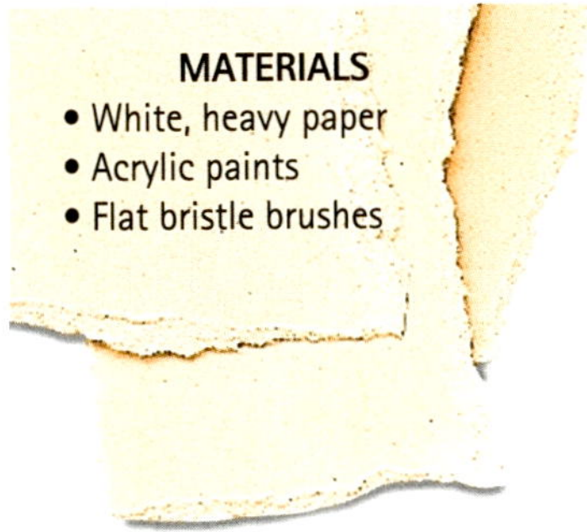

MATERIALS
- White, heavy paper
- Acrylic paints
- Flat bristle brushes

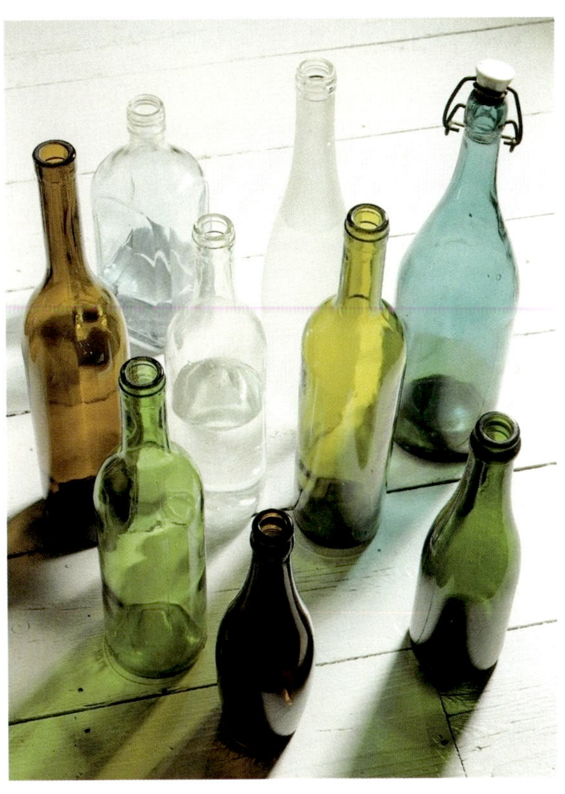

Artificial lighting has been chosen to avoid changes in the shapes of the transparencies and to be able to work at a slow pace while creating divergent shadows.

1

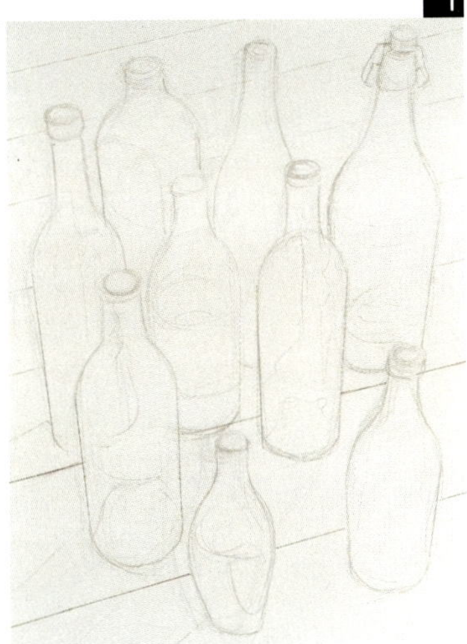

1 The preliminary drawing is done on paper with pencil. It shows the general lines of the transparencies and the shadows.

TECHNIQUES USED

◆ Preliminary drawing ◆
◆ Glazing ◆
◆ Modeling ◆
◆ Impastos ◆
◆ Harmonizing with adjacent complementary colors (green and orange) ◆

A BIRD'S-EYE VIEW
A bird's-eye view has been chosen to capture the full effect of the projected shadows. This decision has resulted in a composition in the shape of an inverted pyramid. There is a great feeling of space. The bottles resemble live people. The long shadows reinforce their place within the space in front of the light projected at a low level.

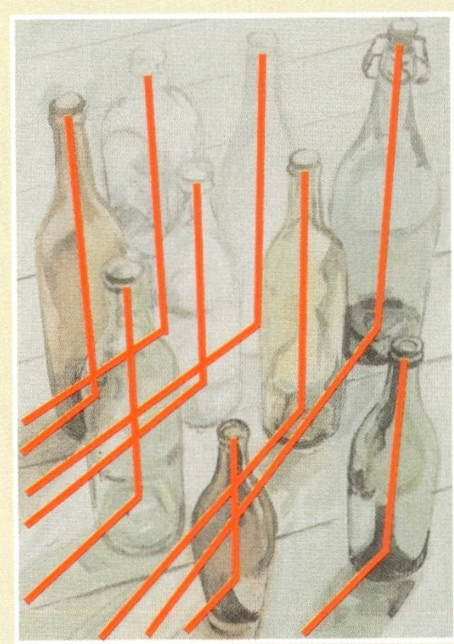

The combination of the shadows with the diagonals of the bottles' axes creates great compositional dynamics.

From general to specific

No matter how fascinating the forms and the colors of the transparencies, they should be planned the same way as any other theme: first the general tones are defined and then the details are worked out. These nine bottles will be modeled little by little, one after the other. First the color of the glass is applied, finishing it later with its reflections and internal contrasts.

Here, the projected shadows are as important as the bottles. Therefore they are included in the process and are not left for the end.

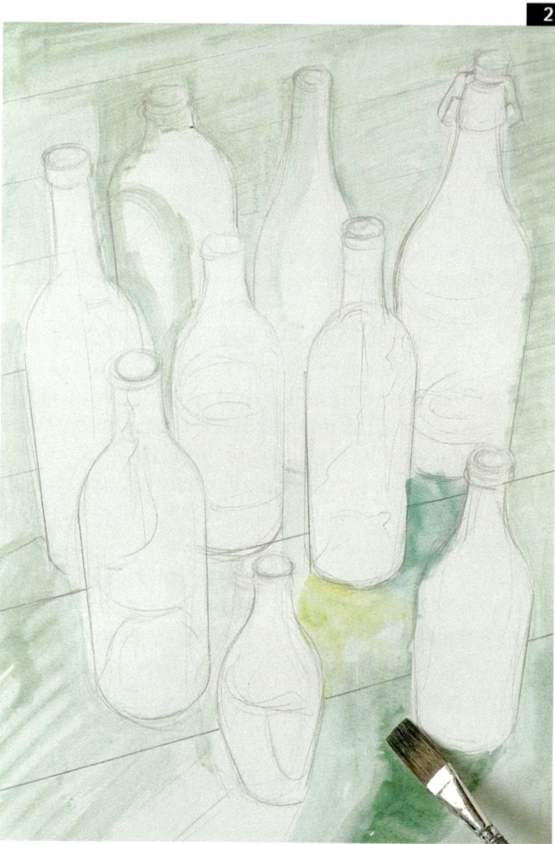

2

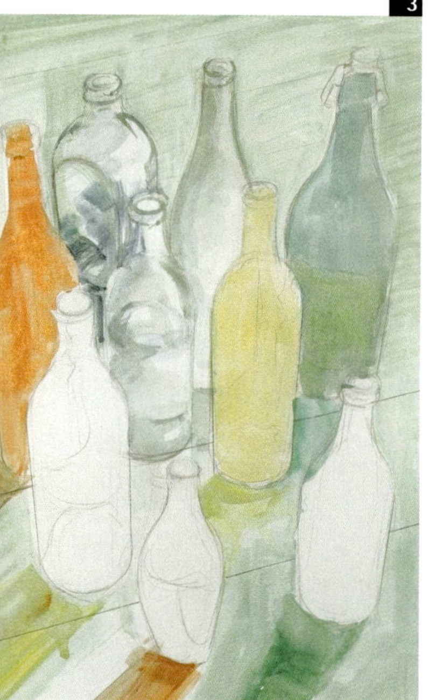

3

2 The first applications of color are general. A very watercolor-like green will define the overall chromatic tendency. The watercolor effect is very appropriate for conveying the feeling of the glass.

3 The first bottles are painted. Notice how their overall tones are not applied evenly. Instead, they are painted by defining the general lines of the shapes that form inside the bottles.

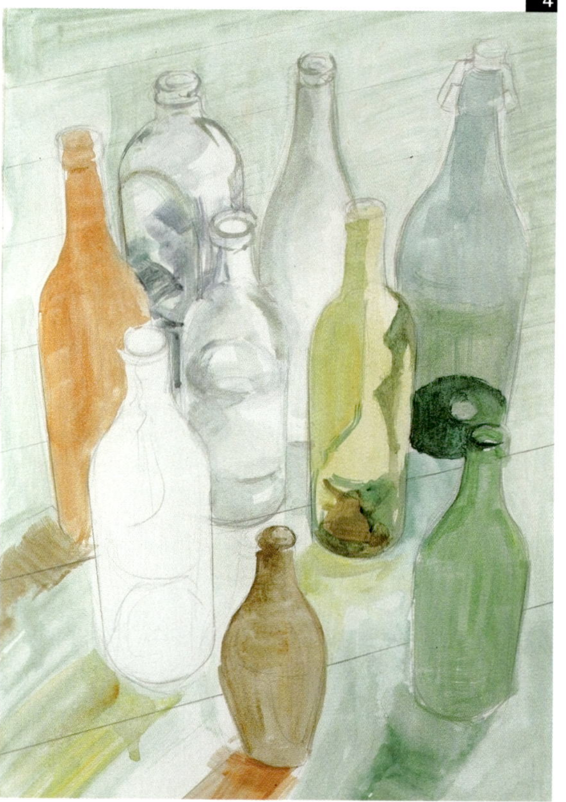

4

4 The painting is viewed as a whole; this is why the bottles are developed at the same time as the shadows. The bottle and its shadow go together. They belong to the same transparency phenomenon, the same way that a shadow is linked to an opaque body.

SUPPORTS FOR ACRYLIC PAINTS

Acrylics, because of their polymer binder, is the medium that best adapts to the greatest variety of supports: canvas, wood, paper, cardboard, metal, plastics, walls, and so on. The other media usually require a specific support as a result of their particular binder or due to their drying process. Acrylics do not require priming, although doing it is a good idea when the support is porous to avoid wasting material and to provide more fluidity.

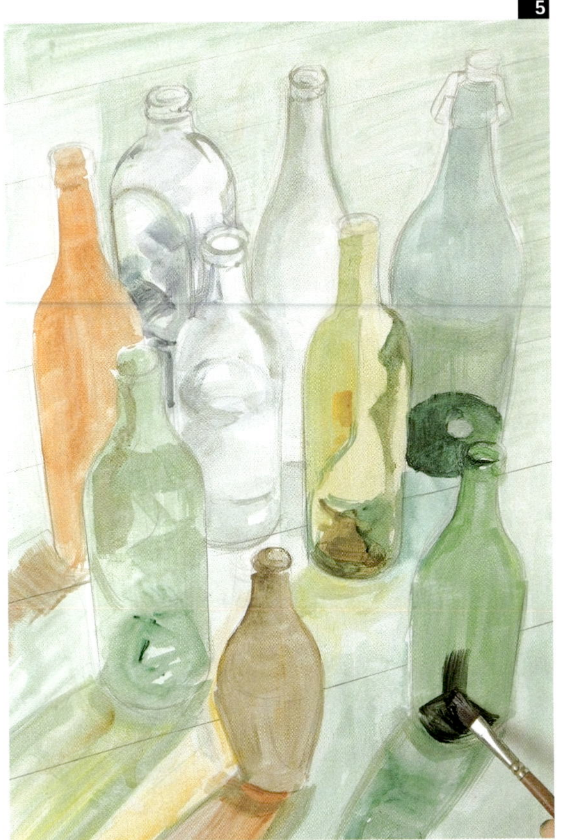

Chiaroscuro in transparent materials

Defining the volume of a transparent body is not created the same way as that of an opaque one. The volume of glass is defined by the outlines and the lines and colors within them, which adapt to the shape of the body and hint at its volume, unless the glass is translucent or very dark.

Contrast is normally the principle that dictates light and shadows, something very similar to the phenomenon of the reflections that we already saw in the still life with jewelry.

Keep in mind that glass is a shiny surface. Therefore, in addition to transparencies they will have reflections. The surface of each bottle will reflect the light and the colors of the bottles that are around them. The color of one bottle goes through another bottle or subtly reflects on its surface.

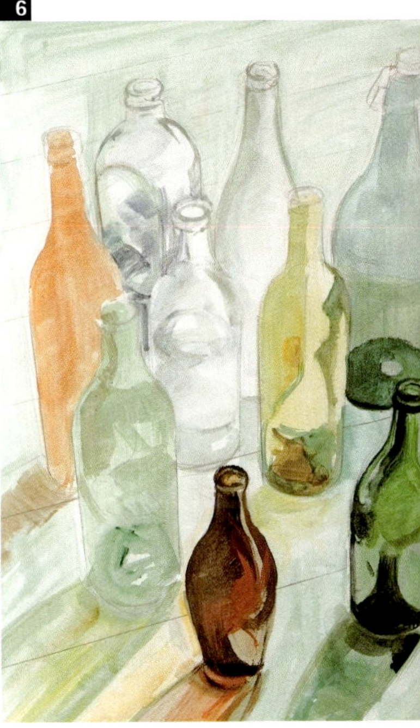

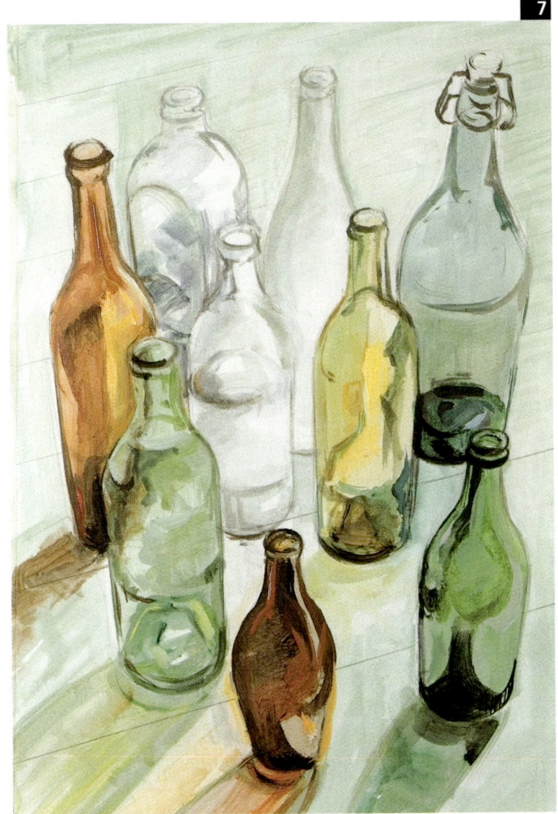

5 Once the general shapes and colors of all the bottles have been defined, a second phase begins in which their reflections and transparencies are laid out in terms of color and form. The line is the most appropriate tool for this task, which in some cases will turn into diluted or graded areas of color.

6 The result of this approach can already be seen in these two bottles. The applications are not arbitrary but the consequence of a process of reflection and observation.

7 Practically all the bottles have been practically painted. Although it may appear that this painting is spontaneous and has been executed quickly, this is not true at all because each brushstroke is the result of a very precise analysis and a series of decisions.

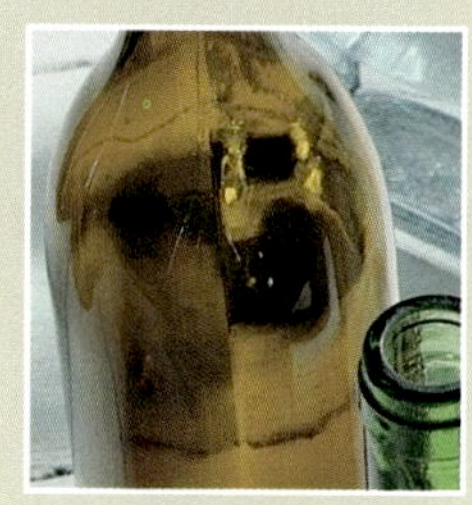
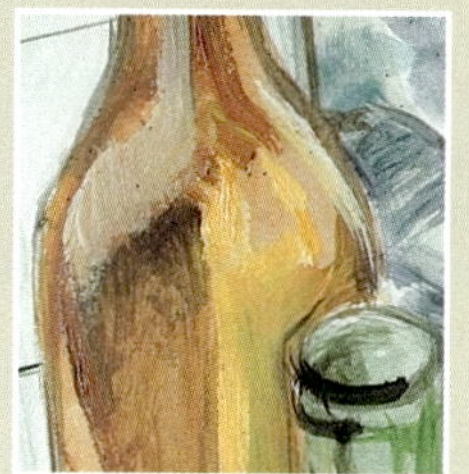
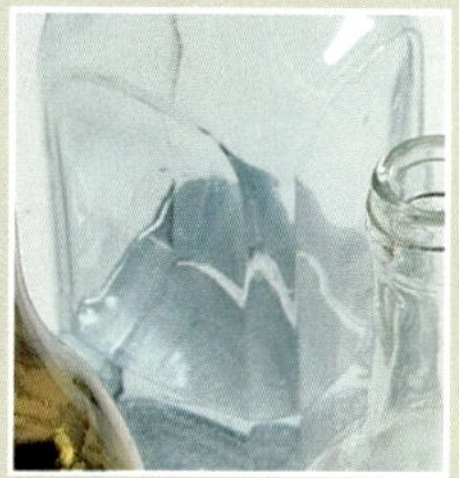
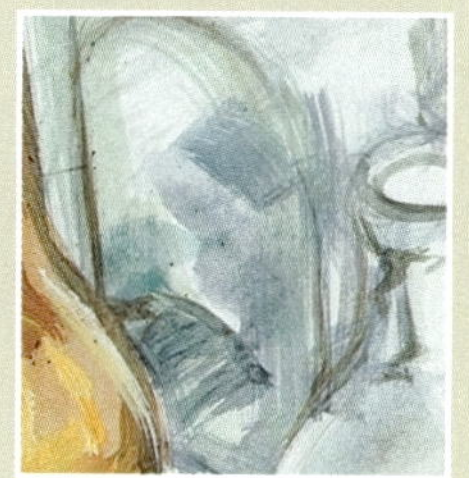
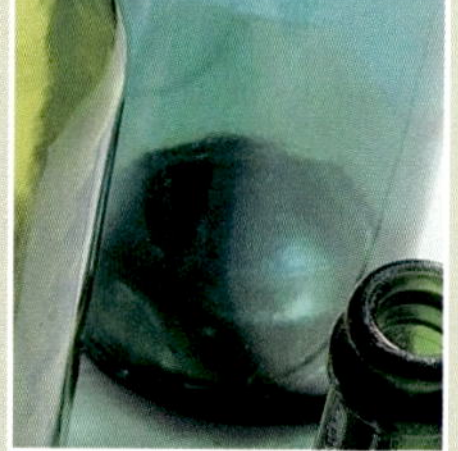
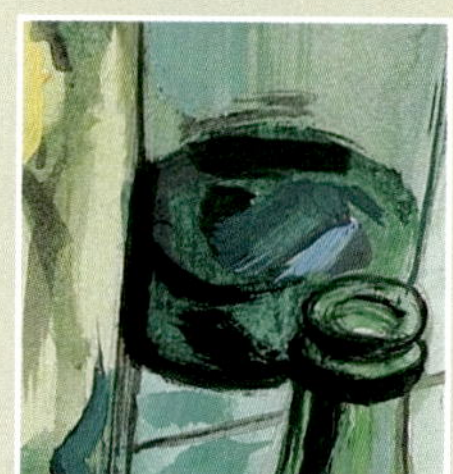
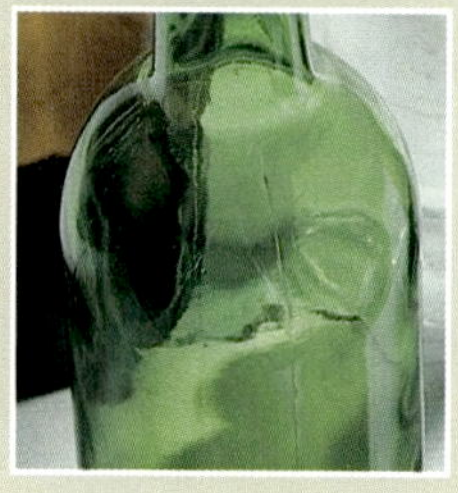
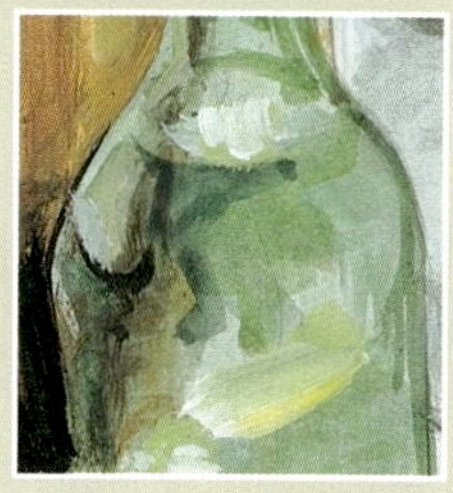
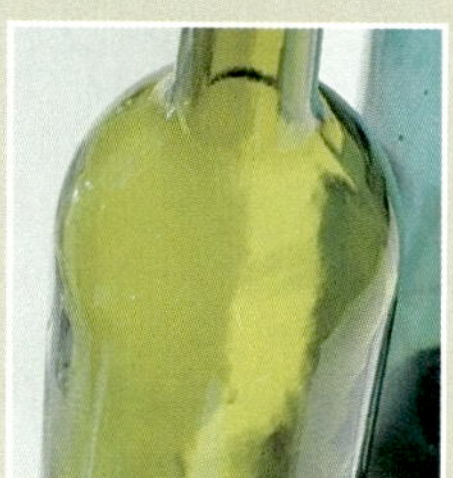
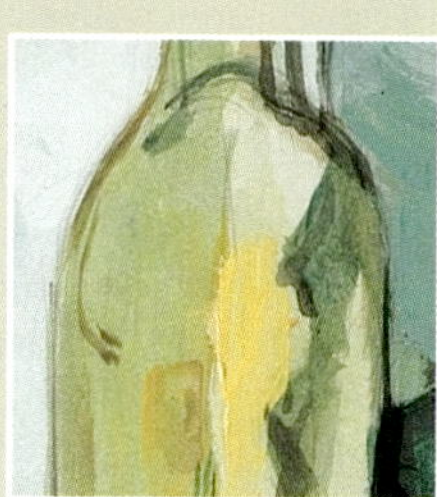

If we observe the details inside each one of the bottles, we will be able to see pictures similar to American abstract expressionism or the contemporary poetic expressionism of Mediterranean countries. This is the true image that captivates the spectator: pure beauty in its most sensitive dimension.

Abstract art inside a bottle

The world is full of abstract images, in nature and in man-made objects. Simply observe the shapes that form in the water, in the sky, or in a bubble. The images that do not tell a story, that are simple combinations of shapes, colors, lines, space, or texture, things that do not describe anything but themselves are considered abstract. This is why the phenomenon of the transparency of the bottles is fascinating, because a universe of incredible beauty is created in its interior. Intricate lines and shapes remind us that not everything has to obey a narrative order and offer us the pleasure of contemplation, the experience of sensitive beauty, without the need of narrative justification.

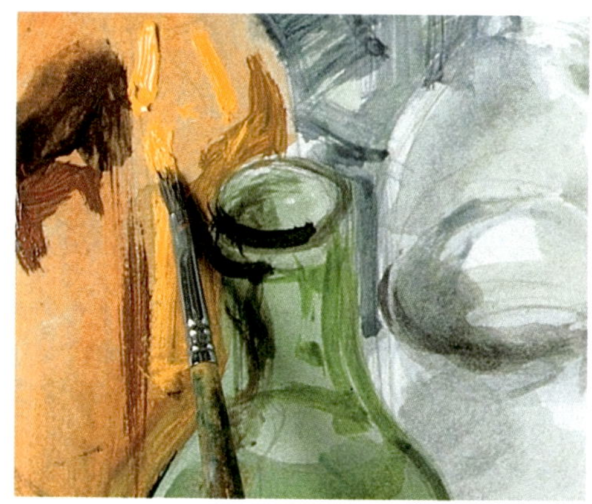

The feeling of transparency is greater as a result of the combination of areas of transparent color with others that are more opaque, even thick, conveying a variety of descriptions that go from what is tangible to what is not, that is, the effect produced by light.

FROM A WATERCOLOR-LIKE EFFECT TO IMPASTO

Acrylic paints can create transparent and very fluid and overlapping effects, just like watercolors, opaque and flat colors like gouache, and hard lines and impastos like oil paints. The only objection that artists have about acrylics is that they are more matte than oils and do not have that special quality of the latter. However, one can always apply varnish to complete the painting.

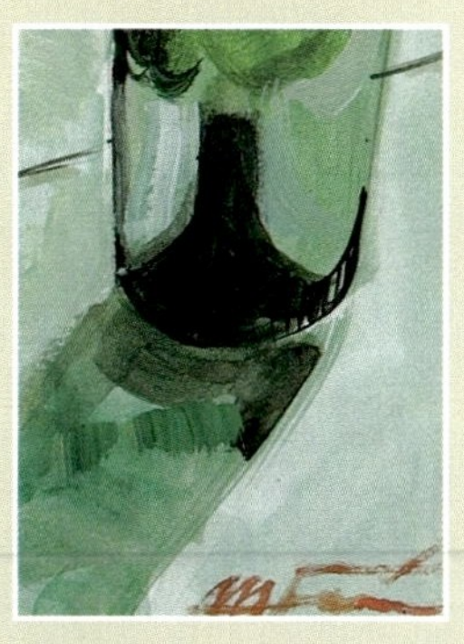

The same combination of light and shadow that appears at the base of this bottle is also present in the projected shadow.

LIGHT IN PROJECTED SHADOWS

Light is present in projected shadows because it passes through the object and projects onto the shadow. If the body were opaque, this phenomenon would not occur. That is why it is very important to represent projected shadows when we paint glass, because the feeling of transparency and the magic of the scene are enhanced, whether the shadows are projected onto another object or onto the paper.

8

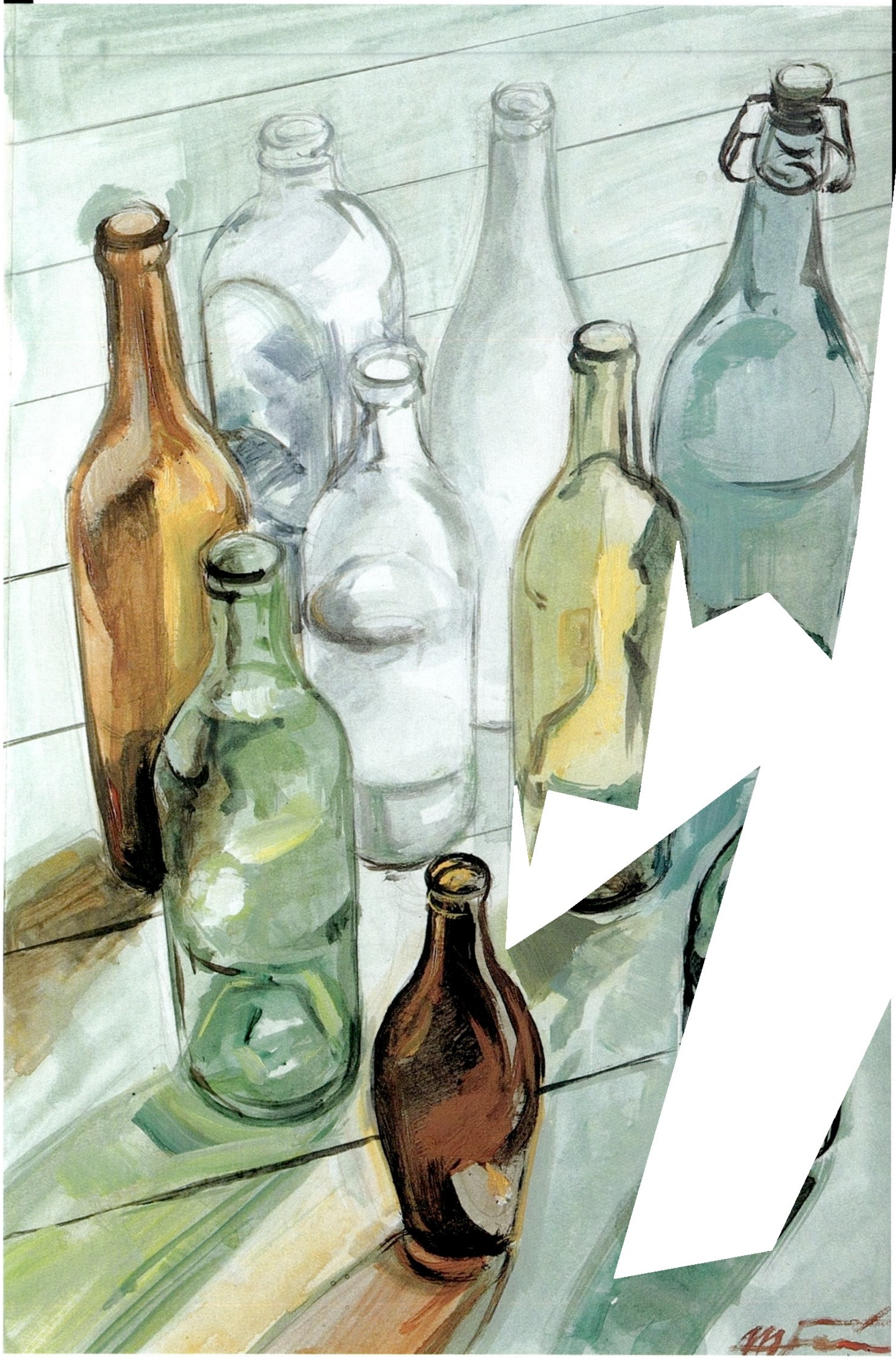

8 The completed painting looks fresher than the real still life because an effort has been made not to darken the glass too much and to maintain that light and luminous green that is so refreshing.

The possibilities of collage

Collage began to be used by avant-garde artists at the beginning of the twentieth century, especially the Dada and cubist painters. This technique is considered classic in painting. Its use in still life depends more on the kind of aesthetic look pursued by the artist than on technical requirements. It works very well with expressive genres like pop art and expressionism and not so well with realistic techniques and styles that are closer to classicism.

Normally, collage is used when the artist wants the material to express itself or when a powerful expressionist effect is pursued. It is also very suitable for "fun" projects and for subjects with a great number of volumes and spatial effects, like the example that we are going to see in the following pages.

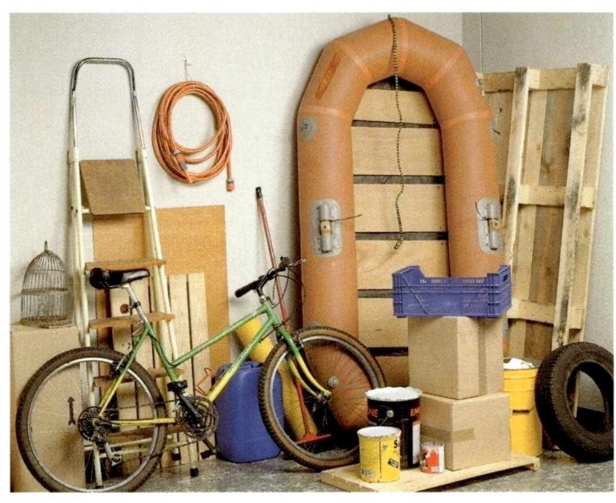

Here we see another corner of a house: a storage room. All kinds of objects and materials are stored in a place like this. Collage has been chosen for this project because it is a cumulative medium. The materials involved will be built up on the plane just like the objects in the scene that we have chosen.

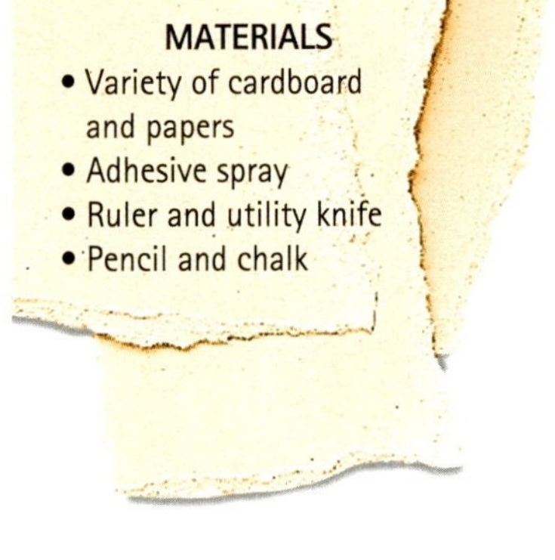

MATERIALS

- Variety of cardboard and papers
- Adhesive spray
- Ruler and utility knife
- Pencil and chalk

TECHNIQUES USED

◆ Collage ◆
◆ Subsequent drawing ◆

1 The first step is to select the materials that will be used. In this case, they will be cardboard and papers of different colors and textures. Even though not all will be used, to start out we will have a wide selection of them, just like a color palette in a different medium.

1

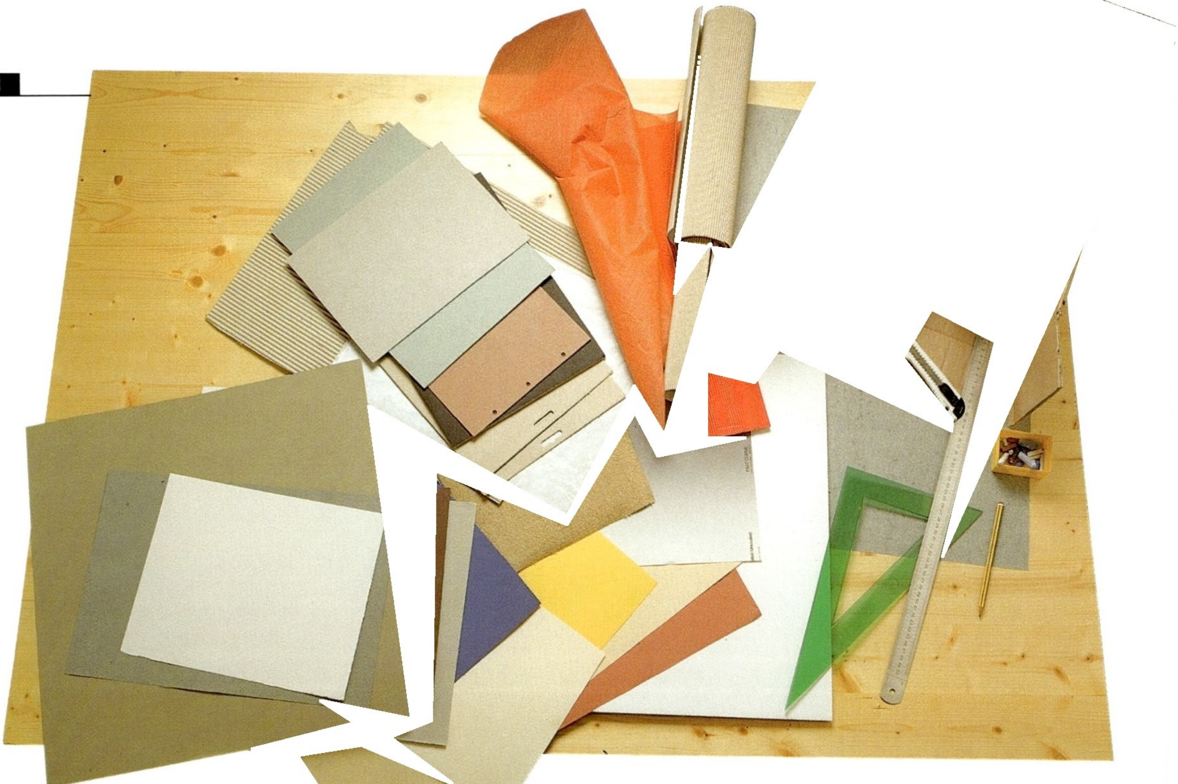

Organizing the work

Although this medium lends itself to quite a free approach, it is very important to plan the work beforehand and to make certain decisions, like the number of objects that will be used, whether or not they will be combined with other media like painting or drawing, and so on.

The first step will be to decide on the materials that will be involved. The use of recycled materials like paper, cardboard, plastic, cans, wood, fabric, and others is very interesting. However, sometimes it is necessary to resort to new materials that are not found around the house but that are very important to achieve the desired result. The type of glue and support used will be dictated by those materials. To work with papers, a lightweight cardboard and spray glue are sufficient. For wood or heavy objects, though, we will need a sturdy board, and probably nails, and carpenter's glue so the objects do not come unglued as a result of the weight. In every case, it is important to be well prepared and to have everything at hand and organized to avoid chaos.

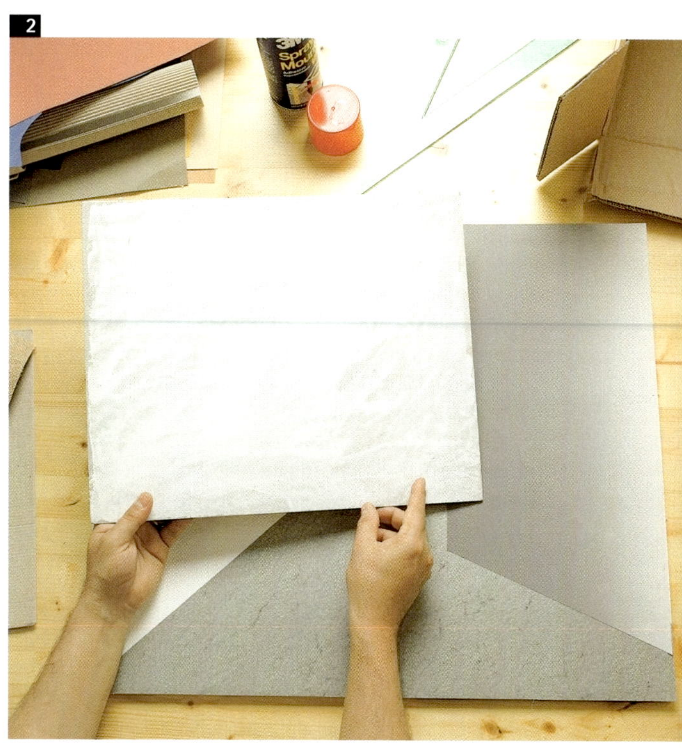

2 The plane of the support has been divided into three large areas according to the space: walls and floor. The base material has been selected for each one of them.

AVOIDING THE "CRAFTY" LOOK
Collage is often used for nonartistic projects as well. Almost everybody has had the experience, for example, of the school project in which pasta, toothpicks, and beans had to be glued onto a template provided by the teacher. This type of work, often of questionable taste, is used to help develop fine motor skills rather than as an artistic process. Therefore, it should not be used as a reference or as a model in understanding this genre. Artistic collage is something different, which we will explore in this final project.

3 This is the first image of the collage. The scene will be developed over this base. There are different kinds of materials: Pantone paper with gradations, a piece of cardboard painted white, corrugated paper, and gray wrapping paper with designs.

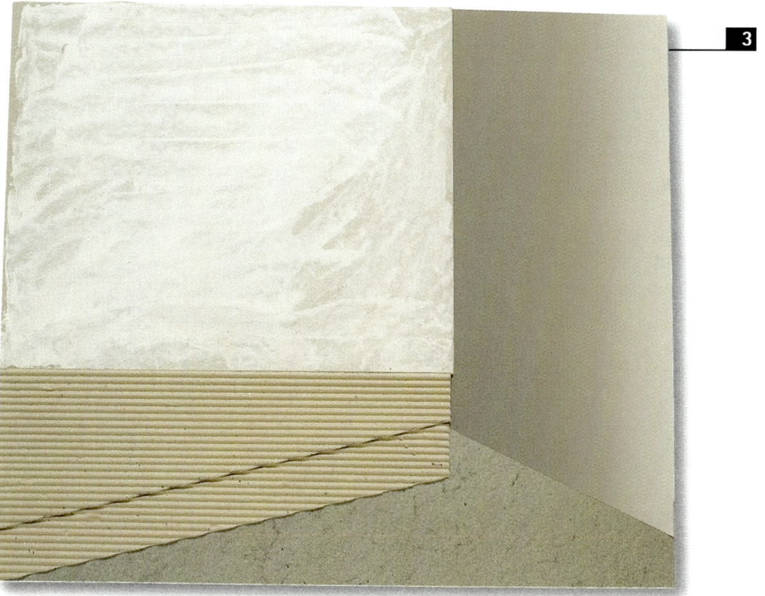

Working spontaneously but with a plan

In this type of work, the project normally is not very well defined but, rather, just a reference—in this case it is a storage room—or a more or less clear idea of a determined object. Each material will suggest a particular action. Sometimes it will be cutting or tearing, crumpling, painting over, and so on. Letting instinct guide you is important because, ultimately, that will be what will discover the message contained within each material. This is what working as we go means, letting instinct carry you away and being open to surprises.

However, this spontaneous work is not done mindlessly. Each step requires thinking. The completed work is reviewed and the decisions are made for the next step. This working method is purely artistic and extremely enriching.

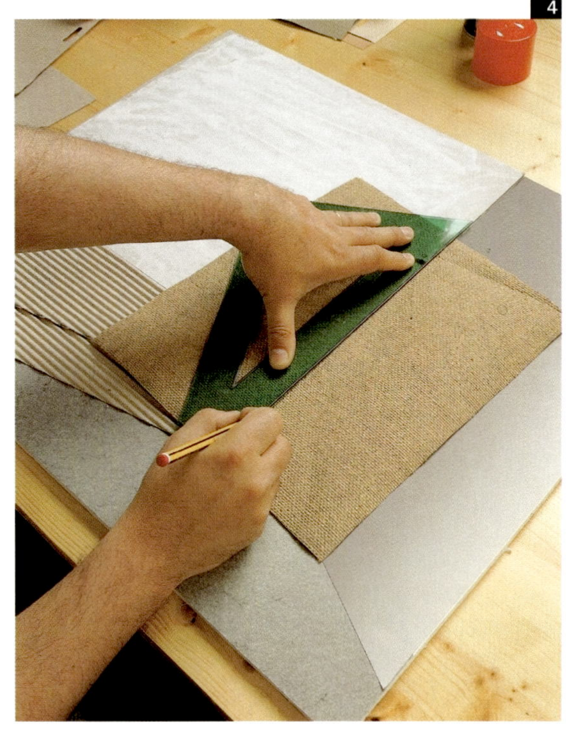

4 It is a good idea to draw the desired shape for the collage before we cut the materials that are to be used.

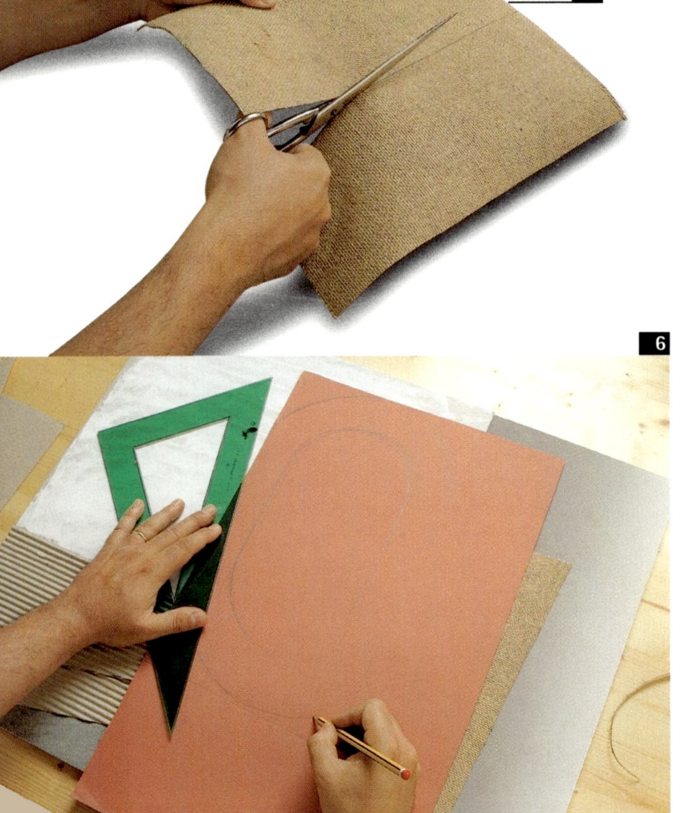

5 Scissors or a utility knife can be used to cut the paper. It can also be torn unevenly to create ragged edges and imperfections deliberately.

6 We can also resort to templates, a compass, a ruler, or any other tool if we want to cut out a shape that requires a clean edge. This is the case of the inflatable boat.

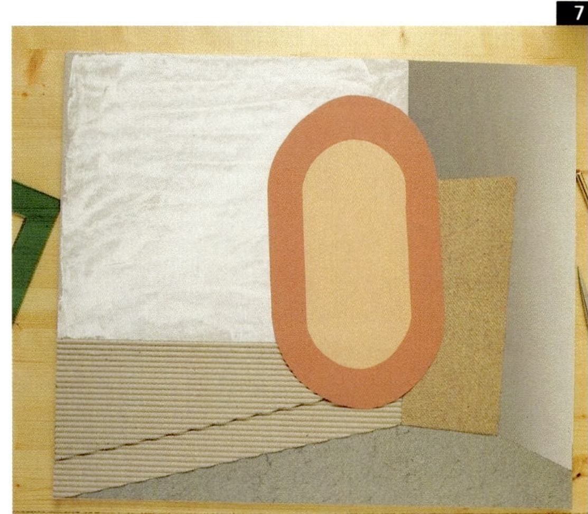

7 This is the second phase of the still life, a little more advanced. The larger elements that have been glued onto the base structure will form part of a second plane.

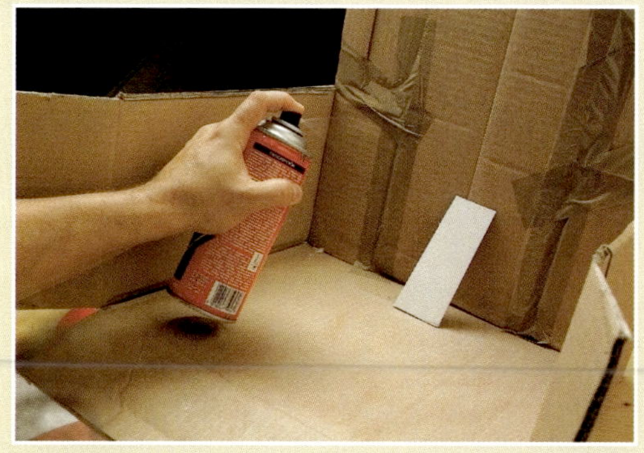

A spray adhesive has been used to create this still life. Precautions have been taken to prepare a small, semienclosed space for the task and to ventilate the workplace properly.

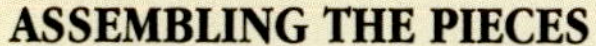

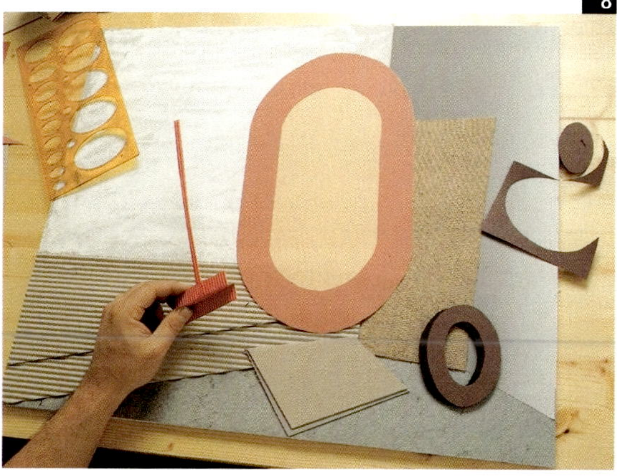

8 More elements of the still life are glued on. Some are flat, for example the piece of wood that functions as both material and texture. Others have more volume, like the red broom made by folding a piece of corrugated paper.

ASSEMBLING THE PIECES

Any type of adhesive can be used for assembling the pieces, depending on what we want to glue. Some things require very strong adhesives, like epoxy, carpenter's glue, or contact cement. One of the most commonly used is latex. This type of plastic glue dissolves in water and can be used with many materials.

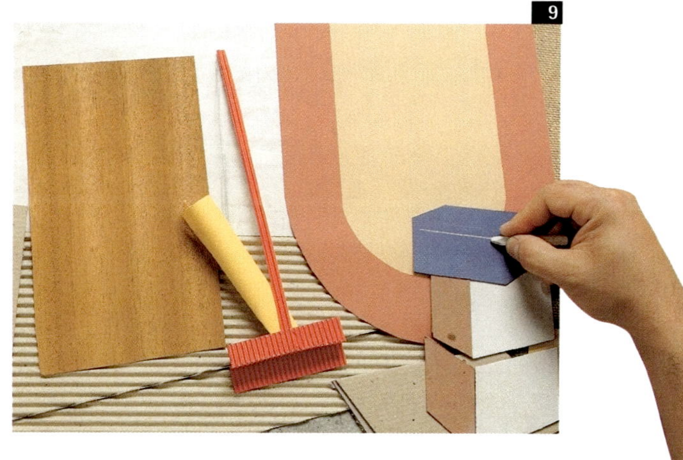

9 Contours, shadows, texture, and other effects are painted on the glued paper. From this point on, drawing and collage are two techniques that will be alternated, complementing each other.

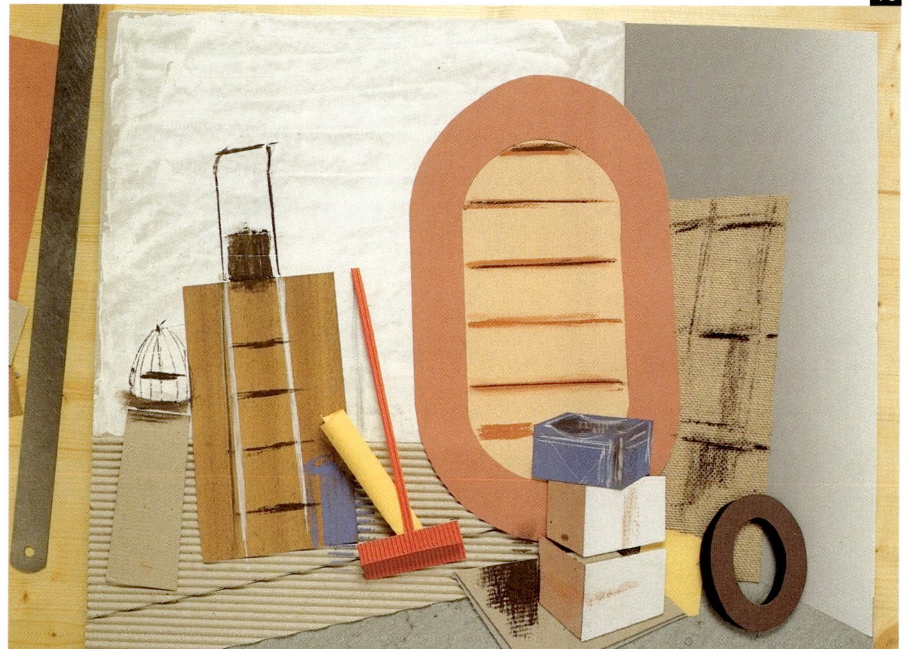

10 The most linear elements of this still life (ladder, bicycle, cage, and so on) will be represented with lines. Another way to do it would be to incorporate similar objects (rope, cable, or wires). However, this idea was discarded to prevent the painting from looking too cluttered.

Drawing and painting over the collage

A collage can look very cold if the hand of the artist is not seen in the creative process. A piece that is too impersonal resembles an illustration or a graphic design project more than a painting or artistic drawing. To avoid that effect, a more artistic approach is used. Lines and paint create the atmosphere, shadows, contours, structures, textures, and spontaneous discoveries that give the work greater quality and personality. This interaction is absolutely enriching.

11

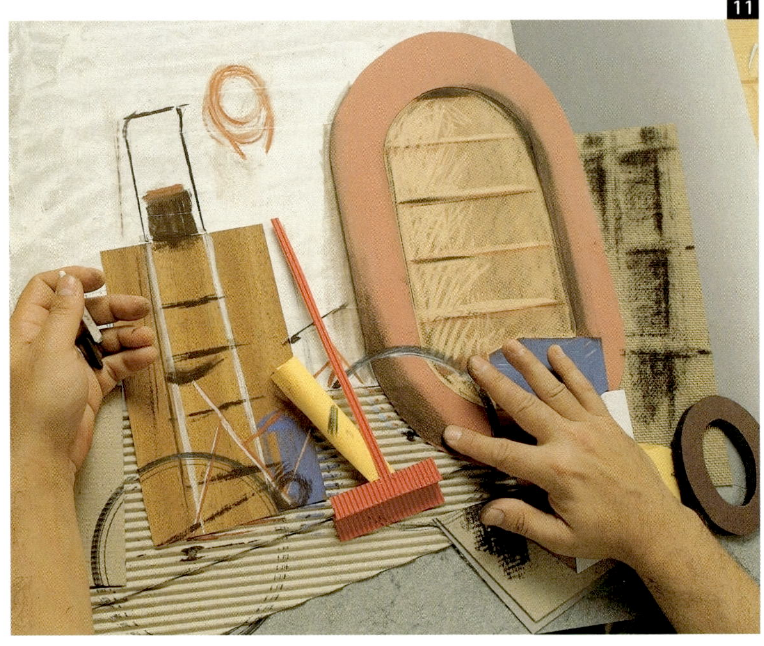

11 The shadows and the drawing of the last elements give the collage greater realism.

12 This is the resulting still life: a fun and fresh work of art, with a certain degree of ingenuity due to the clever materials chosen, the soft color of the grays, and the touches of primary colors red, yellow, and blue.

12

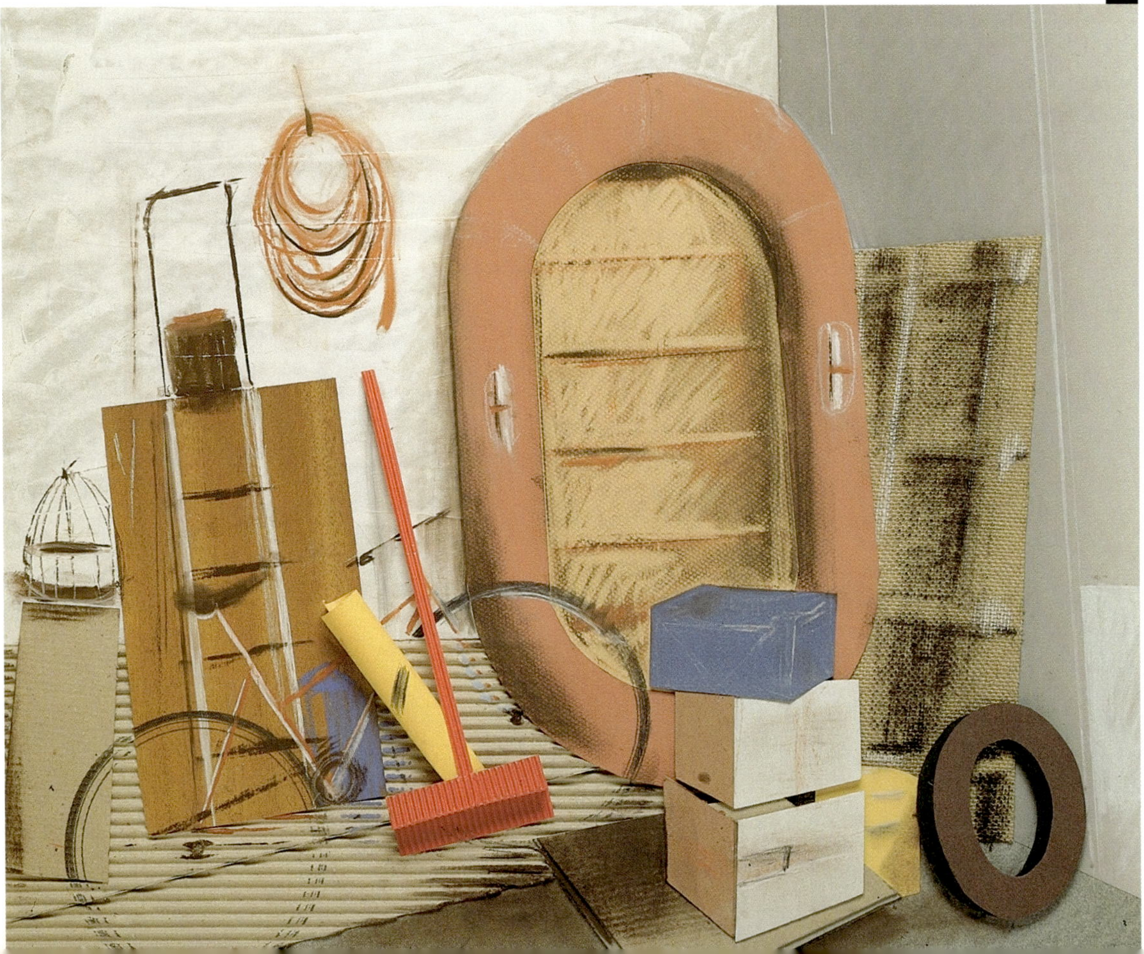

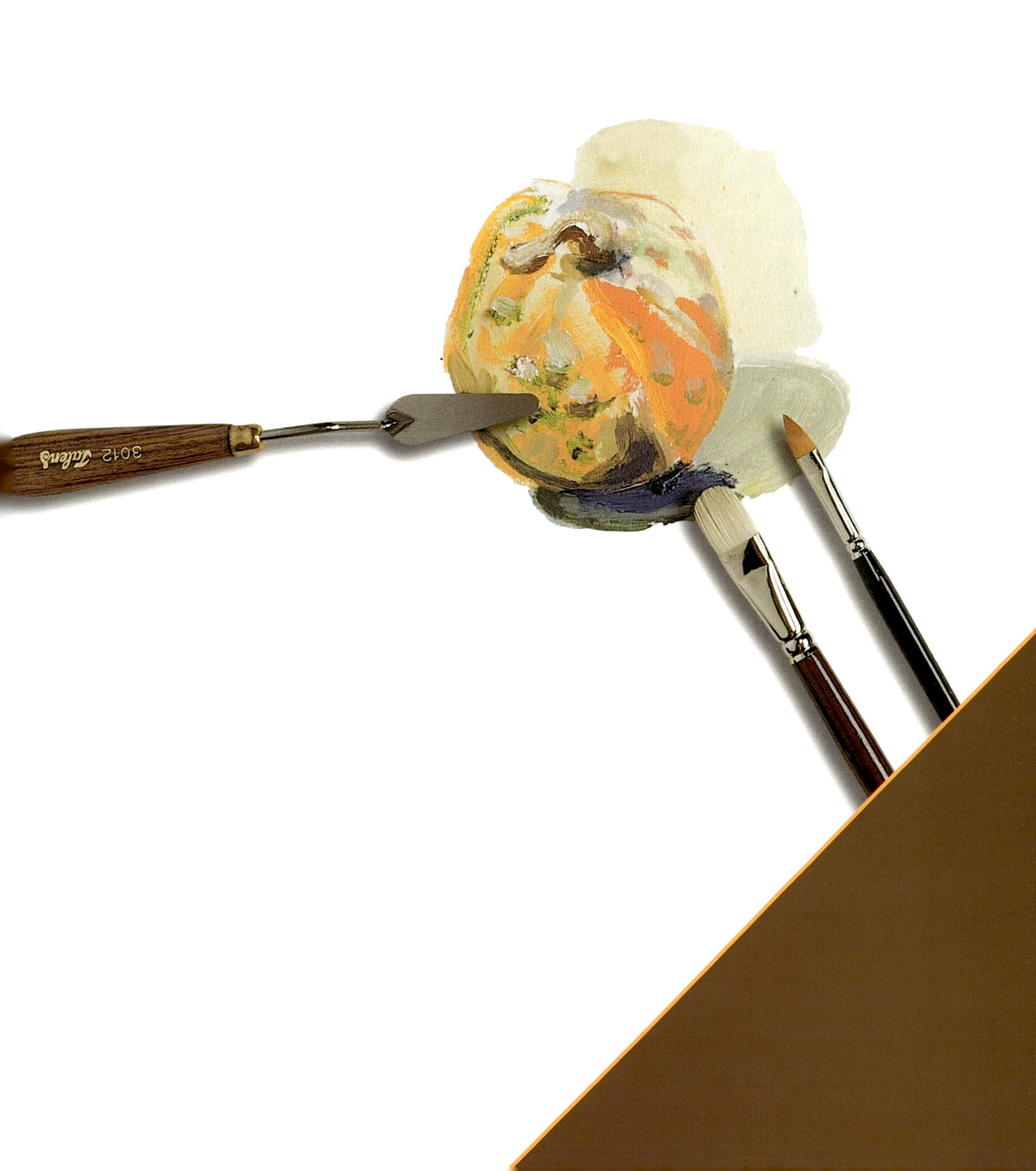
Talens 3012

Related Barron's titles on this subject:

Painter's Corner: Landscape
(ISBN 0-7641-5705-1) Barron's Educational Series, Inc., 2004

The Pastel Artist's Handbook
(ISBN 0-7641-5623-3) Barron's Educational Series, Inc., 2004

Painter's Corner: Anatomy for the Artist
(ISBN 0-7641-5557-1) Barron's Educational Series, Inc., 2002

Art Handbook: Vegetation
(ISBN 0-7641-5353-6) Barron's Educational Series, Inc., 2001

The Basics of Artistic Drawing
(ISBN 0-8120-1929-6) Barron's Educational Series, Inc., 1994

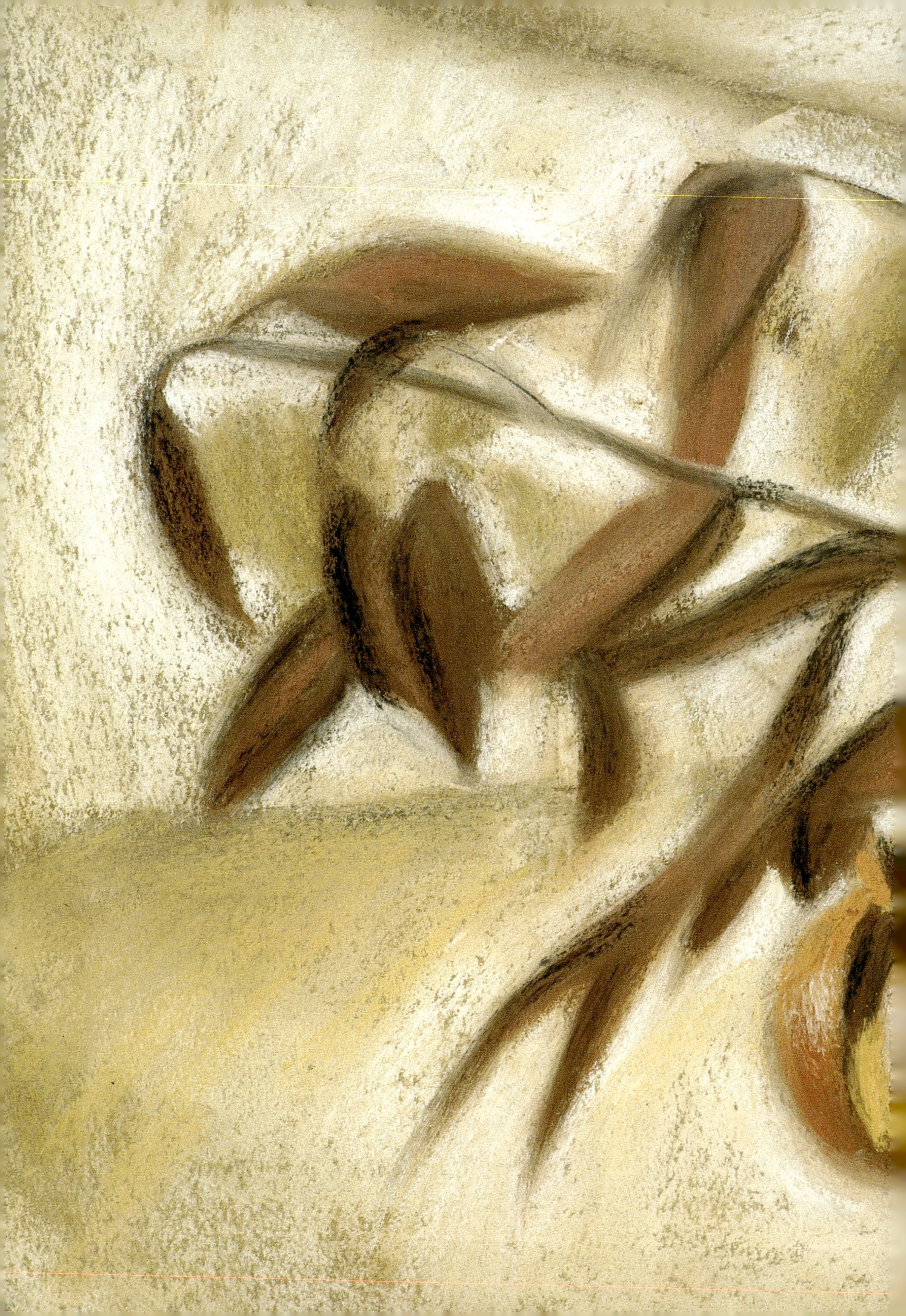